THE HEALTHY PERSONALITY
Readings

Second Edition

THE HEALTHY PERSONALITY
Readings

Second Edition

Edited by
Hung-Min Chiang ● **Abraham H. Maslow**

D. Van Nostrand Company
New York ● Cincinnati ● Toronto ● London ● Melbourne

Preface

Psychological health is an important but elusive concept that still has no single definition acceptable to everyone. What do we actually mean when we say that someone is psychologically healthy? What criteria do we use? Traditionally, psychologists have had a far more difficult time reaching a concensus than physicians have had defining physical health. This difficulty is due to the fact that the idea of a healthy personality is inextricably linked to the question of values and to the conceptual models we use.

For example, if we use a medical model, a person can be judged psychologically healthy as long as he or she is not sick mentally. In this case, no distinction is made between the higher level of psychological well-being and mere absence of disease. If an adjustment mode is used, individuals are accepted as sound and healthy if their behavior is in accordance with social norms. The question of whether the society to which the individual conforms is worthy of such conformity is not involved. In contrast, the humanist model stresses the creative urge of the individual and views the actualization of human potentials as essential.

The realization that the concept of psychological health is inseparable from human values has often led to the belief that the issue falls outside the jurisdiction of science altogether. But the late Abraham H. Maslow disagreed. He was a firm believer in the feasibility of developing a unified theory of positive psychological health based on empirical data. He suggested that we accept values, goals, hopes, and aspirations as legitimate psychological components. To accomodate these essential human experiences he advocated a broader frame of reference for science as well as a new conceptual tool that can do justice to the phenomenon under investigation.

It was with such a long-range goal in mind that the original edition of this book was compiled. In our search for a new image of man, some two dozen articles were brought together under a general rubric of humanistic psychology. In the current edition, many articles have been added to up-date the contents, including an autobiographical sketch by Carl Rogers, Gestalt Therapy by Fritz Perls, and dream research by Stanley Krippner and William Hughes. Also included in this volume is a report on Maslow's workshop, Laboratory in Self-Knowledge, which is printed here for the first time. In order to make room for these additions, however, some papers in the first edition had to be omitted.

As the editor responsible for the current revision, I wish to extend my special thanks to Mrs. Bertha Maslow, who has kindly read the materials related to her late husband in this edition. She also helped me keep abreast of the later works of Abe Maslow, for whom I have an ever deepening respect. I sincerely hope that the present volume is a small step forward in the direction Abe Maslow envisioned for the psychology of personal growth. My paper, A Humanistic Psychologist in the Classroom, is henceforth dedicated to him.

Hung-Min Chiang

Contents

THE
HEALTHY
PERSONALITY
Readings

Second Edition

1

Personality: Normal and Abnormal

GORDON W. ALLPORT

The word *norm* means "an authoritative standard," and, correspondingly, *normal* means abiding by such a standard. It follows that a normal personality is one whose conduct conforms to an authoritative standard, and an abnormal personality is one whose conduct does not do so.

But having said this much we immediately discover that there are two entirely different kinds of standards that may be applied to divide the normal from the abnormal: the one statistical, the other ethical. The one pertains to the average or usual, and the other to the desirable or valuable.

These two standards are not only different, but in many ways they stand in flat contradiction to one another. It is, for example, *usual* for people to have some noxious trends in their natures, some pathology of tissues or organs, some evidences of nervousness and some self-defeating habits; but though usual or avege, such trends are not healthy. Or again, society's authoritative standard for a wholesome sex life is, if we are to accept the Kinsey Report, achieved by only a minority of American males. Here too the usual is not the desirable; what is normal in one sense is not normal in the other sense. And certainly no system of ethics in the civilized world holds up as a model for its children the ideal of becoming a merely average man. It is not the actualities, but rather the potentialities, of human nature that somehow provide us with a standard for a sound and healthy personality.

Fifty years ago this double meaning of *norm* and *normal* did not

Source: Address delivered at the Fifth Interamerican Congress of Psychology, Mexico City, December 1957; sponsored by the Interamerican Society of Psychology; reprinted by permission from the Congress Proceedings.

1

trouble psychology so much as it does today. In those days psychology was deeply involved in discovering average norms for every conceivable type of mental function. Means, modes and sigmas were in the saddle, and differential psychology was riding high. Intoxicated with the new-found beauty of the normal distribution curve, psychologists were content to declare its slender tails as the one and only sensible measure of "abnormality." Departures from the mean were abnormal and for this reason slightly unsavory.

In this era there grew up the concept of "mental adjustment," and this concept held sway well into the decade of the 20s. While not all psychologists equated adjustment with average behavior, this implication was pretty generally present. It was, for example, frequently pointed out that an animal who does not adjust to the norm for his species usually dies. It was not yet pointed out that a human being who does so adjust is a bore and a mediocrity.

Now times have changed. Our concern for the improvement of average human behavior is deep, for we now seriously doubt that the merely mediocre man can survive. As social anomie spreads, as society itself becomes more and more sick, we doubt that the mediocre man will escape mental disease and delinquency, or that he will keep himself out of the clutch of dictators or succeed in preventing atomic warfare. The normal distribution curve, we see, holds out no hope of salvation. We need citizens who are in a more positive sense normal, healthy and sound. And the world needs them more urgently than it ever did before.

It is for this reason, I think, that psychologists are now seeking a fresh definition of what is normal and what is abnormal. They are asking questions concerning the *valuable,* the *right,* and the *good* as they have never asked them before.

At the same time psychologists know that in seeking for a criterion of normality in this new sense they are trespassing on the traditional domain of moral philosophy. They also know that, by and large, philosophers have failed to establish authoritative standards for what constitutes the sound life—the life that educators, parents, and therapists should seek to mold. And so psychologists, for the most part, wish to puruse the search in a fresh way and if they can, avoid the traditional traps of axiology. Let me briefly describe some recent empirical attempts to define normality and afterward attempt to evaluate the state of our efforts to date.

Naturalistic Derivations of "Normality"

During the past few months two proposals have been published that merit serious attention. Both are by social scientists, one a psychologist in the United States, the other a sociologist in England. Their aim is to derive a concept of normality (in the value sense) from the condition of man (in the naturalistic sense). Both seek their ethical imperatives from biology and psychology, not from value-theory directly. In short, they boldly seek the *ought* (the goal to which teachers, counsellors, therapists should strive) from the *is* of human nature. Many philosophers tell us that this is an impossible undertaking. But before we pass judgment let us see what success they have had.

E. J. Shoben asks, "What are the principal psychological differences between man and lower animals?"[1] While he does not claim that his answer is complete, he centers upon two distinctively human qualities. And he makes the extra-psychological assumption that man *should* maximize those attributes that are distinctively human. The first quality is man's capacity for the use of propositional language (symbolization). From this particular superiority over animals Shoben derives several specific guidelines for normality. With the aid of symbolic language, for example, man can delay his gratifications, holding in mind a distant goal, a remote reward, an objective to be reached perhaps only at the end of one's life or perhaps never. With the aid of symbolic language, he can imagine a future for himself that is far better than the present. He can also develop an intricate system of social concepts that leads him to all manner of possible relations with other human beings, far exceeding the rigid symbiotic rituals of, say, the social insects.

A second distinctive human quality is related to the prolonged childhood in the human species. Dependence, basic trust, sympathy and altruism are absolutely essential to human survival, in a sense and to a degree not true for lower animals.

Bringing together these two distinctive qualities, Shoben derives his conception of normality. He calls it "a model of integrative adjustment." It follows, he says, that a sense of *personal responsibility* marks the normal man, for responsibility is a distinctive capacity derived from holding in mind a symbolic image of the future, delaying gratification, and being able to strive in accordance with one's conceptions of the best principles of conduct for oneself. Similarly *social responsibility* is normal; for all these symbolic capacities can interact with the unique factor of trust or altruism. Closely related is the criterion of *democratic social interest* which derives from both symbolization and trust. Similarly, the *possession of ideals* and the necessity for *self control* follow from the same naturalistic analysis. Shoben rightly points out that a *sense of guilt* is an inevitable consequence of man's failure to live according to the distinctive human pattern, and so in our concept of normality we must include both guilt and devices for expiation.

Every psychologist who wishes to make minimum assumptions and who wishes to keep close to empirical evidence, and who inclines toward the naturalism of biological science, will appreciate and admire Shoben's efforts. Yet I imagine our philosopher friends will arise to confound us with some uncomfortable questions. Is it not a distinctively human capacity, they will ask, for a possessive mother to keep her child permanently tied to her apron strings? Does any lower animal engage in this destructive behavior? Likewise, is it not distinctively human to develop fierce in-group loyalties that lead to prejudice, contempt, and war? Is it not possible that the burden of symbolization, social responsibility, and guilt may lead a person to depression and suicide? Suicide, along with all the other destructive patterns I have mentioned, is distinctively human. A philosopher who raises these questions would conclude, "No, you cannot derive the *ought* from the *is* of human nature. What is distinctively human is not necessarily distinctively good."

Let us look at a second attempt to achieve a naturalistic criterion of normality. In a recent book entitled *Towards a Measure of Man*, Paul Halmos prefers to start with the question, "What are the minimum conditions for survival?"[2] When we know these minimum conditions we can declare that any situations falling below this level will lead to abnormality, and tend toward death and destruction. He calls this criterion the *abnorm* and believes we can define it, even if we cannot define normality, because people in general agree more readily on what is bad for man than on what is good for him. They agree on the bad because all mortals are subject to the basic imperative of survival.

The need for survival he breaks down into the need for growth and the need for social cohesion. These two principles are the universal conditions of all life, not merely of human life. *Growth* means autonomy and the process of individuation. *Cohesion* is the basic fact of social interdependence, involving, at least for human beings, initial trust, heteronomy, mating and the founding of family.

Now Halmos believes that by taking an inventory of conditions deleterious to growth and cohesion we may establish the "abnorm." As a start he mentions first and foremost disorders of child training. He says, "continued or repeated interruption of physical proximity between mother and child" and "emotional rejection" of the child by the mother are conditions that harm survival of the individual and the group. In his own terms this first criterion of abnormality lies in a "rupture in the transmutation of cohesion into love." Most of what is abnormal he traces to failures in the principle of cohesion, so that the child becomes excessively demanding and compulsive. Here we note the similarity to such contemporary thinkers as Bowlby, Erikson and Maslow.

The author continues his inventory of the "abnorm" by accepting syndromes that psychiatrists agree upon. For instance, it is abnormal (inimical to survival) if repetition of conduct occurs irrespective of the situation and unmodified by its consequences; also when one's accomplishments constantly fall short of one's potentialities; likewise when one's psychosexual frustrations prevent both growth and cohesion.

It is well to point out that the basic functions of growth and cohesion postulated by Halmos occur time and time again in psychological writing. Bergson, Jung and Angyal are among the writers who agree that normality requires a balance between individuation and socialization, between autonomy and heteronomy. There seems to be considerable consensus in this matter. Let me quote from one of the founders of this Society whose recent death has brought sorrow to us all. Werner Wolff writes:

> When an individual identifies himself to an extreme degree with a group, the effect is that he loses his value. On the other hand, a complete inability to identify has the effect that the environment loses its value for the individual. In both extreme cases the dynamic relationship between individual and environment is distorted. An individual behaving in such a way is called "neurotic." In a normal group each member preserves his individuality but accepts his role as participator also.[3]

While there is much agreement that the normal personality must strike a serviceable balance between growth as an individual and cohesion with society, we do not yet have a clear criterion for determining when these factors are in serviceable balance and when they are not. Philosophers, I fear, would shake their heads at Halmos. They would ask, "How do you know that survival is a good thing?" Further, "Why should all people enjoy equal rights to the benefits of growth and cohe-

sion?'' And, ''How are we to define the optimum balance between cohesion and growth within the single personality?''

Imbalance and Creativity

Halmos himself worries especially about the relation between abnormality and creativity. It was Nietzsche who declared, ''I say unto
you: a man must have chaos yet within him to be able to give birth to a
dancing star.'' Have not many meritorious works of music, literature,
and even of science drawn their inspiration not from balance but from
some kind of psychic chaos? Here, I think, Halmos gives the right
answer. He says in effect that creativity and normality are not identical
values. On the whole the normal person will be creative, but if valuable
creations come likewise from people who are slipping away from the
norm of survival, this fact can only be accepted and valued on the scale
of creativity, but not properly on the scale of normality.

Imbalance and Growth

In this day of existentialism I sense that psychologists are becoming less and less content with the concept of adjustment, and correspondingly with the concepts of ''tension reduction,'' ''restoration of
equilibrium,'' and ''homeostasis.'' We wonder if a man who enjoys
these beatific conditions is truly human. Growth we know is not due to
homeostasis but to a kind of ''transistasis.'' And cohesion is a matter
of keeping our human relationships moving and not in mere stationary
equilibrium. Stability cannot be a criterion of normality since stability
brings evolution to a standstill, negating both growth and cohesion.
Freud once wrote to Fliess that he finds ''moderate misery necessary
for intensive work.''
    A research inspired by Carl Rogers is interesting in this connec-
tion. One series of patients before treatment manifested a zero correlation between their self-image and their ideal self-image. Following
treatment the correlation was +.34, not high but approaching the
coefficient of +.58 that marked a healthy untreated group. Apparently
this magnitude of correlation is a measure of the satisfaction or
dissatisfaction that normal people have with their own personalities.[4]
In other words, a zero correlation between self and ideal self is too low
for normality; it leads to such anguish that the sufferer seeks therapy.

At the same time normal people are by no means perfectly adjusted to themselves. There is always a wholesome gap between self and ideal self, between present existence and aspiration. On the other hand, too high a satisfaction indicates pathology. The highest coefficient obtained, +.90, was from an individual clearly pathological. Perfect correlations we might expect only from smug psychotics, particularly paranoid schizophrenics.

And so whatever our definition of normality turns out to be it must allow for serviceable imbalances within personality, and between person and society.

An Empirical Approach to Soundness

The work of Barron illustrates an approach dear to the psychologist's heart. He lets other establish the criterion of normality, or as he calls it, *soundness,* and then proceeds to find out what *"sound"* men are like. Teachers of graduate students in the University of California nominated a large number of men whom they considered sound, and some of the opposite trend. In testing and experimenting with these two groups, whose identities were unknown to the investigators, certain significant differences appeared.[5] For one thing the sounder men had more realistic perceptions; they were not thrown off by distortions or by surrounding context in the sensory field. Further, on adjective check-lists they stood high on such traits as *integrated pursuit of goals, persistence, adaptability, good nature.* On the Minnesota Multiphasic Personality Inventory they were high in *equanimity, self-confidence, objectivity* and *virility.* Their *self-insight* was superior, as was their *physical health.* Finally, they came from homes where there was *little or no affective rupture*—a finding that confirms Halmos's predictions.

Inventory Approaches

Most authors do not have the benefit of professional concensus on soundness. The simply set forth in a didactic manner the attributes of normality, or health, or soundness, or maturity, or productivity, as they see them. Innumerable descriptive lists result. Perhaps the simplest of these is Freud's. He says the healthy person will be able to "love" and to "work." One of the most elaborate is Maslow's schedule of qualities that include among others: efficient perception of reality, philosophical humor, spontaneity, detachment, and an acceptance of self and others. Such lists are not altogether arbitrary since their authors base them on wide clinical experience, as did Freud, or on a deliberate analysis of case materials, as did Maslow.[6]

There are so many lists of this type now available that a new kind of approach is possible—namely, the combining of these insightful inventories. From time to time I have assigned this task to my students, and while all manner of groupings and re-groupings result, still there are recurrent themes that appear in nearly all inventories. If I were to attempt the assignment myself I should probably start with my own list of three criteria, published 20 years ago, but I would now expand it.[7]

The three criteria I originally listed were:

> i. ego-extension—the capabity to take an interest in more than one's body and one's material possessions. The criterion covers, I think, the attributes that Fromm ascribes to the productive man.
> ii. self-objectification—which includes the ability to relate the feeling tone of the present experience to that of a past experience provided the latter does in fact determine the quality of the former; self-objectification also includes humor which tells us that our total horizon of life is too wide to be compressed into our present rigidities.
> iii. unifying philosophy of life—which may or may not be religious, but in any event has to be a frame of meaning and of responsibility into which life's major activities fit.

To this inventory I now would add:

> iv. the capacity for a warm, profound, relating of one's self to others—which may, if one likes, be called "extroversion of the libido" or "Gemeinschaftsgefühl."
> v. The possession of realistic skills, abilities, and perceptions with which to cope with the practical problems of life.
> vi. a compassionate regard for all living creatures—which includes respect for individual persons and a disposition to participate in common activities that will improve the human lot.

I am aware that psychoanalysts are partial to the criterion of "ego strength": a normal person has a strong ego, an abnormal person a weak ego. But I find this phrase ill defined, and would suggest that my six somewhat more detailed criteria succeed in specifying what we mean by the looser term, "ego strength."

The weakness of all inventories, including my own, is that the philosopher's persistent questions are still unanswered. How does the psychologist know that these qualities comprise normality, that they are good, and that all people should have them? Before I attempt to give a partial answer to our irritating philosopher friend, let me call attention to one additional psychological approach.

Continuity of Symptom and Discontinuity of Process

I refer to a fresh analysis of the problem of continuity-discontinuity. Is abnormality merely an exaggerated normal condition? Is there unbroken continuity between health and disease? Certainly Freud thought so. He evolved his system primarily as a theory of neurosis. But he and his followers came to regard his formulations as a universally valid science of psychology. Whether one is normal or abnormal depends on the degree to which one can manage his relationships successfully. Furthermore, the earlier enthusiasm of psychologists for the normal distribution curve helped to entrench the theory of continuity. The strongest empirical evidence in favor of this view is the occurrence of borderline cases. Descriptively, there is certainly a continuum. We encounter mild neurotics, borderline schizophrenics, hypomanics, and personalities that are paranoid, cycloid, epileptoid. And if scales and tests are employed there are no gaps; scores are continuously distributed.

But—and let me insist on this point—this continuum pertains only to symptoms, to appearances. The *processes (or "mechanisms")* underlying these appearances are not continuous. There is, for example, a polar difference between confronting the world and its problems (which is an intrinsically wholesome thing to do) and escaping and withdrawing from the world (which is an intrinsically unwholesome thing to do). Extreme withdrawal and escape constitute psychosis. But you may ask, do not we all do some escaping? Yes, we do, and what is more, escapism may provide not only recreation but may sometimes have a certain constructive utility, as it has in mild daydreaming. But still the process of escape can be harmless only if the *dominant* process is confrontation. Left to itself escapism spells disaster. In the psychotic this process has the upper hand; in the normal person, on the contrary, confrontation has the upper hand.

Following this line of reasoning we can list other processes that intrinsically generate abnormality, and those that generate normality. The first list deals with catabolic functions. I would mention:

Escape or withdrawal (including fantasy)

Repression or dissociation

Other "ego defences," including rationalization, reaction formation, projection, displacement

Implusivity (uncontrolled)

Restriction of thinking to concrete level

Fixation of personality at a juvenile level

All forms of rigidification

The list is not complete, but the processes in question, I submit, are intrinsically catabolic. They are as much so as are the disease
mechanisms responsible for diabetes, tuberculosis, hyperthyroidism,
or cancer. A person suffering only a small dose of these mechanisms
may appear to be normal, but only if the *anabolic* mechanisms pre-
dominate. Among the latter I would list:

Confrontation (or, if you prefer, "reality testing")

Availability of knowledge to consciousness

Self-insight, with its attendant humor

Integrative action of the nervous system

Ability to think abstractly

Continuous individuation (without arrested or fixated development)

Functional autonomy of motives

Frustration tolerance

I realize that what I have called processes, or mechanisms, are
not in all cases logically parallel. But they serve to make my point, that
normality depends on the dominance of one set of principles, abnormality upon the dominance of another. The fact that all normal people
are occasionally afflicted with catabolic processes does not alter the
point. The normal life is marked by a preponderance of the anabolic
functions; the abnormal by a preponderance of the catabolic.

Conclusion

And now is it possible to gather together all these divergent
threads, and to reach some position tenable for psychology today? Let
us try to do so.

First, I think, we should make a deep obeisance in the direction of moral philosophy and gracefully concede that psychology by itself cannot solve the problem of normality. No psychologist has succeeded in telling us why man ought to seek good health rather than ill; nor why normality should be our goal for all men, and not just for some. Nor can psychologists account for the fact that meritorious creativity may be of value even if the creator himself is by all tests an abnormal person. These and a variety of other conundrums lie beyond the competence of psychology to solve. That moral philosophers have not agreed among themselves upon solutions is also true; but we gladly grant them freedom and encouragement to continue their efforts.

At the same time the lines of research and analysis that I have here reviewed are vitally related to the philosophers quest. After all, it is the psychologists who deal directly with personalities in the clinic, in schools, industry, and in laboratories. It is they who gather the facts concerning normality and abnormality and who try to weave them into their own normative speculations. *A fact and a moral imperative are more closely interlocked than traditional writers on ethics may think.* Among the facts that psychology can offer are the following:

i. Investigations have told us much concerning the nature of human needs and motives, both conscious and unconscious. A grouping of these needs into the broad categories of growth and cohesion is helpful. Much is known concerning the pathologies that result from frustration and imbalance of these needs. It would be absurd for moral philosophers to write imperatives in total disregard of this evidence.

ii. We know much about childhood conditions that predispose toward delinquency, prejudice, and mental disorder. A moralist might do well to cast his imperatives in terms of standards for child training. I can suggest, for example, that the abstract imperative "respect for persons" should be tested and formulated from the point of view of child training.

iii. By virtue of comparative work on men and animals we know much about the motives common to both, but also, as Shoben has shown, about the qualities that are distinctively human. Let the philosophers give due weight to this work.

iv. While I have not yet mentioned the matter, psychology in cooperation with cultural anthropology has a fairly clear picture today of the role of culture in producing and in defining abnormality. We know the incidence of psychosis and neurosis in various populations; we know what conditions are labeled abnormal in some cultures but are regarded as normal in others. We also know, with some accuracy, those conditions that are considered abnormal in all cultures. Since our president, Professor Klineberg, is addressing the Congress on this subject I shall say no more about it; but shall simply point out that these facts are highly relevant to the deliberations of the moral philosopher.

v. Following the lead of Halmos, we may say that biologists, psychologists and sociologists know much about the conditions of individual and group survival. While these facts in themselves do not tell us why we should survive, still they provide specifications for the philosopher who thinks he can answer this riddle.

vi. Still more important, I think, is the empirical work on consensus that is now available. We have cited Barron's method of determining the attributes of men judged to be "sound" as distinguished from those of men judged to be "unsound." While the philosopher is not likely to accept the vote of university professors as an adequate definition of soundness, still he might do well to heed opinions other than his own.

vii. Another type of consensus is obtained from the inventories prepared by insightful writers. These authors have tried, according to their best ability, to summarize as they see them the requirements of normality, health or maturity. They do so on the grounds of extensive experience. As we survey these inventories we are struck both by their verbal differences and by an underlying congruence of meaning that no one has yet succeeded fully in articulating. Here again the philosopher may balk at accepting consensus, and yet he would do well to check his own private reasoning against the conclusions of others no less competent, and probably more clinically experienced, than he.

viii. He would do well, I think, to explore the goals of psychotherapy as stated or implied in leading therapeutic systems. If he were to comb the writings of behavioristic therapists, for example, he might reasonably conclude that *efficiency* (the ability to cope with problems) is the principal goal; in Zen therapy, by contrast, the stress seems to be on restored *cohesion* with the group. Nondirective therapy clearly prizes the goal of *growth;* the desideratum for Goldstein, Maslow, and Jung is *self-actualization;* for Fromm, *productivity;* for Frankl and the logotherapists, *meaningfulness* and *responsibility.* Thus each therapist seems to have in mind a preponderant emphasis which, in terms of value theory, constitutes for him a definition of the good way of life and of health for the personality. While the emphasis differs and the labels vary, still there seems to be a confluence of these criteria. Taken together they remind us of the tributaries to a vast river system, none the less unified for all their differences of source and shape. This confluence is a factor that no moralist can afford to overlook.

ix. Finally, the distinction between the anabolic and catabolic processes in the formation of personality represents a fact of importance. Instead of judging merely the end-product of action, perhaps the moralist would do well to focus his attention upon the processes by which various ends are achieved. Conceivably, the moral law could be written in terms of strengthening anabolic functions in oneself and in others whilst fighting against catabolic functions.

It is true that the preferred method of moral philosophy is to work "from the top down." Apriorism and reason are the legitimate tools of philosophy. Up to now this method has yielded a wide array of moral imperatives, including the following: *so act that the maxim of thy action can become a universal law; be a respecter of persons; seek to reduce your desires; harmonize your interests with the interests of others; thou art nothing, thy folk is everything; thou shalt love the Lord thy God with all thy heart, and with all thy soul, and with all thy mind . . . and thy neighbour as thyself.*
We have no wish to impede this approach from above, for we dare not block the intuitive and rational springs of ethical theory. But I would say—and this is my point of chief insistence—that each of these moral imperatives, and all others that have been or will be devised, can and should be tested and specified with reference to the various forms of psychological analysis that I have here reviewed. By submitting each imperative to psychological scrutiny we can tell whether men are likely to comprehend the principle offered; whether and in what sense it is within their capacity to follow it; what the long-run consequences are likely to be; and whether we find agreement among men in general and among therapists and other meliorists that the imperative is indeed good.
One final word. My discussion of the problem of normality and abnormality has in a sense yielded only a niggardly solution. I have said, in effect, that the criterion we seek has not yet been discovered; nor is it likely to be discovered by psychologists working alone, nor by philosophers working alone. The cooperation of both is needed. Fortunately today psychologists are beginning to ask philosophical questions, and philosophers are beginning to ask psychological questions. Working together they may ultimately formulate the problem aright and, conceivably, solve it.
In the meantime let me state it as my opinion that the work I have reviewed in this paper represents a high level of sophistication, far higher than that which prevailed a short generation ago. Psychologists who in their teaching and counselling follow the lines now laid down will not go far wrong in guiding personalities toward normality.

Notes

1. Shoben, E. J., Jr. 1957. Toward a concept of the normal personality. *American Psychologist*, 12: 183–89.
2. Halmos, P. 1957. *Towards a Measure of Man: the Frontiers of Normal Adjustment.* London: Routledge & Kegan Paul.
3. Wolff, W. 1950. *The Threshold of the Abnormal.* New York: Hermitage House: 131 f.
4. Hall, C., and Lindzey, G. 1957. Cited in *Theories of Personality.* New York: John Wiley & Sons: 492–96.
5. Barron, F. 1954. Personal soundness in university graduate students. *Publications of Personnel Assessment Research,* no. 1. Berkeley: California University Press.
6. Maslow, A. H. 1954. *Motivation and Personality.* New York: Harper Brothers: Chapter 12.
7. Allport, G. W. 1937. *Personality: A Psychological Interpretation.* New York: Henry Holt: Chapter 8.

2

My Philosophy of Interpersonal Relationships and How It Grew

CARL R. ROGERS

In this article I wish to discuss the developments and changes in my attitudes and approaches toward other persons. I will cover not only my professional approach as it has changed over the years, but my personal approach as well.

Let me begin with my childhood. In a narrowly fundamentalist religious home I introjected the value attitudes toward others which were held by my parents. Whether I truly believed in these I cannot be sure. I know that I acted on these values. I think the attitudes toward persons outside our large family can be summed up schematically in this way: Other persons behave in dubious ways which we do not approve in our family. Many of them play cards, go to movies, smoke, dance, drink, and engage in other activities—some unmentionable. So the best thing to do is to be tolerant of them, since they may not know better, and to keep away from any close communication with them and live your life within the family. "Come ye out from among them and be ye separate" is a good Biblical text to follow.

To the best of my recollection this unconsciously arrogant separateness characterized my behavior all through elementary school. I certainly had no close friends. There was a group of boys and girls my age who rode bicycles together on the street behind our house. But I never went to their homes, not did they come to mine.

As to the relations with the others in my family, I thoroughly enjoyed being with and playing with my younger brothers, was jealous

Source: Reprinted by permission from the Journal of Humanistic Psychology, vol. 13, no. 2 (Spring 1973).

of my next older brother, and greatly admired my oldest brother (though the age gap was too great for much communication). I knew my parents loved me, but it would never have occurred to me to share with them any of my personal or private thoughts or feelings because I knew these would have been judged and found wanting. My thoughts, my fantasies, and the few feelings of which I was aware I kept to myself.

I could sum up these boyhood years by saying that anything I would today regard as a close and communicative interpersonal relationship with another was completely lacking during that period. My attitude toward others outside the home was characterized by the distance and the aloofness which I had taken over from my parents.

I attended the same elementary school for seven years. From this point on, until I finished graduate work, I never attended any school for longer than two years, a fact which undoubtedly had its effects on me.

Beginning with high school, I believe my hunger for companionship came a little more into my awareness. But any satisfaction of that hunger was blocked first by the already mentioned attitudes of my parents, and second by circumstances. I attended three different high schools, none for more than two years, commuting long distances by train to each one, so that I never was able to put down any social roots and was never able to participate in any after-school or evening activities with other students. I respected and liked some of my fellow students, and some of them respected and probably liked me—perhaps partly because of my good grades—but there was never time enough to develop a friendship, and certainly I never had any close personal interaction with any of them. I had one date during high school—to attend a senior class dinner.

So, during the important years of adolescence I had no close friend, and only superficial personal contact. I did express some feelings in my English themes during the two terms when I had reasonably understanding teachers. At home I felt increasingly close to my next youngest brother, but an age difference of five years cut down on any deep sharing. I was now more consciously a complete outsider—an onlooker in anything involving personal relationships. I believe my intense scientific interest in collecting and rearing the great night-flying moths was without doubt a partial compensation for the lack of intimate sharing. I realized by now that I was peculiar, a loner, with very little place or opportunity for a place in the world of persons. I was socially incompetent in any but superficial contacts. My fantasies during this period were definitely bizarre, and probably would be classed as schizoid by a diagnostician, but fortunately I never came in contact with a psychologist.

College represented the first break in this solitary experience. I entered the college of argiculture, and almost immediately joined a group of fellows who met in a YMCA class. Starting with this narrow interest we developed into an ongoing, self-directed group carrying on all sorts of activities. Here I first discovered what it meant to have comrades and even friends. There was lively, enjoyable, and interesting discussion of attitudes and ideas about moral and ethical issues. There was even some sharing of personal problems, especially on a one-to-one basis. For two years this group meant a great deal to me, until I shifted to majoring in history in the College of Letters and Science, and gradually lost contact with them.

During this period I suppose I could say that I began my first gropings toward a professional life. I was the leader of a boys club, and enjoyed the experiece. My concept of what to do was limited completely to *activities* in which we could engage—hikes, picnics, swimming, and the like. I don't recall that I ever encouraged, or that we had, any discussions on any matters of interest to the boys. The possibility of communication was evidently beginning to dawn on me so far as my peers were concerned, but I doubt if I ever dreamed of it as a possibility for these twelve-year-olds.

I was also a camp counselor in a camp for underprivileged youngsters during the summer, with 8 counselors and 100 boys under my supervision. The cherry-picking work in which we engaged parttime, and the athletic activities afterward, constituted my idea of a suitable program. Here I have my first memory of a most dubious attempt at a "helping" relationship. Some articles and money had disappeared in our dormitory. The evidence pointed to one boy. So I and several of the counselors took him off by himself to get a confession from him. The term "brainwashing" had not then been invented, but we had real expertise at it. We cajoled, we argued, we persuaded, we were friendly, we were critical—some even prayed for him—but he withstood all our attempts, much to our disappointment. As I look back on this embarrassing scene, I gather that my concept of helping another person was to get him to confess his evil ways so that he might be instructed in the proper way to go.

In other directions, however, I was becoming more of a social being. I began dating girls, fearfully to be sure, but a start. I found I could express myself more freely with older girls, and as a freshman I dated several seniors. I also began going with Helen, the girl who later became my wife, and here an increasingly deep communication of hopes, ideals, aims, gradually began to take place. I discovered that private thoughts and dreams of the future could actually be shared on a mutual basis with another person. It was a very growing experience.

After two years of college Helen and I were separated by distance, but the courtship and frequent contacts continued for two more years before we were married. As I look back I realize this was the first truly caring, close, sharing relationship I had ever formed with anyone. It meant the world to me. During the first two years of marriage we learned a vitally important lesson. We learned, through some chance help, that the elements in the relationship which seemed impossible to share—the secretly disturbing, dissatisfying elements—are the most rewarding to share. This was a hard, risky, frightening thing to learn—and we have relearned it many, many times since. It was a rich and developing experience for each of us.

Meanwhile in graduate school at Union Seminary we were sharing in several courses as well as pursuing our own separate directions—she becoming more of an artist until motherhood occupied much of her time, while I continued my studies. Though I became more and more turned off by the academic courses in religion, there were two experiences which helped to shape my way of relating to others. The first was a self-organized, self-directed seminar of students with no faculty leader. Here we shared responsibility for the topics we considered and the way we wanted to conduct the course. More importantly, we began to share our doubts, our personal problems with our work, and became a mutually trusting group, discussing deep issues which changed the lives of a number of us. The second experience was a course on "Working with Young People" conducted by Goodwin Watson—who is still an active NTL trainer and a progressive leader in education. This course was the first clear realization I had that working closely with individuals might be a profession. It offered me a way out of religious work and as a result of these two experiences I shifted "across the street" (literally) to Teacher's College, Columbia, where Goodwin Watson became my thesis supervisor. I began taking work in clinical psychology. I was also exposed to the thinking of John Dewey, through William Heard Kilpatrick.

My learnings regarding relationships with others had now made tentative steps which were to be important to me later. I had learned that deep sharing with others was possible and enriching. I had learned that in a close relationship the elements which "cannot" be shared are those which are most important and rewarding to share. I had found that a group could be trusted to move in the direction of highly significant and relevant personal learnings. I was even beginning to learn that an individual faculty sponsor could trust the student he was supervising, with only growthful effects. I had discovered that persons in trouble could be helped, but that there were very divergent ideas as to how this could be done.

Meanwhile in my graduate training in clinical psychology I was learning two major ways of relating to individuals who come for help. At Teacher's College the approach was to understand *about* the individual through testing, measurement, diagnostic interviews, and prescriptive advice as to treatment. This cold type of approach was, however, suffused with warmth by the personality of Leta Hollingworth, who taught us more by her person than by her lectures. Later when I interned at the then new and affluent Institute for Child Guidance, I was exposed to a very different atmosphere. Dominated as it was by psychoanalysts, I learned more about the individual—how he cannot be understood without an exhaustive case history 75 pages or more in length which goes into all the personality dynamics of the grandparents, the parents, aunts and uncles, and finally the "patient" himself; possible birth trauma; manner of weaning; degree of dependency; sibling relationships; and on and on. Then there must be the elaborate testing, including the newly imported Rorschach, and finally many interviews with the child before deciding what sort of treatment he should have. It nearly always came out the same: the child was treated psychoanalytically by the psychiatrist, the mother was dealt with in the same fashion by the social worker, and occasionally, the psychologist was asked to tutor the child. Yet I carried on my first therapy case there. It started with tutoring but developed into more and more personal interviews, and I discovered the thrill that comes from observing changes in a person's behavior. Whether those were due to my enthusiasm or my methods I cannot say.

As I look back, I realize that my interest in interviewing and in therapy certainly grew in part out of my early loneliness. Here was a socially approved way of getting really close to individuals, thus filling some of the hungers I had undoubtedly felt. It also offered a chance of becoming close without having to go through the (to me) long and painful process of gradual and deepening acquaintance.

By the time I had completed my work in New York I *knew*—with all the assurance of the newly trained—how to deal with people professionally. In spite of the wide differences between Teacher's College and the Institute, they both helped me arrive at somewhat the same formula which could be stated as follows:

"I will gather an enormous amount of data about this individual:

his history, his intelligence, his special abilities, his personality. Out of all this I can form an elaborate diagnostic formulation as to the causes of his present behavior, his personal and social resources for dealing with his situation, and the prognosis for his future. I will endeavor to interpret all this in simple language to the responsible agencies, to the parents, and to the child if he is capable of understanding it. I will make sound suggestions which, if carried out, will change the behavior, and I will reinforce those suggestions by repeated contact. In all of this I will remain thoroughly objective, professional, and personally aloof from these persons in trouble, except insofar as personal warmth is necessary to build a satisfactory rapport."

This sounds a bit incredible to me now, but I know it is essentially true because I can recall the scorn I felt for one psychiatrist, not an analyst, who simply dealt with problem children as though he *liked* them. He even took them to his home. Clearly he had never learned the importance of being *professional!*

Thus when I went to Rochester, New York, as a member of a "Child Study Department" (really a child guidance clinic for delinquent children and those who were wards of the social agencies because of their poor home environment), I knew what to do. I was so sure, that I remember (painfully) that I told PTA and community groups that our clinic was rather similar to a garage—you brought in a problem, received an expert diagnosis, and were advised how the difficulty could be corrected.

But my views were gradually eroded. Living in a stable community I found I had to live with the consequences of my advice and recommendations—and they did *not* always work out. Many of the children I worked with were housed temporarily in the detention home next door, so I could see them day after day. I was astonished that sometimes, after a particularly "good" interview where I had interpreted to a boy all the causes of his misbehavior, he refused to see me the next day! So I had to win him back to find out what had gone wrong. I began to learn, experientially.

Then as director of the new and independent Rochester Guidance Center, which replaced the Child Study Department, we had more self-referrals. In these cases, we had no authority whatsoever over child or parent and had to build a relationship if we were to be of help.

Then came a few incidents which markedly changed my approach. I have written about the most vivid one, but I will repeat it here. An intelligent mother brought her very seriously misbehaving boy to the clinic. I took the history from her myself. Another psychologist tested the boy. We decided in conference that the central problem was the mother's rejection of her son. I would work with her on this problem. The other psychologist would take the boy on for play therapy. In interview after interview I tried—much more softly and gently now, as a result of experience—to help the mother see the pattern of her rejection and its results in the boy. All to no avail. After about a dozen interviews I told her I thought we both had tried but were getting nowhere, and we should probably call it quits. She agreed. Then as she was leaving the room, she turned and asked, "Do you ever take adults for counseling here?" Puzzled, I replied that sometimes we did. Whereupon she returned to the chair she had just left and began to pour out a story of the deep difficulties between herself and her husband and her great desire for some kind of help. I was bowled over. What she was telling me bore no resemblance to the neat history I had drawn from her. I scarcely knew what to do, but mostly I listened. Eventually, after many more interviews, not only did her marital relationship improve, but her son's problem behavior dropped away as she became a more real and free person. To jump ahead a bit, she was the first client I ever had who continued to keep in occasional touch with me for years afterward, until her boy was doing well in college.

This was a vital learning for me. I had followed *her* lead rather than mine. I had just *listened* instead of trying to nudge her toward a diagnostic understanding I had already reached. It was a far more personal relationship and not nearly so "professional." Yet the results spoke for themselves.

At about this time came a brief two-day seminar with Otto Rank, and I found that in his therapy (not in his theory) he was emphasizing some of the things I had begun to learn. I felt stimulated and confirmed. I employed a social worker, trained in Rankian "relationship therapy" at the Philadelphia School of Social Work, and learned much from her. So my views shifted more and more. This transition is well captured in my book, *Clinical Treatment of the Problem Child,* written in 1937–38, where I devote a long chapter to relationship therapy, though the rest of the book is largely a diagnostic-prescriptive approach.

At Ohio State, where I went in 1940, I was greatly enriched as I tried to teach my views of clinical work to bright and questioning graduate students. Here too, I began to realize that I was saying something new (perhaps even original) about counseling and psychotherapy, and I wrote the book of that title. My dream of recording therapeutic interviews came true and helped to focus my interest on the effect of different responses in the interview. This led to a heavy emphasis on technique—the so-called "nondirective technique."

But I was finding that this new-found trust in my client and his capacity for exploring and resolving his problems reached out uncomfortably into other areas. If I trusted my clients, why didn't I trust my students? If this was fine for the individual in trouble, why not for a staff group facing problems? I found that I had embarked not on a new *method*, but a sharply different *philosophy* of living and relationships.

I worked out some of these issues while at Ohio State, and when I was given an opportunity to start a new Counseling Center at the University of Chicago, setting my own policies and selecting my own staff, I was ready to formulate and act on what was for me a new approach to human relationships. I think I can again state it in summarized fashion.

"I have come to trust persons—their capacity for exploring and understanding themselves and their troubles, and their ability to resolve those problems—in any close, continuing relationship where I can provide a climate of real warmth and understanding."

"I am going to venture to put the same kind of trust in a staff group, endeavoring to build an atmosphere in which each is responsible for the actions of the group as a whole, and where the group has a responsibility to each individual. Authority has been given to me, and I am going to give it completely to the group."

"I am going to experiment with putting trust in students, in class groups, to choose their own directions and to evaluate their progress in terms of their own choosing."

Chicago was a time of great learning for me. I had ample opportunity to test out the hypotheses I have just stated. I greatly expanded the empirical testing of our therapeutic hypotheses which had begun earlier. By 1957 I had developed a rigorous theory of therapy and the therapeutic relationship. I had set forth the "necessary and sufficient conditions for therapeutic personality change," all of them personal *attitudes,* not professional training. This was a rather presumptuous paper, but it presented hypotheses to be tested and sparked much research over the next 15 years, which has in general been confirming.

It was a period when, at the urging of my students, I became acquainted with Martin Buber (first, in his writings, and then personally) and with Soren Kierkegaard. I felt greatly supported in my new approach, which I found to my surprise was a home-grown brand of existential philosophy.

Finally it was a period of great learning in my personal life. A badly bungled therapeutic relationship (really nontherapeutic) thrust me into a deep internal personal crisis and finally into therapy with one of my colleagues. I now learned just what is was like to experience on one day a tremendous surge of fresh insight, only to seem to lose it all the next in a wave of despair. But as I slowly came out of this, I at last learned what many people, fortunately, learn first. I learned that not only could I trust clients, staff, and students, but I could trust myself. Slowly I learned to trust the feelings, the ideas, the purposes which continually emerge in *me*. It was not an easy learning, but a most valuable and continuing one. I found myself becoming more free, more real, more deeply understanding not only in my relationships with my clients but with others too.

All of these learnings I have mentioned carried over increasingly in my relationships with groups—first the workshops we started in Chicago as early as 1946, then in the groups with which I have been so much involved in recent years. They have all been encounter groups, long before the term was coined.

I will quickly cover the years at Wisconsin and La Jolla. At Wisconsin I rediscovered what I had learned at Chicago—that by and large most psychologists are not open to new ideas. Perhaps this is true of me, too, though I have struggled against that defensive tendency. But students, as before were most responsive.

In one experience at Wisconsin, I violated one of the learnings I had so painfully acquired and discovered what disaster that can bring. In the large research team assembled for the task of studying psychotherapy with schizophrenics, I gave over the authority and responsibility to the group. But I did not go far enough in establishing the climate of close, open, interpersonal communication which is fundamental for carrying such responsibility. Then, as serious crises developed, I made the even more fatal mistake of trying to draw back into my own hands the authority I had given the group. Rebellion and chaos were the very understandable result. It was one of the most painful lessons I have ever learned; a lesson in how *not* to carry on participative management of an enterprise.

In La Jolla, my experience has been much happier. A highly congenial group eventually formed the Center for Studies of the Person, a most unusual and exciting experiment. I will try to describe only its interpersonal aspects, because if would be impossible to describe all the activities of its members, which range from Kenya to Rome to Ireland, from New Jersey to Colorado to Seattle, from psychotherapy to writing to esoteric research, from consulting with organizations to leading groups of all kinds, from encouraging learning in group facilitation to igniting revolutions in educational methods. Psychologically we are a close community, supporting each other but criticizing each other just as openly. Though our director has routine responsibilities, no one is in authority over anyone else. Everyone can do as he wishes, alone or in concert with others. Everyone is responsible for his own support. Currently we have only one small grant, and that from a private foundation. We do not like the strings (often initially invisible) which are attached to large or government grants. There is absolutely nothing which holds us together except a common interest in the dignity and capacity of persons and the continuing possibility of deep and real communication with each other. To me, it is a great experiment in building a functioning group (a nonorganization really) entirely around the strength of interpersonal sharing.

But I could easily go on too long in my enthusiasm. There is one other input to my learning which I should like to mention. It was first brought to my attention many years ago by Leona Tyler, who in a personal letter pointed out to me that my thinking and action seemed to be something of a bridge between Eastern and Western thought. This was a surprising idea, but I find that in more recent years I have enjoyed some of the techniques of Buddhism, of Zen, and especially the sayings of Lao-tse, the Chinese sage who lived some 25 centuries ago. Let me read a few of his thoughts to which I resonate very deeply:

> It is as though he listened
> and such listening as his enfolds us in a silence
> in which at last we begin to hear
> what we are meant to be.[1]

One statement combines two of my favorite thinkers. Martin Buber endeavors to explain the Taoist principle of "wu-wei," which is really the action of the whole being, but so effortless when it is most effective that it is often called the principle of "nonaction," a rather misleading term. Buber, in explaining this concept, says:

> To interfere with the life of things means to harm both them and oneself. . . . He who imposes himself has the small, manifest might; he who does not impose himself has the great, secret might. . . .
> The perfected man . . . does not interfere in the life of beings, he does not impose himself on them, but he "helps all beings to their freedom (Lao-tse)." Through his unity, he leads them too, to unity, he liberates their nature and their destiny, he releases Tao in them.[2]

I suppose that my effort with people has increasingly been to liberate "their nature and their destiny."

Or if one is seeking a definition of an effective group facilitator one need look no further than Lao-tse:

A leader is best
When people barely know that he exists
Not so good when people obey and acclaim him
Worst when they despise him. . . .
But of a good leader, who talks little
When his work is done, his aim fulfilled
They will all say, "We did this ourselves."[3]

But perhaps my favorite saying, which sums up many of my deeper beliefs, is another from Lao-Tse:

If I keep from meddling with people, they take care of themselves,
If I keep from commanding people, they behave themselves,
If I keep from preaching at people, they improve themselves,
If I keep from imposing on people, they become themselves.[4]

I will admit that this saying is an oversimplification, yet for me it contains the sort of truth which we have not yet appreciated in our Western culture.

Conclusion

I trust I have made it clear that over the years I have moved a long way from some of the beliefs with which I started: that man is essentially evil; that professionally he is best treated as an object; that help is based on expertise; that the expert could advise, manipulate, and mold the individual to produce the desired result.

Let me, in contrast, try to summarize the learnings in which I currently believe, and by which I would like to live. As I have indicated, I frequently fail to profit by these learnings, failing many times in small ways and occasionally, in enormous blunders, I will list the learnings not in the order in which they occurred to me but in what appears to be a more natural order.

I have come to prize each emerging facet of my experience, of myself. I would like to treasure the feelings of anger and tenderness and shame and hurt and love and anxiety and giving and fear—all the positive and negative reactions which crop up. I would like to treasure the ideas which emerge—foolish, creative, bizarre, sound, trivial—all a part of me. I like the behavioral impulses—appropriate, crazy, achievement-oriented, sexual, murderous. I want to accept each of these feelings, ideas, and impulses as an enriching part of me. I do not expect to act on all of them, but when I accept them all I can be more real. My behavior, therefore, will be much more appropriate to the immediate situation.

On the basis of my experience I have found that if I can help bring about a climate marked by genuineness, prizing, and understanding, then exciting things happen. Persons and groups in such a climate move away from rigidity and toward flexibility, away from static living toward process living, away from dependence toward autonomy, away from being predictable toward an unpredictable creativity, away from defensiveness toward self-acceptance. They exhibit living proof of an actualizing tendency.

Because of this evidence I have developed a deep *trust* in myself, in individuals, and in groups, when we are exposed to such a growth-promoting climate.

Also because of this experience I find that I love to create such an environment in which persons, groups (and even plants) can grow.

I have learned that in any significant or continuing relationship feelings which are persistent had best be expressed. If they are expressed as *feelings*, owned by *me*, the result may be temporarily upsetting but ultimately far more rewarding than any attempt to deny or conceal them.

I believe that for me interpersonal relationships best exist as a rhythm—openness and expression, and then assimilation; flow and change, then a temporary quiet; risk and anxiety, then temporary security. I could not live in a continuous encounter group.

For me, being transparently open is far more rewarding than being defensive. This is difficult to achieve, even partially, but enormously enriching to a relationship.

It is necessary for me to stay close to the earthiness of real experience. I cannot live my life in abstractions. Consequently, real relationships with persons, hands dirtied in the soil, observing the budding of a flower, or viewing the sunset, are necessary to my life. At least one foot must be in the soil of reality.

I like my life best when it faces outward most of the time. I prize the times when I am inward-looking, searching to know myself, meditating and thinking. But in my case this must be balanced by doing things—interacting with people, producing something—whether a flower or a book or a piece of carpentry.

Finally, I have a deep belief, which can only be a hypothesis, that the philosophy of interpersonal relationships which I have helped to formulate, and which is contained in this paper, is applicable to all situations involving persons. I believe it is applicable to therapy, to marriage, to parent and child, to teacher and student, to high status and low status, to persons of one race relating to persons of another. I am even brash enough to believe that it could be effective in situations now dominated by the exercise of raw power—in politics, but especially in our dealings with other nations. I challenge, with all the strength I possess, the current American belief, evident in every phase of our foreign policy, and especially in our insane wars, that "might makes right." That, in my estimation, is the road to self-destruction. I go along with Martin Buber and the ancient oriental sages: "He who imposes himself has the small, manifest might; he who does not impose himself has the great, secret might."*

NOTES

1. Bynner, W., trans. 1962. *The Way of Life According to Lao-tsu.* New York: Capricorn Books.
2. Buber, M. 1957. *Pointing the Way.* New York: Harper & Row.
3. Bynner, op. cit.
4. Friedman, M. 1972. *Touchstones of Reality.* New York: E. P. Dutton.

*An earlier, much longer autobiography of Rogers can be found in *History of Psychology in Autobiography*, vol. 5, edited by E. Boring and G. Lindzey. New York: Appleton-Century-Crofts, 1967.

3

A Theory of Metamotivation: The Biological Rooting of the Value-Life

ABRAHAM H. MASLOW

I

Self-actualizing individuals (more matured, more fully-human),
by definition, already suitably gratified in their basic needs, are now
*motivated in other higher ways, to be called "metamotivations."**

This is to say that they have a feeling of belongingness and
rootedness, they are satisfied in their love needs, have friends and feel
loved and loveworthy, they have status and place in life and respect
from other people, and they have a reasonable feeling of worth and
self-respect. If we phrase this negatively—in terms of the frustration of
these basic needs and in terms of pathology—then this is to say that
self-actualizing people do not (for any length of time) feel anxiety-
ridden, rootless, or isolated, nor do they have crippling feelings of infe-
riority or worthlessness (Maslow, 1954, Chap. 12).

Of course this can be phrased in other ways and this I have done.
For instance, since the basic needs had been assumed to be the only
motivations for human beings, it was possible, and in certain contexts
also useful, to say of self-actualizing people that they were "unmoti-
vated" (Maslow, 1954, Chap. 15). This was to align these people with
the Eastern philosophical view of health as the transcendence of striving or desiring.

It was also possible to describe self-actualizing people as expressing rather than coping, and to stress that they were spontaneous, and
natural, that they were more easily themselves than other people.

*The twenty-eight italicized theses listed here are presented as testable propositions.

Each of these phrasings has its own operational usefulness in particular research contexts. But it is also true that for certain purposes it is best to ask the question, "What motivates the self-actualizing person?"

Clearly we must make an immediate distinction between the ordinary motives of people below the level of self-actualization—that is, people motivated by the basic needs—and the motivations of people who are sufficiently gratified in all their basic needs and therefore are no longer motivated by them primarily, but rather by "higher" motivations. It is therefore convenient to call these higher motives and needs of self-actualizing persons by the name "metaneeds" and also to differentiate the category of motivation from the category of "metamotivation."

(It is now more clear to me that gratification of the basic needs is not a sufficient condition for metamotivation, although it may be a necessary precondition. I have individual subjects in whom apparent basic-need-gratification is compatible with "existential neurosis," meaninglessness, valuelessness, or the like. Metamotivation now seems *not* to ensue automatically after basic-need-gratification. One must speak also of the additional variable of "defenses against metamotivation" [Maslow, 1967]. This implies that, for the strategy of communication and of theory-building, it may turn out to be useful to add to the definition of the self-actualizing person, not only [a] that he be sufficiently free of illness, [b] that he be sufficiently gratified in his basic needs, and [c] that he be positively using his capacities, but also [d] that he be motivated by some values which he strives for or gropes for and to which he is loyal.)

II

All such people are devoted to some task, call, vocation, beloved work ("outside themselves").

Generally the devotion and dedication is so marked that one can fairly use the old words vocation, calling, or mission to describe their passionate, selfless, and profound feeling for their "work." We could even use the words destiny or fate. I have sometimes gone so far as to speak of oblation in the religious sense, in the sense of offering oneself or dedicating oneself upon some altar for some particular task, some cause outside oneself and bigger than oneself, something not merely selfish, something impersonal.

I think it is possible to go pretty far with the notion of destiny or fate. This is a way of putting into inadequate words the feeling that one gets when one listens to self-actualizing people (and some others) talking about their work or task (Maslow, 1965a). One gets the feeling of a beloved job, and, furthermore, of something for which the person is a "natural," something that he is suited for, something that is right for him, even something that he was born for.

It should be said that the above seems to hold true for my female subjects even though in a different sense. I have at lease one woman subject who devoted herself entirely to the task of being the mother, the wife, the housewife and the clan matriarch. Her vocation, one could very reasonably call it, was to bring up her children, to make her husband happy, and to hold together a large number of relatives in a network of personal relations. This she did very well and, as nearly as I could make out, this she enjoyed. She loved her lot completely and totally, never yearning for anything else so far as I could tell, and using all her capacities well in the process. Other women subjects have had various combinations of home life and professional work outside the home which could produce this same sense of dedication to something perceived simultaneously, as both as beloved and also as important and worthwhile doing. In some women, I have also been tempted to think of "having a baby" as fullest self-actualization all by itself, at least for a time.

III

In the ideal instance, inner requiredness coincides with external requiredness, "I want to" with "I must."
I often get the feeling in this kind of situation that I can tease apart two kinds of determinants of this transaction. One can be spoken of as the responses within the person, e.g., "I love babies (or painting, or research, or political power) more than anything in the world. I am fascinated with it. . . . I an inexorably drawn to . . . I need to . . ." This we may call "inner requiredness" and it is felt as a kind of self-indulgence rather than as a duty It is different from and separable from "external requiredness," which is rather felt as a response to what the environment, the situation, requires of the person, as a fire "calls for" putting out, or as a helpless baby demands that one take care of it, or as some obvious injustice calls for righting (Maslow, 1963). Here one feels

more the element of duty, or obligation, or responsibility, of being compelled helplessly to respond no matter what one was planning to do, or wished to do. It is more "I must, I have to, I am compelled" than "I want to."

In the ideal instance, which fortunately also happens in fact in many of my instances, "I want to" coincides with "I must."

I hesitate to call this simply "purposefulness" because that may imply that it happens only out of will, purpose, decision, or calculation, and doesn't give enough weight to the subjective feeling of being swept along, of willing and eager surrender, or yielding to fate and happily embracing it at the same time. Ideally, one also *discovers* one's fate; it is not only made or constructed or decided upon. It is recognized as if one had been unwittingly waiting for it. Perhaps the better phrase would be "Spinozistic" or "Taoistic" choice or decision or purpose— or even will.

The best way to communicate these feelings to someone who doesn't intuitively, directly understand them is to use as a model "falling in love." This is clearly different from doing one's duty, or doing what is sensible or logical. And clearly also "will," if mentioned at all, is used in a very special sense. And when two people love each other fully, then each one knows what it feels like to be magnet and what it feels like to be iron filings, and what it feels like to be both simultaneously.

IV

This ideal situation generates feelings of good fortune and also of ambivalence and unworthiness.

This model also helps to convey what is difficult to communicate in words, that is, their sense of good fortune, of luck, of gratuitous grace, of awe that this miracle should have occurred, of wonder that they should have been chosen, and of the peculiar mixture of pride fused with humility, of arrogance shot through with the pity-for-the-less-fortunate that one finds in lovers.

Of course the possibility of good fortune and success also can set into motion all sorts of neurotic fears, feelings of unworthiness, countervalues, Jonah-syndrome dynamics (Maslow, 1967), etc. These defenses against our highest possibilities must be overcome before the highest values can be wholeheartedly embraced.

V

At this level the dichotomizing of work and play is transcended; wages, hobbies, vacations, etc., must be defined at a higher level.

And then, of course, it can be said of such a person with real meaningfulness that he is being his own kind of person, of being himself, or actualizing his real self. An abstract statement, an extrapolation out from this kind of observation toward the ultimate and perfect ideal would run something like this: This person is the best one in the whole world for this particular job, and this particular job is the best job in the world for this particular person and his talents, capacities, and tastes. He was meant for it, and it was meant for him.

Of course, as soon as we accept this and get the feel of it, then we move over into another realm of discourse, i.e., the realm of being (Maslow, 1962a; Maslow, 1962b), of transcendence. Now we can speak meaningfully only in the language of geing ("The B-language," communication at the mystical level, etc.). For instance, it is quite obvious with such people that the ordinary or conventional dichotomy between work and play is transcended totally (Marcuse, 1955; Maslow, 1965a). That is, there is certainly no distinction between work and play in such a person in such a situation. His work is his play and his play is his work. If a person loves his work and enjoys it more than any other activity in the whole world and is eager to get to it, to get back to it after any interruption, then how can we speak about "labor" in the sense of something one is forced to do against one's wishes?

VI

Such vocation-loving individuals tend to identify (introject, incorporate) with their "work" and to make it into a defining-characteristic of the self. It becomes part of the self.

If one asks such a person, i.e., self-actualizing, work-loving, "Who are you?" or "What are you?" he often tends to answer in terms of his "call," e.g., "I am a lawyer." "I am a mother." "I am a psychiatrist." "I am an artist," etc.

Or, if one asks him, "Supposing you were not a scientist (or a teacher, or a pilot), then what would you be?" Or, "Supposing you were not a psychologist, then what?" It is my impression that his response is apt to be one of puzzlement, thoughtfulness, being taken aback, i.e., not having a ready answer. Or the response can be one of amusement, i.e., it is funny. In effect, the answer is, "If I were not a mother (anthropologist, industrialist), then I wouldn't be *me*. I would be someone else. And I can't imagine being someone else."

This kind of response parallels the confused response to the question, "Supposing you were a woman rather than a man?"

A tentative conclusion is then that in self-actualizing subjects, their beloved calling tends to be perceived as a defining characteristic of the self, to be identified with, incorporated, introjected. It becomes an inextricable aspect of one's being.

VII

The tasks to which they are dedicated seem to be interpretable as embodiments or incarnations of intrinsic values (rather than as a means to ends outside the work itself, and rather than as functionally autonomous). The tasks are loved (and introjected) BECAUSE *they embody these values. That is, ultimately it is the values that are loved rather than the job as such.*

For these people the profession seems to be *not* functionally autonomous, but rather to be a carrier of, an instrument of, or an incarnation of ultimate values. For them the profession of, e.g., law is a means to the end of justice, and not an end in itself. Perhaps I can communicate my feeling for the subtle difference in this way: for one man the law is loved because it *is* justice, while another man, the pure value-free technologist, might love the law simply as an intrinsically lovable set of rules, precedents, procedures without regard to the ends or products of their use.

VIII

These intrinsic values overlap greatly with the B-values, and perhaps are identical with them.

I feel it desirable to use my description of the B-values, not only because it would be theoretically pretty if I could, but also because they are operationally definable in so many different ways (Maslow, 1962b; 1964a, Appendix G). That is to say, they are found at the end of so many different investigative roads, that the suspicion arises that there is something in common between these different paths, e.g., education, art, religion, psychotherapy, peak-experiences, science, mathematics, etc. If this turns out to be so, we may perhaps add as another road to final values, the "cause," the mission, the vocation, that is to say, the "work" of self-actualizing people.

IX

This introjection means that the self has enlarged to include aspects of the world and that therefore the distinction between self and not-self (outside, other) has been transcended.

These B-values or metamotives are not longer *only* intrapsychic or organismic. They are equally inner and outer. The metaneeds, insofar as they are inner, and the requiredness of all that is outside the person move toward becoming indistinguishable, that is, toward fusion.

Certainly simple selfishness is transcended here and has to be defined at higher levels. For instance, we know that it is possible for a person to get more pleasure (selfish? unselfish?) out of food through having his child eat it than through eating it with his own mouth. His self has enlarged enough to include his child. Hurt his child and you hurt him. Clearly the self can no longer be identified with the biological entity which is applied with blood from his heart along his blood vessels. The psychological self can obviously be bigger than its own body.

There are other important consequences of this incorporation of values into the self. For instance, you can love justice and truth in the world or in a person out there. You can be made happier as your friends move toward truth and justice, and sadder as they move away from it. This is easy to understand. But supposing you see yourself moving successfully toward truth, justice, beauty, and virtue? Then of course you may find that, in a peculiar kind of detachment and objectivity toward oneself, for which our culture has no place, you will be loving and admiring yourself, in the kind of healthy self-love that Fromm (1947) has described. You can respect yourself, admire yourself, take tender care of yourself, reward yourself, feel virtuous, loveworthy, respect-worthy. You may then treat yourself with the responsibility and otherness that, for instance, a pregnant woman does, whose self now has to be defined to include not-self. So also may a person with a great talent protect it and himself as if he were a carrier of something which is simultaneously himself and not himself. He may become his own guardian, so to speak.

X

Less evolved persons seem to use their work more often for achieving gratification of lower basic needs, of neurotic needs, as a means to an end, out of habit, or as a response to cultural expectations, etc. However, it is probable that these are differences of degree. Perhaps all human beings are (potentially) metamotivated to a degree.

The conventional categories of career, profession, or work may serve as channels of many other kinds of motivations, not to mention sheer habit or convention or functional autonomy. They may satisfy or seek vainly to satisfy any or all of the basic needs as well as various neurotic needs. They may be a channel for "acting out" or for "defensive" activities as well as for real gratifications.

All these various habits, determinants, motives, and metamotives are acting simultaneously in a very complex pattern which is centered more toward one kind of motivation or determinedness than the others. This is to say that the most highly developed persons we know are metamotivated to a much higher degree, and are basic-need-motivated to a lesser degree than average or diminished people are.

XI

The full definition of the person or of human nature must then include intrinsic values, as part of human nature.

If we then try to define the deepest, most authentic, most constitutionally based aspects of the real self, of the identity, or of the authentic person, we find that in order to be comprehensive we must include not only the person's constitution and temperament, not only anatomy, psychology, neurology, and endocrinology, not only his capacities, his biological style, not only his basic instinctoid needs, but also the B-values, which are also *his* B-values.

XII

These intrinsic values are instinctoid in nature, i.e., they are needed (a) to avoid illness and (b) to achieve fullest humanness or growth. The "illnesses" resulting from deprivation of intrinsic values (metaneeds) we may call metapathologies. The "highest" values, the spiritual life, the highest aspirations of mankind are therefore proper subjects for scientific study and research. They are in the world of nature.

These "illnesses" (which come from deprivation of the B-values or metaneeds or B-facts) are new and have not yet been described as such, i.e., as pathologies, except unwittingly, or by implication, or, as by Frankl (1966), in a very general and inclusive way, not yet teased apart into researchable form. In feneral, they have been discussed through the centuries by religionists, historians, and philosophers under the rubric of spiritual or religious shortcomings, rather than by physicians, scientists, or psychologists under the rubric of psychiatric or psychological or biological "illnesses" or stuntings or diminutions. To some extent also there is some overlap with sociological and political disturbances, "social pathologies," and the like.

I will call these "illnesses" (or, better, diminutions of humanness) "metapathologies" and define them as the consequences of deprivation of the B-values either in general or of specific B-values.

XIII

The metapathologies of the affluent and indulged young come partly from deprivation of intrinsic values, frustrated "idealism," from disillusionment with a society they see (mistakenly) motivated only by lower or animal or material needs.

My hypothesis is that this behavior can be a fusion of continued search for something to believe in, combined with anger at being disappointed. (I sometimes see in a particular young man total despair or hopelessness about even the *existence* of such values.)

Of course, this frustrated idealism and occasional hopelessness is partially due to the influence and ubiquity of stupidly limited theories of motivation all over the world. Leaving aside behavioristic and positivistic theories—or rather non-theories—as simple refusals even to see the problem, i.e., a kind of psychoanalytic denial, then what is available to the idealistic young man and woman?

Not only does the whole of official nineteenth-century science and orthodox academic psychology offer him nothing, but also the major motivation theories by which most men live can lead him only to depression or cynicism. The Freudians, at least in their official writings (though not in good therapeutic practice), are still reductionistic about all higher human values. The deepest and most real motivations are seen to be dangerous and nasty, while the highest human values and virtues are essentially fake, being not what they seem to be, but camouflaged versions of the "deep, dark, and dirty." Our social scientists are just as disappointing in the main. A total cultural determinism is still the official, orthodox doctrine of many or most of the sociologists and anthropologists. This doctrine not only denies intrinsic higher motivations, but comes perilously close sometimes to denying "human nature" itself. The economists, not only in the West but also in the East, are essentially materialistic. We must say harshly of the "science" of economics that it is generally the skilled, exact, technological application of a totally false theory of human needs and values, a theory which recognizes only the existence of lower needs or material needs (Schumacher, 1967; Weisskopf, 1963; Wootton, 1967).

How could young people not be disappointed and disillusioned? What else could be the result of *getting* all the material and animal gratifications and then *not being happy,* as they were led to expect, not only by the theorists, but also by the conventional wisdom of parents and teachers, and the insistent gray lies of the advertisers?

What happens then to the "eternal verities"? to the ultimate truths? Most sections of the society agree in handing them over to the churches and to dogmatic, institutionalized, conventionalized religious organizations. But this is also a denial of high human nature! It says in effect that the youngster who is looking for something will definitely *not* find it in human nature itself. He must look for ultimates to a non-human, non-natural source, a source which is definitely mistrusted or rejected altogether by many intelligent young people today.

XIV

This value-starvation and value-hunger come both from external deprivation and from our inner ambivalence and counter-values.

Not only are we passively value-deprived into metapathology by the environment. We also fear the highest values, both within ourselves and outside ourselves. Not only are we attracted; we are also awed, stunned, chilled, frightened. That is to say, we tend to be ambivalent and conflicted. We defend ourselves against the B-values. Repression, denial, reaction-formation, and probably all the Freudian defense-mechanisms are available and are used against the highest within ourselves just as they are mobilized against the lowest within ourselves. Humility and a sense of unworthiness can lead to evasion of the highest values. So also can the fear of being overwhelmed by the tremendousness of these values. (In another paper [1967] I have called this the Jonah-syndrome and described it more fully.)

XV

The hierarchy of basic needs is prepotent to the metaneeds.

Basic needs and metaneeds are in the same hierarchial-integration, i.e., on the same continuum, in the same realm of discourse. They have the same basic characteristic of being "needed" (necessary, good for the person) in the sense that their deprivation produces "illness" and diminution, and that their "ingestion" fosters growth toward full-humanness, toward greater happiness and joy, toward psychological "success," toward more peak-experiences, and in general toward living more often at the level of being. That is, they are *all* biologically desirable, and *all* foster biological success. And yet, they are also different in definable ways.

First of all, it is clear that the whole hierarchy of the basic needs is prepotent to the metaneeds, or, to say it in another way, the metaneeds are postpotent (less urgent or demanding, weaker) to the basic needs. I intend this as a generalized statistical statement because I find some single individuals in whom a special-talent or a unique sensitivity makes truth or beauty or goodness, for that single person, more important and more pressing than some basic need.

Secondly, the basic needs can be called deficiency-needs, having the various characteristics already described for deficiency-needs, while the metaneeds seem rather to have the special characteristics described for "growth-motivations" (Maslow, 1962a, Chap. 3).

XVI

The metaneeds are equally potent among themselves, on the average—i.e., I cannot detect a generalized hierarchy of prepotency. But in any given individual, they may be and often are hierarchically arranged according to idiosyncratic talents and constitutional differences.

The metaneeds (or B-values, or B-facts) so far as I can make out are not arranged in a hierarchy of prepotency, but seem, all of them, to be equally potent on the *average*. Another way of saying this, a phrasing that is useful for other purposes, is that each individual seems to have his own priorities or hierarchy or prepotency, in accordance with his own talents, temperament, skills, capacities, etc. Beauty is more important than truth to one person, but for his brother it may be the other way about with equal statistical likelihoodl

XVII

It looks as if any intrinsic or B-value is fully defined by most or all of the other B-values. Perhaps they form a unity of some sort, with each specific B-value being simply the whole seen from another angle.
That is, truth, to be fully and completely defined, must be beautiful, good, perfect, just, simple, orderly, lawful, alive, comprehensive, unitary, dichotomy-transcending, effortless, and amusing (Maslow, 1962b). (The formula, "The truth, the whole truth, and nothing but the truth," is certainly quite inadequate.) Beauty, fully defined, must be true, good, perfect, alive, simple, etc.

XVIII

The value-life (spiritual, religious, philosophical, axiological, etc.) is an aspect of human biology and is on the same continuum with the "lower" animal life (rather than being in separated, dichotomized, or mutually exclusive realms). It is probably therefore species-wide, supracultural even though it must be actualized by culture in order to exist.
The spiritual life is part of the human essence. It is a defining-characteristic of human nature, without which human nature is not full human nature. It is part of the Real Self, of one's identity, of one's specieshood, of full-humanness. To the extent that pure expressing of oneself, or pure spontaneity, is possible, to that extent will the metaneeds also be expressed. "Uncovering" or Taoistic or existential therapeutic or logotherapeutic (Frankl, 1966), or "ontogogic" techniques (Bugental, 1965), should uncover and strengthen the metaneeds as well as the basic needs.
Depth-diagnostic and therapeutic techniques should ultimately also uncover these same metaneeds because, paradoxically, our "highest nature" is also our "deepest nature." The value life and the animal life are not in two separate realms as most religions and philoso-

phies have assumed, and as classical, impersonal science has also assumed. The spiritual life (the contemplative, "religious," philosophical, or value-life) is within the jurisdiction of human thought and is attainable in principle by man's own efforts. Even though it has been cast out of the realm of reality by the classical, value-free science which models itself upon physics, it can be reclaimed as an object of study and technology by humanistic science.

Let me also make quite explicit the implication that metamotivation is species-wide, and is, therefore, supracultural, common-human, not created arbitrarily by culture. Since this is a point at which misunderstandings are fated to occur, let me say it so: the metaneeds seem to me to be instinctoid, that is, to have an appreciable hereditary, species-wide determination. But they are potentialities, rather than actualities. Culture is definitely and absolutely needed for their actualization; but also culture can fail to actualize them, and indeed this is just what most known cultures actually seem to do and to have done throughout history. Therefore, there is implied here a supracultural factor which can criticize any culture from outside and above that culture, namely, in terms of the degree to which it fosters or suppresses self-actualization, full-humanness, and metamotivation (Maslow, 1964b).

The so-called spiritual (or transcendent, or axiological) life is clearly rooted in the biological nature of the species. It is a kind of "higher" animality whose precondition is a healthy "lower" animality, i.e., they are hierarchically-integrated (rather than mutually exclusive). But this higher, spiritual "animality" is so timid and weak, and so easily lost, is so easily crushed by stronger cultural forces, that it can become widely actualized *only* in a culture which approves of human nature, and therefore actively fosters its fullest growth.

XIX

Pleasures and gratifications can be arranged in hierarchy of levels from lower to higher. So also can hedonistic theories be seen as ranging from lower to higher, i.e., metahedonism.

The B-values, seen as gratifications of metaneeds, are then also the highest pleasures or happiness that we know of.

I have suggested elsewhere (1966) the need for and usefulness of being conscious that there is a hierarchy of pleasures, ranging from, e.g., relief from pain, through the contentment of a hot tub, the happiness of being with good friends, the joy of great music, the bliss of having a child, the ecstasy of the highest love-experiences, on up to the fusion with the B-values.

Such a hierarchy suggests a solution of the problem of hedonism, selfishness, duty, etc. If one includes the highest pleasures among the pleasures in general, then it becomes true in a very real sense that fully-human people also seek only for pleasure, i.e., metapleasure. Perhaps we can call this "metahedonism" and then point out that at this level there is then no contradiction between pleasure and duty since the highest obligations of human beings are certainly to truth, justice, beauty, etc., which however are also the highest pleasures that the species can experience. And of course at this level of discourse the mutual exclusiveness between selfishness and unselfishness has also disappeared. What is good for us is good for everyone else, what is gratifying is praiseworthy, our appetites are now trustworthy, rational, and wise, what we enjoy is good for us, seeking our own (highest) good is also seeking the general good, etc.

XX

Since the spiritual life is instinctoid, all the techniques of "subjective biology" apply to its education.

The spiritual life (B-values, B-facts, metaneeds, etc.) can in principle be introspected. It has "impulse voices" or "inner signals" which, though weaker than basic needs, can yet be "heard," and which therefore comes under the rubric of the "subjective biology" I have described (Maslow, 1965b, 1967).

In principle, therefore, all the principles and exercises which help to develop (or teach) our sensory awarenesses, our body awarenesses, our sensitivities to the inner signals (given off by our needs, capacities, constitution, temperament, body, etc.)—all these apply also, though less strongly, to our inner metaneeds, i.e., to the education of our yearnings for beauty, law, truth, perfection, etc. I have used the term "experientially empty" to describe those persons whose inner signals are either absent or remain unperceived. Perhaps we can also invent some such term as "experientially rich" to describe those who are so sensitive to the inner voices of the self that even the metaneeds can be consciously introspected and enjoyed.

It is this experiential richness which in principle should be "teachable" or recoverable, I feel confident, at least in degree, perhaps with the proper use of psychedelic chemicals, with Esalen-type, non-verbal methods,* with meditation and contemplation techniques, with further study of the peak-experiences, or of B-cognition, etc.

XXI

But B-values seem to be the same as B-facts. Reality then is ultimately fact-values or value-facts.

The traditional dichotomizing of *is* and *ought* turns out to be characteristic of lower levels of living, and is transcended at the highest level of living, where fact and value fuse. For obvious reasons, those words which are simultaneously descriptive and normative can be called "fusion words" (Maslow, 1967).

At this fusion level "love for the intrinsic values" is the same as "love of ultimate reality." Devotion *to* the facts here implies love *for* the facts. The sternest effort at objectivity or perception, i.e., to reduce as much as possible the contaminating effect of the observer, and of his fears and wishes and selfish calculations, yields an emotional, esthetic, and axiological result, a result pointed toward and approximated by our greatest and most perspicuous philosophers, scientists, artists, and spiritual inventors and leaders.

Contemplation of ultimate values becomes the same as contemplation of the nature of the world. Seeking the truth (fully defined) may be the same as seeking beauty, order, oneness, perfection, rightness (fully defined) and truth may then be sought *via* any other B-value. Does science then become indistinguishable from art? love? religion? philosophy? Is a basic scientific discovery about the nature of reality also a spiritual or axiological affirmation?

XXII

Not only is man PART *of nature, and it part of him, but also he must be at least minimumly isomorphic with nature (similar to it) in*

---

*The Esalen Institute at Big Sur, California, specializes in such methods. The tacit assumption underlying this new kind of education is that both the body and the "spirit" can be loved, and that they are synergic and hierarchically rather than mutually exclusive, i.e., one can have both.

order to be viable in it. It has evolved him. His communion with what transcends him therefore need not be defined as non-natural or super-natural. It may be seen as a "biological" experience.

Perhaps man's thrilling to nature (perceiving it as true, good, beautiful, etc.) will one day be understood as a kind of self-recognition or self-experience, a way of being oneself and full functional, a way of being at home, a kind of biological authenticity, of "biological mysticism," etc. Perhaps we can see mystical or peak-fusion not only as communion with that which is most worthy of love, but also as fusion with that which *is,* because he belongs there, being truly part of what is, and being, so to speak, a member of the family:

> . . . one direction in which we find increasing confidence is the conception that we are basically one with the cosmos instead of strangers to it (Gardner Murphy).

This *biological* or evolutionary version of the mystic experience or the peak-experience—here perhaps no different from the spiritual or religious experience—reminds us again that we must ultimately outgrow the obsolescent usage of "highest" as the opposite of "lowest" or "deepest." Here the "highest" experience ever described, the joyful fusion with the ultimate that man can conceive, can be seen simultaneously as the deepest experience of our ultimate personal animality and specieshood, as the acceptance of our profound biological nature as isomorphic with nature in general.

XXIII

The B-values are not the same as our personal attitudes toward these values, nor our emotional reactions to them. The B-values induce in us a kind of "requiredness feeling" and also a feeling of unworthiness.

The B-values had better be differentiated from our human attitudes toward these B-values, at least to the extent that is possible for so difficult a task. A listing of such attitudes toward ultimate values (or reality) included: love, awe, adoration, humility, reverence, unworthiness, wonder, amazement, marveling, exaltation, gratitude, fear, joy, etc. (Maslow, 1964a, p. 94). These are clearly emotional-cognitive reactions within a person witnessing something not the same as himself, or at least verbally separable. Of course, the more the person fuses with the world in great peak or mystic experiences, the less of these intra-self reactions there would be and the more the self would be lost as a separable entity.

XXIV

The vocabulary to describe motivations must be hierarchical, especially since metamotivations (growth-motivations) must be characterized differently from basic needs (deficiency-needs).

This difference between intrinsic values and our attitudes toward these values also generates a hierarchical vocabulary for motives (using this word most generally and inclusively). In another place I have called attention to the levels of gratification, pleasures, or happiness corresponding to the hierarchy of needs to metaneeds (Maslow, 1966). In addition to this, we must keep in mind that the concept of "gratification" itself is transcended at the level of metamotives or growth-motives, where satisfactions can be endless. So also for the concept of happiness which can also be altogether transcended at the highest levels. It may then easily become a kind of cosmic sadness or soberness or non-emotional contemplation. At the lowest basic need levels we can certainly talk of being driven and of desperately craving, striving, or needing, when, e.g., cut off from oxygen or experiencing great pain. As we go on up the hierarchy of basic needs, words like desiring, wishing, or preferring, choosing, wanting become more appropriate. But at the highest levels, i.e., of metamotivation, all these words become subjectively inadequate, and such words as yearning for, devoted to, aspiring to, loving, adoring, admiring, worshipping, being drawn to or fascinated by, describe the metamotivated feelings more accurately.

XXV

The B-values call to behavioral expression or "celebration" as well as inducing subjective states.

We must agree wit Heschel's (1965, p. 117) stress on "celebration" which he describes as "an act of expressing respect or reverence for that which one needs or honors. . . . Its essence is to call attention to the sublime or solemn aspects of living. . . . To celebrate is to share in a greater joy, to participate in an eternal drama."

It is well to notice that the highest values are not only receptively enjoyed and contemplated, but that they often also lead to expressive and behavioral responses, which of course would be easier to investigate than subjective states.

XXVI

There are certain educational and therapeutic advantages in differentiating the realm (or level) or being from the realm (or level) of deficiencies, and in recognizing language differences at these levels.

I have found it most useful for myself to differentiate between the realm of being (B-realm) and the realm of deficiencies (D-realm), that is, between the eternal and the "practical." Simply as a matter of the strategy and tactics of living well and fully and of choosing one's life instead of having it determined for us, this is a help.

I have found this vocabulary useful also in teaching people to be more aware of values of being, of a language of being, of the ultimate facts of being, of the life of being, of unitive consciousness, etc. The vocabulary is certainly clumsy and sometimes grates on the sensibilities, but it does serve the purpose (Maslow, 1964a, Appendix I: An example of B-analysis).

XXVII

"Intrinsic conscience" and "intrinsic guilt" are ultimately biologically rooted.

Stimulated by Fromm's discussion of "humanistic conscience" (1941) and Horney's (1939) reconsideration of Freud's "superego," other humanistic writers have agreed that there is an "intrinsic conscience" beyond the supergo, as well as "intrinsic guilt" which is a deserved self-punishment for betrayal of the intrinsic self.

I believe that the biological rooting of metamotivation theory can clarify and solidify these concepts further.

One's personal biology is beyond question a *sine qua non* component of the "Real Self." Being oneself, being natural or spontaneous, being authentic, expressing one's identity, all these are also biological statements since they imply the acceptance of one's constitutional, temperamental, anatomical, neurological, hormonal, and in-stinctoid-motivational nature. Such a statement is in both the Freudian line and in the Neo-Freudian line (not to mention Rogerian, Jungian, Sheldonian, Goldsteinian, *et el.*). It is a cleansing and a correction of what Freud was groping toward and of necessity glimpsed only vaguely. I therefore consider it to be in the *echt*-Freudian or "*epi*-Freudian" tradition. I think Freud was trying to say something like this with his various instinct theories. I believe also that this statement is an acceptance of, plus an improvement upon, what Horney was trying to say with her concept of a Real Self.

If my more biological interpretation of an intrinsic self is corroborated, then it would also support the differentiation of neurotic guilt from the intrinsic guilt which comes from defying one's own nature and from trying to be what one is not.

XXVIII

Many of the ultimate religious functions are fulfilled by this theoretical structure.

From the point of view of the eternal and absolute that mankind has always sought, it may be that the B-values could also, to some extent, serve this purpose. They are *per se,* in their own right, not dependent upon human vagaries for their existence. They are perceived, not invented. They are trans-human and trans-individual. They exist beyond the life of the individual. They can be conceived to be a kind of perfection. They could conceivably satisfy the human longing for certainty.

And yet they are also human in a specifiable sense. They are not only his, but him as well. The command adoration, reverence, celebration, sacrifice. They are worth living for and dying for. Contemplating them or fusing with them gives the greatest joy that a human being is capable of.

And so for other functions that the organized religions have tried to fulfill. Apparently all, or almost all, the characteristically religious experiences that have ever been described in any of the traditional religions, in their own local phrasings, whether theist or non-theist, Eastern or Western, can be assimilated to this theoretical structure and can be expressed in an empirically meaningful way, i.e., phrased in a testable way.

REFERENCES

Bugental, J. 1965. *The Search for Authenticity.* New York: Holt, Rinehart & Winston.

Frankl, V. 1966. Self-transcendence as a human phenomenon. *Journal of Humanistic Psychology,* 6: 97–106.

Fromm, E. 1941. *Escape from Freedom.* New York: Farrar & Rinehart.

———. 1947. *Man for Himself.* New York: Holt, Rinehart & Winston.

Heschel, A. 1965. *Who Is Man?* Stanford, California: Stanford University Press.

Horney, K. 1939. *New Ways in Psychoanalysis.* New York: W. W. Norton.

Marcuse, H. 1955. *Eros and Civilization.* Boston: Beacon Press.

Maslow, A. H. 1954. *Motivation and Personality.* New York: Harper & Row.

———. 1962a. *Toward a Psychology of Being.* New York: Van Nostrand.

———. 1962b. Notes on being-psychology. *Journal of Humanistic Psychology,* 2: 47–71.

———. 1964a. *Religions, Values, and Peak-Experiences.* Columbus: Ohio State University Press.

———, and Gross, L. 1964b. Synergy in society and in the individual. *Journal of Individual Psychology,* 20: 153–64.

———. 1965a. *Eupsychian Management:* A Journal. Homewood, Illinois: Irwin-Dorsey.

———. 1965b. Criteria for judging needs to be instinctoid. In M. R. Jones, ed., *Human Motivation: A Symposium.* Lincoln: University of Nebraska Press.

———. 1966. *The Psychology of Science: A Reconnaissance.* New York: Harper & Row.

———. 1966. Comments on Dr. Frankl's Paper. *Journal of Humanistic Psychology,* 6: 107–12.

———. 1967. Neurosis as a failure of personal growth. *Humanitas,* 3: 153–69.

Schumacher, E. F. 1967. Economic development and poverty. *Manas,* 15 February: 1–8.

Weisskopf, W. 1963. Economic growth and human well-being. *Manas,* 21 August: 1–8.

Wootton, G. 1967. *Workers, Unions and the State.* New York: Schocken.

For a more extensive bibliography, see A. H. Maslow's *Toward a Psychology of Being,* 2nd edition. New York: Van Nostrand. 1968; *The Farther Reaches of Human Nature.* New York: Viking, 1971.

A complete list of works (1932–1972) by Maslow can be found in *Abraham H. Maslow: A Memorial Volume.* Monterey, California: Brooks/Cole, 1972.

4

Here and Now Therapy

FRITZ PERLS

Implicit in the emphasis of orthodox psychotherapy is the point of view that the neurotic is a person who once had a problem, and that the resolution of this past problem is the goal of psychotherapy. The whole approach to treatment through memory and the past indicates this assumption, which runs directly counter to everything we observe about neurosis and the neurotic. From the Gestalt viewpoint the neurotic is not merely a person who once *had* a problem, he is a person who has a *continuing* problem, here and now, in the present. Although it may well be that he is acting the way he is today "because" of things that happened to him in the past, his difficulties today are connected with the ways he is acting today. He cannot get along in the present, and unless he learns how to deal with problems as they arise, he will not be able to get along in the future.

The goal of therapy, then, must be to give him the means with which he can solve his present problems and any that may arise tomorrow or next year. That tool is self-support, and this he achieves by dealing with himself and his problems with all the means presently at his command, right now. If he can become *truly aware* at every instant of himself and his actions on whatever level—fantasy, verbal or physical—he can see how he is producing his difficulties, he can see what his present difficulties are, and he can help himself to solve them in the present, in the here and now. Each one he solves makes easier the solution of the next, for every solution increases his self-support.

Source: From The Gestalt Approach to Therapy by Fritz Perls, Palo Alto, California: Science and Behavior Books, 1973. Reprinted by permission of the author and the publisher.

If therapy is successful the patient will inevitably have taken care of the tag ends of his past unsolved problems, because these tag ends are bound to cause trouble in the present, and so they are bound to come up in the course of the therapeutic session, disguised in any number of different ways—disassociations, nervous habits, fantasies, etc. But these tag ends of the past are also current problems which inhibit the patient's participation in the present.

The neurotic is, by accepted definition, a person whose difficulties make his present life unsuccessful. In addition, by our definition, he is a person who chronically engages in self-interruption, who has an inadequate sense of identity (and thus cannot distinguish properly between himself and the rest of the world), who has inadequate means of self-support, whose psychological homeostasis is out of order, and whose behavior arises from misguided efforts in the direction of achieving balance.

Within this general framework, we can see what must be done. The neurotic finds it difficult to participate fully in the present—his past unfinished business gets in his way. His problems exist in the here and now—and yet too often only part of him is here to cope with them. Through therapy, he must learn to live in the present, and his therapeutic sessions must be his first practice at this hitherto unaccomplished task. Gestalt therapy is therefore a "here and now" therapy, in which we ask the patient during the session to turn all his attention to what he is doing at the present, during the course of the session—right here and now.

Gestalt therapy is an experiential therapy, rather than a verbal or an interpretive therapy. We ask our patients not to talk about their traumas and their problems in the removed area of the past tense and memory, but to *re-experience* their problems and their traumas—which are their unfinished situations in the present—in the here and now. If the patient is finally to close the book on his past problems, he must close it in the present. For he must realize that if his past problems were really past, they would no longer be problems—and they certainly would not be present.

In addition, as an experiential therapy, the Gestalt technique demands of the patient that he experience as much of himself as he can, that he experience himself as fully as he can in the here and now. We ask the patient to become aware of his gestures, of his breathing, of his emotions, of his voice, and of his facial expressions as much as of his pressing thoughts. We know that the more he becomes aware of himself, the more he will learn about what his self is. As he experiences the ways in which he prevents himself from "being" now—the ways in which he interrupts himself—he will also begin to experience the self he has interrupted.

In this process, the therapist is guided by what he observes about the patient. Here let it suffice to say that the therapist should be sensitive to the surface the patient presents so that the therapist's broader awareness can become the means by which the patient is enabled to increase his own.

The basic sentence with which we ask our patients to begin therapy, and which we retain throughout its course—not only in words, but in spirit—is the simple phrase: "Now I am aware." The now keeps us in the present and brings home the fact that no experience is ever possible except in the present. And the present, itself, is of course an ever changing experience. Once the now is used, the patient will easily use the present tense throughout, work on a phenomenological basis and, as I will show later, provide the material of past experience which is required to close the gestalt, to assimilate a memory, to right the organismic balance.

The "I" is used as an antidote to the "it" and developes the patient's sense of responsibility for his feelings, thoughts and symptoms. The "am" is his existential symbol. It brings home whatever he experiences as part of his being, and, together with his now, of his becoming. He quickly learns that each new "now" is different from the previous one.

The "aware" provides the patient with the sense of his own capacities, and abilities, his own sensoric and motor and intellectual equipment. It is not the conscious—for that is purely mental—it is the experience sifted, as it were, only through the mind and through words. The "aware" provides something in addition to the conscious. Working, as we do, with what the patient has, his present means of manipulation, rather than with what he has not developed or what he has lost, the "aware" gives both therapist and patient the best picture of the patient's present resources. For awareness always takes place in the present. It opens up possibilities for action. Routine and habits are established functions, and any need to change them requires that they should be brought into the focus of awareness afresh. The mere idea of changing them presupposes the possibility of alternative ways of thinking and acting. Without awareness, there is no cognition of choice. Awareness, contact, and present are merely different aspects of one and the same process—self-realization. It is here and now that we become aware of all our choices, from small pathological decisions (is this pencil lying straight enough?) to the existential choice of devotion to a cause or avocation.

How does this "now I am aware," this here and now therapy work in action? Let us take the example of a neurotic whose unfinished business is the unfinished labor of mourning a dead parent. Aware or unaware, such a patient fantasizes that his guiding parent is still around; he acts as if the parent were still alive and conducts his life by outdated directions. To become self-supportive and to participate fully in the present as it is, he has to give up this guidance; he has to part, to say a final good-bye to his progenitor. And to do this successfully, he has to go to the deathbed and face the departure. He has to transform his thoughts about the past into actions in the present which he experiences as if the now were the then. He cannot do it merely by re-recounting the scene, he must re-live it. He must go through and assimilate the interrupted feelings which are mostly of intense grief, but which may have in them elements of triumph or guilt or any number of other things. It is insufficient merely to recall a past incident, one has to *psychodramatically* return to it. Just as talking about oneself is a resistance against experiencing oneself, so the memory of an experience—simply talking about it—leaves it isolated as a deposit of the past—as lacking in life as the ruins of Pompei. You are left with the opportunity to make some clever reconstructions, but you don't bring them back alive. The neurotic's memory is more than simply a hunting ground for the archeologists of man's behavior we call psychoanalysts. It is the uncompleted event, which is still alive and interrupted, waiting to be assimilated and integrated. It is here and now, in the present, that this assimilation must take place.

The psychoanalyst, out of the vast stores of his theoretical knowledge, might explain to the patient: "You are still tied to your mother because you feel guilty about her death. It was something you wished for in childhood and repressed, and when your wish came true, you felt like a murderer." And there may be elements of truth in what he says. But this kind of symbolic or intellectual explanation does not affect the patient's feelings, for these are the result not of his sense of guilt, but of his interruption of it when his mother died. If he had permitted himself fully to experience his guilt then, he would not feel distressed now. In Gestalt therapy we therefore require that the patient psychodramatically talk to his dead mother.

Because the neurotic finds it difficult to live and experience himself in the present, he will find it difficult to stick to the here and now technique. He will interrupt his present participation with memories of the past, and he will persist in talking about them as if they were indeed past. He finds it less difficult to associate than to concentrate and, in concentrating, to experience himself. Whether concentrating on his body sensations or his fantasies—although at first he will find this a miserable task—his unfinished business makes concentration a major project for him. He no longer has a clear sense of the order of his needs—he tends to give them all equal value. He is like the young man Stephen Leacock once spoke about who got on his horse and galloped off madly in all directions.

It is not a desire to make his life miserable that lies behind our request to make him capable of concentrations. If he is to move towards full participation in the present, to take the first step towards productive living, he must learn to direct his energies—that is, to concentrate. He will be able to move from "now I need this" to "now I need that," only if he truly experiences each now and each need.

In addition, the concentration technique (focal awareness) provides us with a tool for therapy in depth, rather than in breadth. By concentrating on each symptom, each area of awareness, the patient learns several things about himself and his neurosis. He learns what he is actually experiencing. He learns how he experiences it. And he learns how his feelings and behavior in one area are related to his feelings and behavior in other areas.

Let me return for a moment to that classical psychosomatic manifestation, the headache. Patients frequently list this as one of their most annoying symptoms. They complain that their headaches bother them and now, when they come for treatment, they want to bother us with their symptoms. They are, of course, welcome to do so. But we in turn bother them—we ask them to take more responsibility and less aspirin. We do this by asking them to discover through experiencing how they produce their headaches. (The "aha" experience of discovery is one of the most powerful agents for cure). We ask them first to localize the pain and to stay, or sit, or lie with the tension. We ask them to concentrate on the pain, not to dispose of it. In the beginning only a few will be able to stand the tension. Most patients will tend to interrupt immediately with explanations, associations, or by pooh-poohing what we are doing. Consequently, the therapist has to work through one way of interrupting after another, and he has to change these interruptions into "I" functions. This means that even before we work on the headache itself, we have already done a considerable amount of integration. Suppose, for example, the therapist asks the patient to stay with his pains and the patient says, as often happens, "this is all nonsense." If he learns to say, instead, "what you are try-ing to do is all nonsense," he is taking a tiny step forward. With such a small step we have transformed a minute particle of "it" into a *contact function,* into a self-expression. We might even follow up his statement and ask the patient to elaborate on it. This would give him an op-portunity to come out with a lot of his unspoken skepticism, distrust, and so on, and all of these are part of the unfinished businesses that are preventing his total participation in the present.

But finally the patient will be able to stay with his headache, and with his pains, which he can now localize. This staying with is opening up the possibility for development of contact with the self. If he stays with his pains he may find that he has been contracting some muscles or that he feels a numbness. Let us say that he discovers his pains are associated with muscle contractions. Then we will ask him to exag-gerate the contracting. He will then see how he can voluntarily create and intensify his own pains. He might then say, as a result of his dis-coveries up to now, "It's as if I were screwing up my face to cry." The therapist might then ask, "Would you like to cry?" And then, if we ask him to direct that remark directly to us, to say it to our face, he might well burst out crying and weeping. "I won't cry, damn you! Leave me alone, leave me alone!" Apparently, then, his headache was an inter-ruption of the need to cry. It has become apparent that he has lost his need to interrupt his crying by giving himself headaches. At best, the patient may lose his need to cry, too, for if the therapy can be concentrated on this one factor for a long enough period of time, he may be able to work through the past interruptions that also led to the need to cry in the present. But even before this stage, progress has been made. The patient has transformed a partial involvement (headache) into a total involvement (weeping). He has transformed a psychosomatic symptom into an expression of the total self, because in his short outburst of despair he was wholly and totally involved. So through the concentration technique the patient has learned how to participate fully in at least one present experience. He has learned at the same time something about his process of self-interruption and the ways in which these self-interruptions are related to the totality of his experience. He has discovered one of his means of manipulation.

The neurotic is, as we said, self-interrupter. All schools of psychotherapy take this fact into account. Freud, as a matter of fact, built his therapy around a recognition of this phenomenon. Of all the possible forms of self-interruption he chose a very decisive one, which he called the Censor. He said, "Do not interrupt the free flow of your associations." But he also assumed that the Censor was the servant of embarrassment, and thus spoke Freud: "Do not be embarrassed." Precisely with these two taboos he interrupted the patient's experience of his embarrassment and his experience of its dissolution. This results in a desensitization, an inability to experience embarrassment, or even (and this applies still more to patients in Reichian theraph) in overcompensating brazenness. What has to be tackled in therapy is not the censored material but the censoring itself, the form that self-interruption takes. Again, we cannot work from the inside out, but only from the outside in.

The therapeutic procedure (which is the re-establishment of the self by integrating the dissociated parts of the personality) must bring the patient to the point where he no longer interrupts himself, that is, to the point where he is no longer neurotic. How can we do this without making the mistake of interrupting the interruption? We have previously mentioned Freud's command, "do not censor," which is in itself a censoring of the censor, an interruption of the process of censoring. What we have to do is notice and deal with the *hows* of every interruption, rather than with the censor—which is Freud's postulated *why* of interruption. If we deal with the interruptions per se, we deal with the direct clinical picture, with the experience the patient is living through. Again, we deal with the surface that presents itself. There is no need to guess and to interpret. We hear the interruption of a sentence or we notice that the patient holds his breath or we see that he is making a fist, as if to hit someone, or swinging his legs as if to kick, or we observe how he interrupts contact with the therapist by looking away.

Is he aware of these self-interruptions? This must be our first question to him in such a situation. Does he know that this is what he is doing? As he becomes more aware of the ways in which he interrupts himself, he will inevitably become more aware of what he is interrupting. As our example of the headache showed, it was in staying with his interruption, his headache, that he discovered how he was using this mechanism to interrupt his own crying. This example shows how, by concentrating on the interruption per se—on the hows of it, not its whys—the patient comes to an awareness of the fact that he is interrupting himself, and becomes aware of what he is interrupting. He also becomes able to dissolve his interruptions and to live through and finish up one unfinished experience.

The neurotic mechanisms of introjection, projection, and retroflection are themselves mechanisms of introjection, and often developed in response to interruptions from the outside world. In the normal process of growth, we learn through trial and error, through testing our lives and our world as freely and uninterruptedly as possible.

Imagine a kitten climbing a tree. It is engaged in experimenting. It balances itself, it tests its strength and its agility. But the mother cat will not leave it alone; she insists that it come down. "You may break your neck, you naughty kitten," she hisses. How this would interrupt the kitten's pleasure in growing! It would even interrupt the growth process itself. But cats, of course, do not behave so stupidly. They leave the pursuit of safety to the human beings.

On the contrary, the cat, like any other animal and any sensible human being, will consider it the essence of up-bringing to facilitate the transformation of external into self-support. The newly born kitten can neither feed, transport nor defend itself. For all this it needs its mother. But it will develop the means to do these things itself, partly through developing its inborn instincts, and partly through environmental teaching. In the human being, the transition from external to self-support is, of course, more complicated. Consider only the need to change diapers, to dress, to cook, to choose a vocation, or to gain knowledge.

Since we are forced to learn so much more through education than by using our inherited instincts, much of the animal's intuition as to what is the right procedure is missing. Instead, the "right" procedure is established by composite fantasies which are handed over and modified from generation to generation. They are mostly support functions for social contact, such as manners and codes of behavior (ethics), means of orientation (reading, weltanschauungen), standards of beauty (aesthetics), and social position (attitudes). Often, however, these procedures are not biologically oriented, thus disrupting the very root of our existence and leading to degeneration. Psychiatric case histories show over and over how our depreciatory orientation towards sex can produce neurosis. But whether these procedures are anti-biological or anti-personal or anti-social, they are interruptions in the ongoing processes which, if left alone, would lead to self-support.

Such interruptions are the nightmares of Junior's upbringing. There are the *interruptions of contact,* the "don't touch that!" and the "don't do that!" that fly around his ears day in and day out. Or "leave me alone! Can't I have a moment's peace," interrupt his wish to interrupt mamma. His *withdrawals* are also interrupted. "You stay here now, keep your mind on your homework and don't dream," or "you can't go out to play until you finish your dinner."

Shall we then follow a policy of utter non-interruption? Like any other animal, Junior has to test the world, to find his possibilities, to try to expand his boundaries, to experiment with how far he can go. But at the same time he has to be prevented from doing serious harm to himself or others. He has to learn to cope with interruptions.

The real trouble begins when the parents interfere with the child's maturation, either by spoiling him and interrupting his attempts to find his own bearings or by being overprotective, and destroying his confidence in his ability to be self-supportive within the limits of his development. They regard the child as a possession to be either preserved or exhibited. In the latter case, they will tend to create precocity by making ambitious demands on the child, who at that time lacks sufficient inner support to fulfill them. In the former case, they will tend to block maturation by giving the child no chance to make use of the inner supports he has developed. The first child may grow up self-sufficient, the second dependent—neither self-supportive.

Our patients come to us having incorporated their parent's interruptions into their own lives—and this is introjection. Such patients are the ones who say to us, for example, "grown men don't cry!" They come to us having disowned the offending parts of themselves—the ones that were interrupted in their childhood—this is projection. "These darn headaches! Why do I have to suffer from them!" They may turn the qualities their parents called bad, and the display of which they interrupted, against themselves. This is retroflection. "I must control myself. I must not let myself cry!" They may have become so confused by their parents' interruptions that they give up their identity completely and forget the difference and the connection between their internal needs and the external means of satisfying them. This result is confluence. "I always get a headache when people yell at me."

Through making our patients aware, in the here and now, by concentration, of what these interruptions are, of how these interruptions affect them, we can bring them to real integrations. We can dissolve the endless clinch in which they find themselves. We can give them a chance to be themselves, because they will begin to experience themselves; this will give them a true appreciation both of themselves and others, and will enable them to make good contact with the world, because they will know where the world is. Understanding means, basically, seeing a part in its relation to the whole. For our patients, it means seeing themselves as part of the total field and thus becoming related both to themselves and to the world. This is good contact.

REFERENCES

The reader who wishes additional information about Gestalt therapy may find the following list of readings helpful.

Fagan, J., and Shepherd, I. L., eds., 1970. *Gestalt Therapy Now*. Palo Alto, California: Science and Behavior Books.

Perls, F. S. 1969. *Gestalt Therapy Verbatim*. Lafayette, California: Real People.

———. 1969. *In and Out the Garbage Pail*. Layfayette, California: Real People.

———. 1973. *The Gestalt Therapy and Eye-Witness to Therapy*. Palo Alto, California: Science and Behavior Books.

Polster, E., and Polster, M. 1973. *Gestalt Therapy Integrated*. New York: Brunner Mazel.

Shepard, M. 1975. *Fritz*. New York: Dutton.

Stevens, J. O. *Gestalt Is*. Moab, Utah: Real People, 1975.

5

To Be and Not To Be: Contributions of Existential Psychotherapy

ROLLO MAY

The fundamental contribution of existential therapy is its understanding of man as *being*. It does not deny the validity of dynamisms and the study of specific behavior patterns in their rightful places. But it holds that drives of dynamisms, by whatever name one calls them, can be understood only in the context of the structure of the existence of the person we are dealing with. The distinctive character of existential analysis is, thus, that it is concerned with *ontology,* the science of being, and with *Dasein,* the existence of this particular being sitting opposite the psychotherapist.

Before struggling with definitions of *being* and related terms, let us begin existentially by reminding ourselves that what we are talking about is an experience every sensitive therapist must have countless times a day. It is the experience of the instantaneous encounter with another person who comes alive to us on a very different level from what we know *about* him. "Instantaneous" refers, of course, not to the actual time involved but to the quality of the experience. We may know a great deal about a patient from his case record, let us say, and may have a fairly good idea of how other interviewers have described him. But when the patient himself steps in, we often have a sudden, sometimes powerful, experience of here-is-a-new-person, an experience that normally carries with it an element of surprise, not in the sense of perplexity or bewilderment, but in its etymological sense of being "taken from above." This is of course in no sense a criticism

Source: From Existence *edited by Rollo May, Ernest Angel, and Henri Ellenberger,* © *1958. Reprinted by permission from Basic Books, Inc., Publishers, New York.*

of one's colleagues' reports; for we have this experience of encounter even with persons we have known or worked with for a long time.[1] The data we learned *about* the patient may have been accurate and well worth learning. But the point rather is that *the grasping of the being of the other person occurs on a quite different level from our knowledge of specific things about him.* Obviously a knowledge of the drives and mechanisms which are in operation in the other person's behavior is useful; a familiarity with his patterns of interpersonal relationships is highly relevant; information about his social conditioning, the meaning of particular gestures and symbolic actions is of course to the point, and so on *ad infinitum.* But all these fall on to a quite different level when we confront the overarching, most real fact of all—namely, the immediate, living person himself. When we find that all our voluminous knowledge about the person suddenly forms itself into a new pattern in this confrontation, the implication is not that the knowledge was wrong; it is rather that it takes its meaning, form, and significance from the reality of the person of whom these specific things are expressions. Nothing we are saying here in the slightest deprecates the importance of gathering and studying seriously all the specific data one can get about the given person. This is only common sense. But neither can one close his eyes to the experiential fact that this data forms itself into a configuration given in the encounter with the person himself. This also is illustrated by the common experience we all have had in interviewing persons; we may say we do not get a "feeling" of the other person and need to prolong the interview until the data "breaks" into its own form in our minds. We particularly do not get this "feeling" when we ourselves are hostile or resenting the relationship—that is, keeping the other person out—no matter how intellectually bright we may be at the time. This is the classical distinction between *knowing* and *knowing about.* When we seek to know a person, the knowledge *about* him must be subordinated to the overarching fact of his actual existence.

In the ancient Greek and Hebrew languages the verb "to know" is the same word as that which means "to have sexual intercourse." This is illustrated time and again in the King James translation of the Bible—"Abraham knew his wife and she conceived . . ." and so on. Thus the etymological relation between knowing and loving is exceedingly close. Though we cannot go into this complex topic, we can at

---

1. We may have it with friends and loved ones. It is not a once-and-for all experience; indeed, in any developing, growing relationship it may—probably should, if the relationship is vital—occur continually.

least say that knowing another human being, like loving him, involves a kind of union, a dialectical participation with the other. This Binswanger calls the "dual mode." One must have at least a readiness to love the other person, broadly speaking, if one is to be able to understand him.

The encounter with the being of another person has the power to shake one profoundly and may potentially be very anxiety-arousing. It may also be joy-creating. In either case, it has the power to grasp and move one deeply. The therapist understandably may be tempted for his own comfort to abstract himself from the encounter by thinking of the other as just a "patient" or by focusing only on certain mechanisms of behavior. But if the technical view is used dominantly in the relating to the other person, obviously one has defended himself from anxiety at the price not only of the isolation of himself from the other but also of radical distortion of reality. For one does not then really *see* the other person. It does not disparage the importance of technique to point out that technique, like data, must be subordinated to the fact of the reality of two persons in the room.

This point has been admirably made in a slightly different way by Sartre. If we "consider man," he writes, "as capable of being analyzed and reduced to original data, to determined drives (or 'desires'), supported by the subject as properties of an object," we may indeed end up with an imposing system of substances which we may then call mechanisms or dynamisms or patterns. But we find ourselves up against a dilemma. Our human being has become "a sort of indeterminate clay which would have to receive [the desires] passively—or he would be reduced to a simple bundle of these irreducible drives or tendencies. In either case the *man* disappears; we can no longer find 'the one' to whom this or that experience has happened."[2]

2. Jean-Paul Sartre, *Being and Nothingness*, trans. by Hazel Barnes (1956), p. 561. Sartre goes on, ". . . either in looking for the *person* we encounter a useless, contradictory metaphysical substance—or else the being whom we seek vanishes in a dust of phenomena bound together by external connections. But what each of us requires in this very effort to comprehend another is that he should never resort to this idea of substance, which is inhuman because it is well this side of the human" (p. 52). Also, "If we admit that the person is a totality, we can not hope to reconstruct him by an addition or by an organization of the diverse tendencies which we have empirically discovered in him. . . ." Every attitude of the person contains some reflection of this totality, holds Sartre. "A jealousy of a particular date in which a subject posits himself in history in relation to a certain woman, signifies for the one who knows how to interpret it, the total relation to the world by which the subject constitutes himself as a self. In other words this *empirical attitude* is by itself the expression of the 'choice of an intelligible character.' There is no mystery about this" (p. 58).

To Be and Not To Be

It is difficult enough to give definitions of "being" and *Dasein,* but our task is made doubly difficult by the fact that these terms and their connotations encounter much resistance. Some readers may feel that these words are only a new form of "mysticism" (used in its disparaging and quite inaccurate sense of "misty") and have nothing to do with science. But this attitude obviously dodges the whole issue by disparaging it. It is interesting that the term "mystic" is used in this derogatory sense to mean anything we cannot segmentize and count. The odd belief prevails in our culture that a thing or experience is not real if we cannot make it mathematical, and somehow it must be real if we can reduce it to numbers. But this means making an abstraction out of it—mathematics is the abstraction par excellence, which is indeed its glory and the reason for its great usefulness. Modern Western man thus finds himself in the strange situation, after reducing something to an abstraction, of having then to persuade himself it is real. This has much to do with the sense of isolation and loneliness which is endemic in the modern Western world; for the only experience we let ourselves believe in as real is that which precisely is not. Thus we deny the reality of our own experience. The term "mystic," in this disparaging sense, is generally used in the service of obscurantism; certainly avoiding an issue by derogation is only to obscure it. Is not the scientific attitude rather, to try to see clearly what it is we are talking about and then to find whatever terms or symbols can best, with least distortion, describe this reality? It should not so greatly surprise us to find that "being" belongs to that class of realities, like "love" and "consciousness" (for two other examples), which we cannot segmentize or abstract without losing precisely what we set out to study. This does not, however, relieve us from the task of trying to understand and describe them.

A more serious source of resistance is one that runs through the whole of modern Western society—namely, the psychological need to avoid and, in some ways, repress, the whole concern with "being." In contrast to other cultures which may be very concerned with being—particularly Indian and Oriental—and other historical periods which have been so concerned, the characteristic of our period in the West, as Marcel rightly phrases it, is precisely that the awareness of "the sense of the ontological—the sense of being—is lacking. Generally speaking, modern man is in this condition; if ontological demands worry him at all, it is only dully, as an obscure impulse."[3] Marcel

3. Gabriel Marcel, *The Philosophy of Existence* (1949), p. 1.

points out what many students have emphasized, that this loss of the sense of being is related on one hand to our tendency to subordinate existence to function: a man knows himself not as a man or self but as a ticket-seller in the subway, a grocer, a professor, a vice president of A. T. & T., or by whatever his economic function may be. And on the other hand, this loss of the sense of being is related to the mass collectivist trends and widespread conformist tendencies in our culture. Marcel then makes this trenchant challenge: *"Indeed I wonder if a psychoanalytic method, deeper and more discerning than any that has been evolved until now, would not reveal the morbid effects of the repression of this sense and of the ignoring of this need."*[4]

"As for defining the word 'being,' " Marcel goes on, "let us admit that it is extremely difficult; I would merely suggest this method of approach: being is what withstands—or what would withstand—an exhaustive analysis bearing on the data of experience and aiming to reduce them step by step to elements increasingly devoid of intrinsic or significant value. (An analysis of this kind is attempted in the theoretical works of Freud.)"[5] This last sentence I take to mean that when Freud's analysis is pushed to the ultimate extreme, and we know, let us say, everything about drives, instincts, and mechanisms, we have everything *except* being. Being is that which remains. It is that which constitutes this infinitely complex set of deterministic factors into a person *to whom* the experiences happen and who possesses some element, no matter how minute, of freedom to become aware that these forces are acting upon him. This is the sphere where he has the potential capacity to pause before reacting and thus to cast some weight on whether his reaction will go this way or that. And this, therefore, is the sphere where he, the human being, is never merely a collection of drives and determined forms of behavior.

The term the existential therapists use for the distinctive character of human existence is *Dasein*. Binswanger, Kuhn, and others designate their school as *Daseinsanalyse*. Composed of *sein* (being) plus *da* (there), *Dasein* indicates that man is the being who *is there* and implies also that he *has* a "there" in the sense that he can know he is there and can take a stand with reference to that fact. The "there" is moreover not just any place, but the particular "there" that is mine, the particular point *in time* as well as space of my existence at this

4. *Ibid.* Italics mine. For data concerning the "morbid effects of the repression" of the sense of being, cf. Fromm, *Escape from Freedom,* and David Riesman, *The Lonely Crowd.*

5. *Ibid.,* p. 5.

given moment. Man is the being who can be conscious of, and therefore responsible for, his existence. It is this capacity to become aware of his own being which distinguishes the human being from other beings. The existential therapists think of man not only as "being-in-it-self," as all beings are, but also as "being-for-itself." Binswanger and other authors in the chapters that follow speak of *"Dasein* choosing" this or that, meaning "the person-who-is-responsible-for-his-existence choosing. . . ."

The full meaning of the term "human being" will be clearer if the reader will keep in mind that "being" is a participle, a verb form imply-ing that someone is in the process of *being something*. It is unfortunate that, when used as a general noun in English, the term "being" con-notes a static substance, and when used as a particular noun such as *a* being, it is usually assumed to refer to an entity, say, such as a soldier to be counted as a unit. Rather, "being" should be understood, when used as a general noun, to mean *potentia,* the source of potentiality; "being" is the potentiality by which the acorn becomes the oak or each of us becomes what he truly is. And when used in a particular sense, such as *a* human being, it always has the dynamic connotation of someone in process, the person being something. Perhaps, therefore, *becoming* connotes more accurately the meaning of the term in this country. We can understand another human being only as we see what he is moving toward, what he is becoming; and we can know ourselves only as we "project our *potentia* in action." The significant tense for human beings is thus the *future*—that is to say, the critical question is what I am pointing toward, becoming, what I will be in the immediate future.

Thus, being in the human sense is not given once and for all. It does not unfold automatically as the oak tree does from the acorn. For an intrinsic and inseparable element in being human is self-conscious-ness. Man (or *Dasein*) is the particular being who has to be aware of himself, be responsible for himself, if he is to become himself. He also is that particular being who knows that at some future moment he will not be; he is the being who is always in a dialectical relation with nonbeing, death. And he not only knows he will sometime not be, but he can, in his own choices, slough off and forfeit his being. "To be and not to be"—the "and" in our subtitle to this section is not a typo-graphical error—is not a choice one makes once and for all at the point of considering suicide; it reflects to some degree a choice made at every instant. The profound dialectic in the human being's awareness of his own being is pictured with incomparable beauty by Pascal:

Man is only a reed, the feeblest reed in nature, but he is a thinking reed. There is no need for the entire universe to arm itself in order to annihilate him: a vapour, a drop of water, suffices to kill him. But were the universe to crush him, man would yet be more noble than that which slays him, because he knows that he dies, and the advantage that the universe has over him; of this the universe knows nothing.[6]

In the hope of making clearer what it means for a person to experience his own being, we shall present an illustration from a case history. This patient, an intelligent woman of twenty-eight, was especially gifted in expressing what was occurring within her. She had some for psychotherapy because of serious anxiety spells in closed places, severe self-doubts, and eruptions of rage which were sometimes uncontrollable.[7] An illegitimate child, she had been brought up by relatives in a small village in the southwestern part of the country. Her mother, in periods of anger, often reminded her as a child of her origin, recounted how she had tried to abort her, and in times of trouble had shouted at the little girl, "If you hadn't been born, we wouldn't have to go through this!" Other relatives had cried at the child, in family quarrels, "Why didn't you kill yourself?" and "You should have been choked the day you were born!" Later, as a young woman, the patient had become well-educated on her own initiative.

In the fourth month of therapy she had the following dream: "I was in a crowd of people. They had no faces; they were like shadows. It seemed like a wilderness of people. Then I saw there was someone in the crowd who had compassion for me." The next session she reported that she had had, in the intervening day, an exceedingly important experience. It is reported here as she wrote it down from memory and notes two years later.

I remember walking that day under the elevated tracks in a slum area, feeling the thought, "I am an illegitimate child." I recall the sweat pouring forth in my anguish in trying to accept that fact. Then I understood what it must feel like to accept, "I am a Negro in the midst of privileged

6. Pascal's *Penseés,* Gertrude B. Burfurd Rawlings, trans. and ed. (Peter Pauper Press), p. 35. Pascal goes on, "Thus all our dignity lies in thought. By thought we must raise ourselves, not by space and time, which we cannot fill. Let us strive, then, to think well,—therein is the principle of morality." It is perhaps well to remark that of course by "thought" he means not intellectualism nor technical reason but self-consciousness, the reason which also knows the reasons of the heart.

7. Since our purpose is merely to illustrate one phenomenon, namely, the experience of the sense of being, we shall not report the diagnostic or other details of the case.

whites," or "I am blind in the midst of people who see." Later on that
night I woke up and it came to me this way, "I accept the fact that I am
an illegitimate child." *But* "I am not a child anymore." So it is, "I am
illegitimate." That is not so either: "I was born illegitimate." Then what
is left? What is left is this, *"I Am."* This *act* of contact and acceptance
with "I am," once gotten hold of, gave me (what I think was for me the
first time) the experience "Since I am, I have the right to be."

What is this experience like? It is a primary feeling—it feels like
receiving the deed to my house. It is the experience of my own aliveness
not caring whether it turns out to be an ion or just a wave. It is like when
a very young child I once reached the core of a peach and cracked the
pit, not knowing what I would find and then feeling the wonder of finding
the inner seed, good to eat in its bitter sweetness. . . . It is like a sail-
boat in the harbor being given an anchor so that, being made out of
earthly things, it can by means of its anchor get in touch again with the
earth, the ground from which its wood grew; it can lift its anchor to sail
but always at times it can cast its anchor to weather the storm or rest a
little. . . . It is my saying to Descartes, *"I Am, therefore* I think, I feel, I
do."

It is like an axiom in geometry—never experiencing it would be
like going through a geometry course not knowing the first axiom. It is
like going into my very own Garden of Eden where I am beyond good
and evil and all other human concepts. It is like the experience of the
poets of the intuitive world, the mystics, except that instead of the pure
feeling of and union with God it is the finding of and the union with my
own being. It is like owning Cinderella's shoe and looking all over the
world for the foot it will fit and realizing all of a sudden that one's own
foot is the only one it will fit. It is a "Matter of Fact" in the etymological
sense of the expression. It is like a globe before the mountains and
oceans and continents have been drawn on it. It is like a child in grammar
finding the *subject* of the verb in a sentence—in this case the subject being one's own life span. It is ceasing to feel like a theory toward one's
self. . . .

We shall call this the "I-am" experience.[8] This one phase of a
complex case, powerfully and beautifully described above, illustrates

---

8. Some readers will be reminded of the passage in Exodus 3:14 in which Moses, after
Yahweh had appeared to him in the burning bush and charged him to free the Israelites
from Egypt, demands that the God tell his name. Yahweh gives the famous answer, "I
am that I am." This classical, existential sentence (the patient, incidentally, did not consciously know this sentence) carries great symbolic power because, coming from an arc-
haic period, it has God state that *the quintessence of divinity is the power to be.* We are
unable to go into the many rich meanings of this answer, nor the equally intricate transla-

the emergence and strengthening of the sense of being in one person. The experience is etched the more sharply in this person because of the more patent threat to her being that she had suffered as an illegitimate child and her poetic articulateness as she looked back on her experience from the vantage point of two years later. I do not believe either of these facts, however, makes her experience different in fundamental quality from what human beings in general, normal or neurotic, go through.

We shall make four final comments on the experience exemplified in this case. First, the "I-am" experience is not in itself the solution to a person's problems; it is rather the *precondition* for their solution. This patient spent some two years thereafter working through specific psychological problems, which she was able to do on the basis of this emerged experience of her own existence. In the broadest sense, of course, the achieving of the sense of being is a goal of all therapy, but in the more precise sense it is a relation to one's self and one's world, an experience of one's own existence (including one's own identity), which is a prerequisite for the working through of specific problems. It is, as the patient wrote, the "primary fact," a *ur* experience. It is not to be identified with any patient's discovery of his or her specific powers—when he learns, let us say, that he can paint or write or work successfully or have successful sexual intercourse. Viewed from the outside, the discovery of specific powers and the experience of one's own being may seem to go hand in hand, but the latter is the underpinning, the foundation, the psychological precondition of the former. We may well be suspicious that solutions to a person's specific problems in psychotherapy which do not presuppose this "I-am" experience in greater or lesser degree will have a pseudo quality. The new "powers" the patient discovers may well be experienced by him as merely compensatory—that is, as proofs that he is of significance despite the fact that he is certain on a deeper level that he is not, since he still lacks a basic conviction of "*I Am,* therefore I think, I act." And we could well wonder whether such compensatory solutions would not represent rather the patient's simply exchanging one defense system for another, one set of terms for another, without ever experiencing himself as existing. In the second state the patient, instead of blowing up a anger,

---

tion problems, beyond pointing out that the Hebrew of the sentence can be translated as well, "I shall be what I shall be." This bears out our statement above that being is in the future tense and inseparable from becoming; God is creative *potentia,* the essence of the power to become.

"sublimates" or "introverts" or "relates," but still without the act being rooted in his own existence.

Our second comment is that this patient's "I-am" experience is not to be explained by the transference relationship. That the positive transference, whether directed to therapist or husband,[9] is obviously present in the above case is shown in the eloquent dream the night before in which there was one person in the barren, depersonalized wilderness of the crowd who had compassion for her. True, she is showing in the dream that she could have the "I-am" experience only if she could trust some other human being. But this does not account for the experience itself. It may well be true that for any human being the possibility of acceptance by and trust for another human being is a necessary condition for the "I-am" experience. But the awareness of one's own being occurs basically on the level of the grasping of one's self; it is an experience of *Dasein,* realized in the realm of self-awareness. It is not to be explained *essentially* in social categories. The acceptance by another person, such as the therapist, shows the patient that he no longer needs to fight his main battle on the front of whether anyone else, or the world, can accept him; the acceptance *frees* him to experience his own being. This point must be emphasized because of the common error in many circles of assuming that the experience of one's own being will take place automatically if only one is accepted by somebody else. This is the basic error of some forms of "relationship therapy." The attitude of "If-I-love-and-accept-you, this-is-all-you-need," is in life and in therapy an attitude which may well minister to increased passivity. The crucial question is what the individual himself, in his own awareness of and responsibility for his existence, does with the fact that he can be accepted.

The third comment follows directly from the above, that *being* is a category which cannot be reduced to introjection of social and ethical norms. It is, to use Nietzsche's phrase, "beyond good and evil." To the extent that my sense of existence is authentic, is precisely *not* what others have told me I should be, but is the one Archimedes point I have to stand on from which to judge what parents and other authorities demand. Indeed, *compulsive and rigid moralism arises in given persons precisely as the result of a lack of a sense of being.* Rigid

---

9. We omit for purposes of the above discussion the question whether this rightly should be called "transference" or simply human trust at this particular point in this case. We do not deny the validity of the concept of transference rightly defined, but it never makes sense to speak of something as "just transference," as though it were all carried over simply from the past.

moralism is a compensatory mechanism by which the individual persuades himself to take over the external sanctions because he has no fundamental assurance that his own choices have any sanction of their own. This is not to deny the vast social influences in anyone's morality, but it is to say that the ontological sense cannot be wholly reduced to such influences. The ontological sense *is not a superego* phenomenon. By the same token the sense of being gives the person a basis for a self-esteem which is not merely the reflection of others' views about him. For if your self-esteem must rest in the long run on social validation, you have, not self-esteem, but a more sophisticated form of social conformity. It cannot be said too strongly that the sense of one's own existence, though interwoven with all kinds of social relatedness, is in basis not the product of social forces; it always presupposes *Eigenwelt,* the "own world" (a term which will be discussed below).

Our fourth comment deals with the most important consideration of all, namely that the "I-am" experience must not be identified with what is called in various circles the "functioning of the ego." That is to say, it is an error to define the emergence of awareness of one's own being as one phase of the "development of the ego." We need only reflect on what the concept of "ego" has meant in classical psychoanalytic tradition to see why this is so. The ego was traditionally conceived as a relatively weak, shadowy, passive, and derived agent, largely an epiphenomenon of other more powerful processes. It is "derived from the Id by modifications imposed on it from the external world" and is "representative of the external world."[10] "What we call the ego is essentially passive," says Groddeck, a statement which Freud cites with approval.[11] The developments in the middle period of psychoanalytic theory brought increased emphasis on the ego, to be sure, but chiefly as an aspect of the study of defense mechanisms; the ego enlarged its originally buffeted and frail realm chiefly by its negative, defensive functions. It "owes service to three masters and is consequently menaced by three dangers: the external world, the libido of the Id, the severity of the Super-ego."[12] Freud often remarked that the

10. Healy, Bronner and Bowers, *The Meaning and Structure of Psychoanalysis* (1930), p. 38. We give these quotations from a standard summary from the classical middle period of psychoanalysis, not because we are not aware of refinements made to ego theory later, but because we wish to show the essence of the concept of the ego, an essence which has been elaborated but not basically changed.

11. *Ibid.,* p. 41.

12. *Ibid.,* p. 38.

ego does very well indeed if it can preserve some semblance of harmony in its unruly house.

A moment's thought will show how great is the difference between this ego and the "I-am" experience, the sense of being which we have been discussing. The latter occurs on a more fundamental level and is a precondition for ego development. The ego is a *part* of the personality, and traditionally a relatively weak part, whereas the sense of being refers to one's whole experience, unconscious as well as conscious, and is by no means merely the agent of awareness. The ego is a reflection of the outside world; the sense of being is rooted in one's own experience of existence, and if it is a mirroring of, reflection of, the outside world alone, it is then precisely not one's own sense of existence. My sense of being is *not* my capacity to see the outside world, to size it up, to assess reality; it is rather my capacity to see myself as a being in the world, *to know myself as the being who can do these things.* It is in this sense a precondition for what is called "ego development." The ego is the *subject* in the subject-object relationship; the sense of being occurs on a level prior to this dichotomy. Being means not "I am the subject," but "I am the being who can, among other things, know himself as the subject of what is occurring." The sense of being is not in origin set against the outside world but it must include this capacity to set one's self against the external world if necessary, just as it must include the capacity to confront non-being, as we shall indicate later. To be sure, both what is called the ego and the sense of being presuppose the emergence of self-awareness in the child somewhere between the first couple of months of infancy and the age of two years, a developmental process often called the "emergence of the ego." But this does not mean these two should be identified. The ego is said normally to be especially weak in childhood, weak in proportion to the child's relatively weak assessment of and relation to reality; whereas the sense of being may be especially strong, only later to diminish as the child learns to give himself over to conformist tendencies, to experience his existence as a reflection of others' evaluation of him, to lose some of his originality and primary sense of being. Actually, the sense of being—that is, the ontological sense—is presupposed for ego development, just as it presupposed for the solution of other problems.[13]

---

13. If the objection is entered that the concept of the "ego" at least is more precise and therefore more satisfactory scientifically than this sense of being, we can only repeat what we have said above, that precision can be gained easily enough on paper. But the

We are of course aware that additions and elaborations are occurring in ego theory of late decades in the orthodox psychoanalytic tradition. But one cannot strengthen such a weak monarch by decking him with additional robes, no matter how well-woven or intricately tailored the robes may be. The real and fundamental trouble with the doctrine of the ego is that it represents, par excellence, the subject-object dichotomy in modern thought. Indeed, it is necessary to emphasize that *the very fact that the ego is conceived of as weak, passive, and derived is itself an evidence and a symptom of the loss of the sense of being in our day, a symptom of the repression of the ontological concern.* This view of the ego is a symbol of the pervasive tendency to see the human being primarily as a passive recipient of forces acting upon him, whether the forces be identified as the Id or the vast industrial juggernaut in Marxian terms or the submersion of the individual as "one among many" in the sea of conformity, in Heidegger's terms. The view of the ego as relatively weak and buffeted about by the Id was in Freud a profound symbol of the fragmentation of man in the Victorian period and also a strong corrective to the superficial voluntarism of that day. But the error arises when this ego is elaborated as the basic norm. The sense of being, the ontological awareness, must be assumed below ego theory if that theory is to refer with self-consistency to man as man.

We now come to the important problem of *non-being* or, as phrased in existential literature, *nothingness.* The "and" in the title of this section, "To Be *and* Not To Be," expresses the fact that non-being is an inseparable part of being. To grasp what it means to exist, one needs to grasp the fact that he might not exist, that he treads at every moment on the sharp edge of possible annihilation and can never escape the fact that death will arrive at some unknown moment in the future. Existence, never automatic, not only can be sloughed off and forfeited but is indeed at every instant threatened by non-being. Without this awareness of non-being—that is, awareness of the threats to one's being in death, anxiety, and the less dramatic but persistent threats of loss of potentialities in conformism—existence is vapid, unreal, and characterized by lack of concrete self-awareness. But with the confronting of non-being, existence takes on vitality and im-

---

question always is the bridge between the concept and the reality of the person, and the scientific challenge is to find a concept, a way of understanding, which does not do violence to reality, even though it may be less precise.

mediacy, and the individual experiences a heightened consciousness of himself, his world, and others around him.

Death is of course the most obvious form of the threat of non-being. Freud grasped this truth on one level in his symbol of the death instinct. Life forces (being) are arrayed at every moment, he held, against the forces of death (non-being), and in every individual life the latter will ultimately triumph. But Freud's concept of the death instinct is an ontological truth and should not be taken as a deteriorated psychological theory. The concept of the death instinct is an excellent example of our earlier point that Freud went beyond technical reason and tried to keep open the tragic dimension of life. His emphasis on the inevitability of hostility, aggression, and self-destructiveness in existence also, from one standpoint, has this meaning. True, he phrased these concepts wrongly, as when he interpreted the "death instinct" in chemical terms. The use of the word "thanatos" in psychoanalytic circles as parallel to libido is an example of this deteriorated phraseology. These are errors which arise from trying to put ontological truths, which death and tragedy are, into the frame of technical reason and reduce them to specific psychological mechanisms. On that basis Horney and others could logically argue that Freud was too "pessimistic" and that he merely rationalized war and aggression. I think that is a sound argument against the usual oversimplified psychoanalytic interpretations, which are in the form of technical reason; but it is not a sound argument against Freud himself, who tried to preserve a real concept of tragedy, ambivalent though his frame of reference was. He had indeed a sense of non-being, despite the fact that he always tried to subordinate it and his concept of being to technical reason.

It is also an error to see the "death instinct" only in biological terms, which would leave us hobbled with a fatalism. The unique and crucial fact, rather, is that the human being is the one who *knows* he is going to die, who anticipates his own death. The critical question thus is how he relates to the fact of death: whether he spends his existence running away from death or making a cult of repressing the recognition of death under the rationalizations of beliefs in automatic progress or providence, as is the habit of our Western society, or obscuring it by saying "one dies" and turning it into a matter of public statistics which serve to cover over the one ultimately important fact, that he himself at some unknown future moment will die.

The existential analysts, on the other hand, hold that the confronting of death gives the most positive reality to life itself. It makes the individual existence real, absolute, and concrete. For "death as an irrelative potentiality singles man out and, as it were, individualizes him to make him understand the potentiality of being in others [as well as in himself], when he realizes the inescapable nature of his own death."[14] Death is, in order words, the one fact of my life which is not relative but absolute, and my awareness of this gives my existence and what I do each hour an absolute quality.

Nor do we need to go as far as the extreme example of death to see the problem of non-being. Perhaps the most ubiquitous and ever-present form of the failure to confront non-being in our day is in *conformism,* the tendency of the individual to let himself be absorbed in the sea of collective responses and attitudes, to become swallowed up in *das Man,* with the corresponding loss of his own awareness, potentialities, and whatever characterizes him as a unique and original being. The individual temporarily escapes the anxiety of non-being by this means, but at the price of forfeiting his own powers and sense of existence.

On the positive side, the capacity to confront non-being is illustrated in the ability to accept anxiety, hostility, and aggression. By "accept" we mean here to tolerate without repression and so far as possible to utilize constructively. Severe anxiety, hostility, and agression are states and ways of relating to one's self and others which would curtail or destroy being. But to preserve one's existence by running away from situations which would produce anxiety or situations of potential hostility and aggression leaves one with the vapid, weak, unreal sense of being—what Nietzsche meant in his brilliant description we quoted in the previous chapter of the "impotent people" who evade their aggression by repressing it and thereupon experience "drugged tranquillity" and free-floating resentment. Our point does

14. This is an interpretation of Heidegger, given by Werner Brock in the introduction to *Existence and Being* (Regnery, 1949), p. 77. For those who are interested in the logical aspects of the problem of being vs. non-being, it may be added that the dialectic of "yes vs. no," as Tillich points out in *The Courage to Be,* is present in various forms throughout the history of thought. Hegel held that non-being was an integral part of being, specifically in the "antithesis" stage of his dialectic of "thesis, antithesis, and synthesis." The emphasis on "will" in Schilling, Schopenhauer, Nietzsche, and others as a basic ontological category is a way of showing that being has the power of "negating itself without losing itself." Tillich, giving his own conclusion, holds that the question of how being and non-being are related can be answered only metaphorically: "Being embraces both itself and non-being." In everyday terms, being embraces non-being in the sense that we can be aware of death, can accept it, can even invite it in suicide, in short, can by self-awareness emcompass death.

not at all imply the sloughing over of the distinction between the *neurotic* and *normal* forms of anxiety, hostility, and aggression. Obviously the one constructive way to confront neurotic anxiety, hostility, and aggression is to clarify them psychotherapeutically and so far as possible to wipe them out. But that task has been made doubly difficult, and the whole problem confused, by our failure to see the normal forms of these states—"normal" in the sense that they inhere in the threat of non-being with which any being always has to cope. Indeed, is it not clear that *neurotic* forms of anxiety, hostility, and aggression develop precisely because the individual has been unable to accept and deal with the *normal* forms of these states and ways of behaving? Paul Tillich has suggested far-reaching implications for the therapeutic process in his powerful sentence, which we shall quote without attempting to elucidate, "The self-affirmation of a being is the stronger the more non-being it can take into itself."

6

On the Tantra*

ALAN WATTS

April 10, 1968

You yourself are the eternal energy which appears as this universe.
You didn't come into this world. You came out of it, like a wave from
the ocean. You are not a stranger here. On the contrary, everything
that happens to you, everything that you experience, is your karma:
your own doing. This, though expressed in differing ways, is the
central philosophy of both Hinduism and Buddhism, cradled alike in
the culture of ancient India.

Obviously, this "you yourself" is not the superficial personality
or ego that we know as John or Jane Doe, which does not feel itself
directly responsible for growing hair or beating a heart, much less for
blowing the wind or shining the stars. The Hindu and Buddhist
sadhanas (or spiritual disciplines) are ways of awakening to the actual
sensation of oneself as a process vaster by far than what is ordinarily
felt to be "I"—that very limited center of conscious attention and voli-
tion which we call the person or ego.

As in watching anything intently—such as the form of a beautiful
woman—one's attention becomes fastened upon particular details, so

*Tantra is a class of esoteric Yogic teachings in Hinduism, Janism, and Buddhism. It
postulates that the human body is a microcosm through which spiritual truth must be at-
tained. In the Tantric practices of Tibetan Buddhism, for instance, the body and mind are
accepted as a proper medium, rather than an obstacle, for the realization of the universal
self. [Ed.]

the basic energy of this universe becomes fascinated with particular plots and patterns, and thus identifies itself with each and every "I"— whether human, animal, or vegetable. But in each instance of doing this, it temporarily forgets that it is *what* there is, *all* that there is, the "which than which there is no whicher" for ever and ever.

Thus every individual is, as it were, God in disguise, playing hide-and-seek with himself through the ages of eternity. "God" is not, in this Hindu view, the universal monarch and governor of Jewish and Christian theology, but rather the Player and Actor of the world, playing all the parts of life so rapidly and intensely that he forgets himself and becomes identified with each one of them. Every role he assumes is also audience to all the others, and the play is performed so convincingly that the audience takes it "for real."

According to Indian philosophy, there are two principal ways by which you may become free from this fascination and so remember your original identity as the source and ground of the universe.

The first and better known is by renunciation of pleasure, by detachment and asceticism, as a means of breaking fascination with the particular forms of life. The self-tormented fakir on his bed of nails is trying to attain to a state in which nothing—but nothing—in life can throw him. He returns to center by plumbing the sensation of pain to its depths, attaining final freedom from the fear of suffering and death.

The second, less known, way—called Tantra—is the opposite: not withdrawal from life but the fullest possible acceptance of one's desires, feelings, and situation as a human being. If you are the Godhead, the universal self, fascinated with the particular existence of John Doe, then just *be* that and *do* that to the full. Explore the fascination of desire, love, and lust to its limit. Accept and enjoy without reservation the ego that you seem to be.

Thus, the follower of the Tantric way plunges himself into just those things which the ascetic renounces: sexuality, food and drink, and all the involvements of worldly life. He does not, however, do this in the half-hearted and timid spirit of the ordinary pleasure seeker. He abandons himself to the pleasure-pain of ordinary sensual experience with the utmost concentration on the finest vibrations of feeling, and learns to play these sensations as one plays with the breath on a flute.

Through this intense exploration of sensory experience he discovers two things. First, that existence or energy is at root a simple alternation or vibration of on and off, yes and no, now you see it/now you don't, which is capable of infinite complication, as all numbers can be represented with the symbols 0 and 1. He learns that the "yes" or "on" element of energy cannot be experienced without contrast with the "no" or "off," and therefore that darkness and death are by no means the mere absence of light and life, but rather their origin. In this way the fear of death and nothingness is entirely overcome.

Because of this startling discovery, so alien to our normal common sense, he worships the divinity under its female rather than its male form—for the female is symbolically representative of the negative, dark, and hollow aspect of the world, without which the masculine, positive, light, and solid aspect cannot be manifested or seen. The very word "Tantra" is connected with the art of weaving, and denotes the interdependence of warp and woof in woven cloth: the one cannot hold together without the other.

Second, he discovers that existence is basically a kind of dancing or music—an immensely complex energy pattern which needs no explanation other than itself—just as we do not ask what is the *meaning* of fugues by Bach or sonatas by Mozart. We do not dance to reach a certain point on the floor, but simply to dance. Energy itself, as William Blake said, is eternal delight—and all life is to be lived in the spirit of rapt absorption in an arabesque of rhythms.

Tantric imagery in painting, sculpture, and ritual has, therefore, particular themes which exemplify its own way of experiencing the world. It shows the male and female divinities joined in a meditative form of sexual union in which each worships the other as his and her origin. It shows the god or goddess as a many-headed or multi-armed being, a sort of cosmic centipede, portraying every individual as a limb of the central and eternal self. It also employs patterns of meaningless letters and chants of meaningless sounds (mantras) to suggest and help one to realize the essentially musical and dancing spirit of the universe.

Some understanding of Tantra is therefore a marvelous and welcome corrective to certain excesses of Western civilization. We overaccentuate the positive, think of the negative as "bad," and thus live in a frantic terror of death and extinction which renders us incapable of "playing" life with an air of noble and joyous detachment. Failing to understand the musical quality of nature, which fulfills itself in an eternal present, we live for a tomorrow which never comes—like an orchestra racing to attain the finale of a symphony. But through understanding the creative power of the female, of the negative, of empty space, and of death, we may at least become completely alive in the present.

REFERENCES

The reader who wishes additional information about Tantric Yoga may find the following list of readings helpful.

Gunther, Herbert V., and Trungpa, C. 1975. *The Dawn of Tantra.* Berkeley: Shambhala.

Migot, A. 1954. Buddhist Yoga and Tibetan Tantric techniques. In P. A. Sorokin, ed., *Forms and Techniques of Altruistic and Spiritual Growth.* Boston: Beacon.

Zimmer, H. 1960. On the significance of the Indian Tantric Yoga. In J. Campbell, ed., *Spiritual Disciplines.* New York: Pantheon.

Several very informative articles on Tantra can also be found in a new bi-monthly journal, *The Laughing Man,* 1976, vol. 1, no. 2. (Box 2200, Clearlake Highlands, California 95422).

7

The Absolute and the Relative: Two Aspects of Dynamic Experience

JAMES B. KLEE

I

By the absolute aspect of dynamic experience I mean the "thing-in-itself" quality which is accepted in the naive realism of everyday living. By dynamic experience I am trying to indicate that motivation, or value generally, is part of the experience itself, is intrinsic to the experience and is not superimposed by some drive or force external to the experience. Experience itself is forceful and self-driven. The emphasis, however, in this description of naive experience is not on either the objective reality of the alleged referent of experience or the subjective reality of the experiencer. This dichotomization of experience into organism and environment is legitimate only from the point of view of an external observer during the experience or before and/or after the experience relative to the experiencer. The absoluteness of experience concerns the immediacy of the dynamic experience. The experience is absolute as long as the object is not identified as such and the perceiver is not conscious of his relationship to the object as perceiver; or it is absolute as long as the relation of the simultaneousness of object and perceiver itself has become the absolute of experience. The absolute is that which Northrop calls "the immediately apprehended differentiated aesthetic continuum" with both "terms," the object and the subject, reduced to one, experience. Whatever you may wish to call this absoluteness of dynamic experience, this statement of im-

Source: Reprinted by permission from Darshana International, vol. IV, nos. 1, 2 (Moradabad, India, 1964).

mediate relationship, is irrelevant. James Joyce has suggested the use of the term "epiphany" in the brief discussion of aesthetics in *Stephan Hero* and this may well be accepted because of the seemingly miraculous element in all experience. The point remains that recognition must be given to this existential consciousness. Of all that which from a relativistic aspect could have been the particular relationships of organism and environment, only the only experience did in fact occur and that is the given, that is the condition of existence and for good or bad you're stuck with it. Perhaps the thinker could have had other thoughts and perhaps other contents were available yet the particular thought as the combination of specific thinker and content was absolute and irrevocable. The particular experience experienced, the experiencer goes on from there.

This absoluteness of immediate apprehension, or the epiphany of aesthetic reality, this dynamic experience in itself is easy to recognize in one's response to inventions, scientific discoveries, moral statements (categorical imperatives), political or economic principles, historical events, the act of love, and to works of art, for these have a discreteness, a "standing alone" quality which frequently tends to prevent comparisons or other types of relational activity with other areas of experience. In a sense no continuum or choice scale is immediately recognized. These events have the arresting and numbing quality of a thorough seduction. For the moment, the individual is captivated and encapsulated from all the rest of the world. He becomes selfless and seems to exist neither in time or space for indeed such questions about subject or object, time or space, are not likely to arise. He is the experience and vice versa, and seems to move in a relatively effortless way towards—satiation. This is most frequently called the aesthetic experience. And yet it is but an aspect of the whole of experience and as such can be treated as noncorrelative. It is but one factor in the matrix of experience, a factor which enables the uniqueness of each experience, a moment of the exact time and space which makes the past past and the object always that object, the subject always that subject, and no other. Such is the dimension in which all experience is discrete, unique, and limited in time and space. By such is meant the absolute.

II

If art helps us to define the absolute, so madness brings us to a closer understanding of the relative. For whereas we sometimes can

accept the aesthetic, the immediacy of the work of art, we fight acceptance of the products of the deluded and call it madness. We say no to
the possessions, the compulsions, the hallucinations. We deny their
uniqueness, their absoluteness and immediacy, and place them in relation to something that can be accepted. We say these are the products
of diseased minds, of sick brains and glands, of distorting heat waves,
of propaganda and suggestion, or drugs and poisons, of the experience
of frustration, conflict, and trauma. For these other categories are acceptable. The unacceptable is thus related to the sick organism, to the
false culture, to the disproportionate environment: we feel safe once
again. And we may be at that, sometimes. For in the relational dimension there is mobility, change, and the chance to choose. One is not
captivated entirely; one can compare, discriminate, and select. It is
possible to move from or toward, increase or decrease one over the
other. Then there is the chance to get out of trouble or into still more.
There is freedom to the n—1 absolutes available within the perspective
allowed. One has gone from the principle of pleasure to the principle of
reality; but when no choice continuum is offered, when there are no
degrees of freedom, then one is frustrated in that dimension. We may
try to fight as long as there is some dimly sensed hope, but when that
too disappears that dimension is dead for us and we are left just a little
less alive.

Of course for him who is "adjusted" to his madness, who accepts
his mission, who no longer questions his lot, the same epiphanous
structure of experience is evident as in the case of the experience
called aesthetic. There is no need to distinguish between abnormality
in the absolute dimension of experience. The madman like the priest
accepts his calling. In fact it is not unusual for the inventive genius to
claim the voice of God as the only authority. For the new absolute is
not derivative, has no ultimate sanction beyond its being, its epiphany.
Each individual, including the reader, must refer to his own insight for
an ostensive definition.

To some extent experience in madness and aesthetic experience
differ only as a matter of taste. There is no difference that cannot be
questioned. Each may be accepted for itself and that is the point. It is
only in so far as we see that each leads to consequences of different
value to us that any distinction between the two may be noticed. Madness too frequently is self-limiting, and as such defeats its protective
function by ultimately removing or devaluating that which it would
protect. The question which madness does not answer or answers but
poorly is: "Madness, then what?" In fact any inability to answer the

question: "Then what?" is revealing of madness; to the degree that the answer evades this question, to that degree there is madness.

That is the only test of the abnormal. The normal epiphany of experience is, like most science and art, open ended. Growth may still occur, selection take place, change be accepted with grace and interest. Life can expand in depth and scope, in richness of action and experience. The completion of one leads to the opening of the next, not to boredom, self-destruction, or fear. Theoretically, if the paths chosen were completely normal, there should be no termination to life. Even at present there is usually continuity of life on into the future somewhere of some species. And that life can be called normal, the healthy life. No, it is not in the absolute dimension that the difference between normal and abnormal lies. It is only in the relative dimension that such a consideration gains significance. Then why do we continue to make the mistake of judging the absolute as good and bad, healthy and diseased, normal and abnormal? I do not know entirely the probable answer to this but the fact is that we do confuse these and I would like to point to a few crucial areas where this confusion causes no end of needless suffering to those so misinformed. This includes all of us.

III

Actually a good part of the difficulty starts in the confusions relating to the nature and scope of one's own experience and particularly as it is extended to the interpretation of one's relation to others. This is especially obvious when one is in an authoritative relation to another as expert, leader, or parent. True, good and evil exists for us in our pain and misery, joy and exaltation. Yet the thing-in-itself is not good or bad but only in its relationships. Any one thing is sometimes good and sometimes evil and only the extremely misexperienced can ultimately fail to see this. Very recently some things like love were good, others like sex were bad. Yet how can this be if one is of the other? We admired the highly motivated but despised the over emotional yet the intense disregard of emotion is nothing but the negative aspect of high motivation. To do any one thing intensively is for that time to neglect and obviate all other values. Too often we developed pairs of names to designate the good and bad aspects of a thing separately, yet failed to realize we were but naming the same thing twice instead of the different relationships which were the actual basis of the differentiations. The epiphanous experience in and of itself is always ambivalent. Only the context enables the discrimination of its relative values. The psychoanalyst has long been aware of this ambivalence and of course it has been long recognized as the "golden mean," "tao," or "way."

From birth, and possibly from even before, such choices are apparent and are usually mishandled by those in the dominant political (power) relationship to the developing individual. For the authority in attempting to choose for someone else sets up rules or lists by which to ease this task for himself. No longer can he permit others the exercise of taste for obviously his tastes are his own and not the others'. An authority then, if *he* is to control the actions of others, must resort to standards and external sanctions. Only in this way can he maintain *his* special privilege. And yet if dynamic experience or taste is the basis of choice how mad he must be to think he can in any way choose for another. Because of his often superhuman sense of power and its complement of obligation he feels it his responsibility, which, of course it would be if he were omniscient. Yet does not the parent think he knows better in relation to the child, the child to the dog, the teacher to the student, the lawyer to his client, the doctor to his patient, the governor to his people, the priest to his parish? The superior, the expert, because it is what he knows is his own absolute experience is misled to believe it is all that is to be known and so offers a rule, a list of sanctions and values. And because the recipient is likely to be unaware of such origins in the absolutes and relationships in the experience of the authority, he can only apply the rules to the thing and so probably is doubly mistaken and confused.

The last statement is somewhat misleading for the submitter does not experience the list or rule of things entirely without relationships. In fact, the matter is far worse than one might suspect. The additional trouble lies in that there is always and very definitely a relationship but it is to the authority and not to the situation that the relationship is established. To borrow from Norbert Wiener (out of Heisenberg) the concept of the "evil eye," the authority by trying to establish an experience of relationships to some situation succeeds only in establishing it to himself. But when asked for what he has done this he will usually deny that was his intent and answer instead that he was trying for the development of independent and responsible experience in the existence of the other. As such, all authority is truly mad. At best the expert, the individual, who, because of more experience has some advantage, can only lead by example and guidance and not by command and instruction if both of these dilemmas are to be circumvented.

Specific examples of this type of difficulty are extremely easy to find for they are most of our life. The mother who is anxious for the welfare of her newly born child prevents it from putting strange objects in its mouth for fear of contaminative results to the infant. She has just established that habit when the time for weaning arrives and she must now cope with a child which rejects what is for it, the "bad" strange objects, its new solid food. Simultaneously this rejection of what was learned to be avoided incurs the loss of his mother's affections for which the avoidance relationship has been established in the first place. He soon ceases to trust the evidence of his senses and in his turn seeks signs of eternal truth instead of reliable knowledge. Again strictures regarding sexuality, especially for females, cause them to abhor the act for the first third of their existence but then they discover after receiving the ring that it takes the next third of existence to overcome this former set of values to what formerly was bad is now good. No wonder that so many reach the menopause thoroughly confused. The student in submitting to "basic disciplines" soon abandons thinking about the subject matter of the discipline and instead thinks primarily of how to please his superior, the teacher. And since his own original work is likely to be highly unbasic or individual and not in strict conformity with the "basic discipline" he too ceases to trust in his own experience and seeks sanctions in a white coat, collar, or skin color. Yet when out of school he discovers that he must learn to choose for himself. We can only pray he hasn't learned the original lesson too well. Of course one could continue to develop food aversions, frigidity, or slavish professionalism instead of fighting through the handicap. Such individuals are frequently comfortable in their selves even though to others they are dull and a threat to the freedom of everyone. It is possible to let the ambivalent remain bad always or good always. One *can* place the blame or praise elsewhere and so not have to choose now one way now another according to the relative circumstances. I just suggest that since choice is *possible,* and if we wish to have a democratic society with a self-choosing and responsible people, we can do much to make such choosing *probable.* We do not *have to* give in to totalitarian measures. They are not necessary.

IV

On the more intimate level of the belief in one's own experiences the same sorts of consideration apply. Actually of course one need not apply principles to experience since, as experience is unique—"solid," discrete, or absolute—principle or form can be found to be intrinsic to it in the first place. It is this of which I speak.

The individual accepts or rejects his own immediate experience to the degree that he is able to reject or accept the declarations of authority. This is particularly noticeable in the case where the two may be found to conflict. Perhaps such conflict does not exist in the vast majority of cases. This may even be the case for most of us a good part of the time. After all, we all eat much the same food (if given the chance), we all sleep, drink, etc. It may even seem at first that to give up total totalitarian control of our more dependable experiences, just to make room for the vagaries of a few individuals or our own rare contradictory experiences, may be too great a price for the immediate security which the totalistic system apparently would offer. The anxiety which at first glance seems to be the alternative may easily spur the defeated individual to re-establish a security system far worse than the one so hesitantly left behind. And the despair following defeat certainly seems horrible at first. Such anxiety, the "dizziness of freedom" as Kierkegaard put it, should never be underestimated. Anxiety is always the first payment towards the price of freedom. Yet the longer the first step is postponed the more difficult it may appear to be to take it. And the main point is overlooked, anyway. If such motives or dynamic experiences (anger, eating, love) are so dependable in the first place, would it not be wiser to recognize that it is not necessary to insist upon them? Can we not see that they will so likely insure themselves that any systematic organization can be developed democratically and need not be imposed from above? The stupidity and madness of totalitarian discipline lie in the fact that in the hysterical haste to regulate and constantify life one loses sight of the truth that life contains in itself sufficient limitation and self-discipline as to obviate the need for regulation if given half a chance. Life itself is its own discipline, contains its own order, is self-regulating. More order in and of itself within the life structure is unnecessary.

Perhaps the story is apocryphal, but an acquaintance once said he came across Mondrian in the Metropolitan Museum of Art, seated before a Breughel making sketches for one of his "compositions." In the Breughel could be seen the order he was abstracting. But it could not have been the other way. What is necessary is to expand and enrich living, to bring more into the scope of living. This will not occur if we deliberately cut off the paths to the future by distracting attention to the internal disorder which is disordered only by our misunderstandings and fear and by the unconsidered vagaries of existence which have induced or elicited it. Actually the cues to further internal order are outside the system and these can only be found by continual expansion, not by involution and contraction. Creativity and invention, although they restructure the experience at hand, do so only because of the additional experience of other sorts which create new contexts and dimensions of experience. They do not come from more of the same for all that provides are the permutations and combinations of what one already has. In the latter case the need for *creativity* is obviated. If what one had at hand solved one's problems entirely one would have no problems to begin with. The staticity, the balance, the homeostasis, the ordered discipline sought under authoritarian ideals is found only in the unperpetuating machine. As such it is regular and trustworthy provided it is well maintained. But it is insufficient in the long run, leading only to the boredom of self-imposed impoverishment and to the destruction caused by one's own excess of timidity.

V

As a matter of fact it would seem that wherever ambivalence or conflict arises within a problem it can only be solved by reference to at least a third point of reference. Just as a plane needs to be fixed in space by at least one more point than the two necessary to a line, so any complementary schism needs an additional referent in order to avert mutual destruction. This has usually been popularly recognized in any situation where civil warfare threatens in either the individual or social dimension. It frequently takes an external enemy to bring the individual together with himself, to reunite the quarreling family, to bring the nation together, to restructure the idea. However, it is not necessary that the "third force" be negative and threatening; a common goal can unite the split group or individual. And in fact that is the essential aspect even under negative pressure. For in the latter case, unless there were a place to which or a way in which they could go together, pressure in and of itself need only have a purely chance result. It would even seem that only by a third external factor can any problem, insolvable within the stated limits, be solved. Every trick puzzle bears this out as do all the psychological experimentations on "direction" in thinking. Once a split has occurred into mutual or complementary oppositions, reconciliation must always be through re-organization via the mediation of at least a third factor. Besides, if this were not so, there could be no division or differentiation in the first place. For as indicated above it is the contexts that enable discrimination and for a context to exist there must be at least one more absolute than the thing contexted to provide the relationship.

But what is more, the neglect of the self-regulation of living structures is not dissipated entirely unless the authoritarian control is absolute and perfect. Usually the ignored capacities find enough nourishment on their own to continue independently. The remaining viability is amazingly tough and is likely to fight back as Toynbee's internal proletariat or Freud's unconscious "id" well suggest. As such psychoanalysts as Wilhelm Reich and Carl Jung and the other scientists who have a sense of the continuity of things and their expansive evolution and development have pointed out, the chaos and lack of discipline of which we are most afraid and confronting which we are most anxious and insecure we have ourselves created. For it is but complementary to the restrictive discipline we have attempted to impose. In a sense, whenever one makes a thing disproportionately some one definite thing, one also creates its opposite through neglect or repression. One creates one's own nemesis in dialectical fashion. Only by a grasp of the thing in its entirety can one go on from there. Otherwise one remains in a state of internecine warfare, which will bring either the group or the individual to its own destruction long before its time. In our fear of burning the candle at both ends we burn it in the middle and thus fall apart the sooner.

I do not intend that this has to be of *necessity* in some mystical fashion for that would be as dogmatically limiting as the tendencies to which this argument is offered in opposition. The "failure of nerve," the neurotic hesitancy, the search for perfection of experience before action is equally as destructive and for the same reasons. Rather the whole evidence of evolution is suggestive of the fact that the complementary, that which is left out in the plans of the present, usually finds reinforcement somewhere or it would not be extant in the first place. One would not have neurosis if the things fought against were not sufficiently nourished by one's environment to enable their viability. There would not be the anguish of frustration and the conflict within the individual, the misery of civil warfare between the peoples of a state or states, or the waste of warfare of mankind against the other creatures of his environment, if the opposition were not in some measure in and of itself successful and valuable.

If we were perfect, if we had the exclusive solution, there would be no anxiety, no doubt, no disease. But in fact there has always been something else left to be desired and in an expanding universe one would have to have colossal conceit, superhuman knowledge and experience, to ever not feel that something remains unexplored in this universe. Every art, every science, every system has at one time or another found itself unnecessarily limited by its own conceit and has admitted its humility or has perished. This is as much a fact of experience as any "hard fact" in any field of endeavor. There is little reason to believe that this state of affairs will ever change.

And the recognition of this is in experience itself. Sometimes we deny those murmurings of things to come which are before, nay in and of our eyes. Yet these are in our experience as absolute as that which we do accept, that which we do affirm. As we throw off the totalistic and authoritarian aspects of our experience these new items emerge, not because they are newly created but because they were there all along and have for reasons relating to their evolution only now reached sufficient proportions to be taken cognizance of. Or perhaps we have lost fear of the earlier contents of experience by acceptance of their implicit organization, we have been liberated for what we had potential in us all along. Within the potentially expanding experience of the individual is all that he *can* use, all that he could use to regulate *his* life and set an example in the experience of others. That all that he may need is not *in* his own experience at a particular absolute moment is the tragedy of existence, is the source of his forlornness, his loneliness, his anguish and despair. Yet, to believe that another's experience can do it for him is to deny his own experience, is only to lead to an acceleration of his own destruction and that of the others, too.

REFERENCES

Klee, J. B. 1951. *Problems of Selective Behavior.* Lincoln: University of Nebraska.

———. 1960. Religion as facing forward in-time. *Existential Inquiries,* vol. 1, no. 2: 19–32.

———. and Schrickel, H. G. 1963. Prolegomena to a psychology of signs: I. The symbolistic revolution. *Psychologia,* 6: 193–206.

———. History—death and life. In *Introductory Experiential Psychology,* H. F. Stewart, Jr., and J. D. Thomas (eds.). Dubuque, Iowa: Kendall/Hunt, 1970.

8

Psychoanalysis and Zen Buddhism

ERICH FROMM

The aim of Zen is enlightenment: the immediate, unreflected grasp of reality, without affective contamination and intellectualization, the realization of the relation of myself to the Universe. This new experience is a repetition of the pre-intellectual, immediate grasp of the child, but on a new level, that of the full development of man's reason, objectivity, individuality. While the child's experience, that of immediacy and oneness, lies *before* the experience of alienation and the subject-object split, the enlightenment experience lies after it.

The aim of psychoanalysis, as formulated by Freud, is that of making the unconscious conscious, of replacing Id by Ego. To be sure, the content of the unconscious to be discovered was limited to a small sector of the personality, to those instinctual drives which were alive in early childhood, but which were subject to amnesia. To lift these out of the state of repression was the aim of the analytic technique. Furthermore, the sector to be uncovered, quite aside from Freud's theoretical premises, was determined by the therapeutic need to cure a particular symptom. There was little interest in recovering unconsciousness outside of the sector related to the symptom formation. Slowly the introduction of the concept of the death instinct and eros and the development of the Ego aspects in recent years have brought about a certain broadening of the Freudian concepts of the contents of the unconscious. The non-Freudian schools greatly widened the sector of the unconscious to be uncovered. Most radically Jung, but also Adler, Rank, and the other more recent so-called neo-Freudian authors have

Source: From Zen Buddhism and Psychoanalysis, *by D. T. Suzuki, Erich Fromm, and Richard DeMartino, pp. 134–41.* © *1960 by Erich Fromm. Reprinted by permission of Harper & Row.*

contributed to this extension. But (with the exception of Jung), in spite of such a widening, the extent of the sector to be uncovered has remained determined by the therapeutic aim of curing this or that symptom; or this or that neurotic character trait. It has not encompassed the whole person.

However, if one follows the original aim of Freud, that of making the unconscious conscious, to its last consequences, one must free it from the limitations imposed on it by Freud's own instinctual orientation, and by the immediate task of curing symptoms. If one pursues the aim of the full recovery of the unconscious, then this task is not restricted to the instincts, nor to other limited sectors of experience, but to the total experience of the total man; then the aim becomes that of overcoming alienation, and of the subject-object split in perceiving the world; then the uncovering of the unconscious means the overcoming of affective contamination and cerebration; it means the derepression, the abolition of the split within myself between the universal man and the social man; it means the disappearance of the polarity of conscious vs. unconscious; it means arriving at the state of the immediate grasp of reality, without distortion and without interference by intellectual reflection; it means overcoming of the craving to hold on to the ego, to worship it; it means giving up the illusion of an indestructible separate ego, which is to be enlarged, preserved and as the Egyptian pharaohs hoped to preserve themselves as mummies for eternity. To be conscious of the unconscious means to be open, responding, to *have* nothing and to *be*.

This aim of the full recovery of unconsciousness by consciousness is quite obviously much more radical than the general psychoanalytic aim. The reasons for this are easy to see. To achieve this total aim requires an effort far beyond the effort most persons in the West are willing to make. But quite aside from this question of effort, even the visualization of this aim is possible only under certain conditions. First of all, this radical aim can be envisaged only from the point of view of a certain philosophical position. There is no need to describe this position in detail. Suffice it to say that it is one in which not the negative aim of the absence of sickness, but the positive one of the presence of well-being is aimed at, and that well-being is conceived in terms of full union, the immediate and uncontaminated grasp of the world. This aim could not be better described than has been done by Suzuki in terms of "the art of living." One must keep in mind that any such concept as the art of living grows from the soil of a spiritual humanistic orientation, as it underlies the teaching of Buddha, of the prophets, of Jesus, of Meister Eckhart, or of men such as Blake, Walt Whitman, or Bucke. Unless it is seen in this context, the concept of "the art of living" loses all that is specific, and deteriorates into a concept that goes today under the name of "happiness." It must also not be forgotten that this orientation includes an ethical aim. While Zen transcends ethics, it includes the basic ethical aims of Buddhism, which are essentially the same as those of all humanistic teaching. The achievement of the aim of Zen, as Suzuki has made very clear in the lectures in this book, implies the overcoming of greed in all forms, whether it is the greed for possession, for fame, or for affection; it implies overcoming narcissistic self-glorification and the illusion of omnipotence. It implies, furthermore, the overcoming of the desire to submit to an authority who solves one's own problem of existence. The person who only wants to use the discovery of the unconscious to be cured of sickness will, of course, not even attempt to achieve the radical aim which lies in the overcoming of repressedness.

But it would be a mistake to believe that the radical aim of the de-repression has no connection with a therapeutic aim. Just as one has recognized that the cure of a symptom and the prevention of future symptom formations is not possible without the analysis and change of the character, one must also recognize that the change of this or that neurotic character trait is not possible without pursuing the more radical aim of a complete transformation of the person. It may very well be that the relatively disappointing results of character analysis (which have never been expressed more honestly than by Freud in his "Analysis, Terminable or Interminable?") are due precisely to the fact that the aims for the cure of the neurotic character were not radical enough; that well-being, freedom from anxiety and insecurity, can be achieved only if the limited aim is transcended, that is, if one realizes that the limited, therapeutic aim cannot be achieved as long as it remains limited and does not become part of a wider, humanistic frame of reference. Perhaps the limited aim can be achieved with more limited and less time-consuming methods, while the time and energy consumed in the long analytic process are used fruitfully only for the radical aim of "transformation" rather than the narrow one of "reform." This proposition might be strengthened by referring to a statement made above. Man, as long as he has not reached the creative relatedness of which *satori* is the fullest achievement, at best compensates for inherent potential depression by routine, idolatry, destructiveness, greed for property or fame, etc. When any of these compensations break down, his sanity is threatened. The cure of the potential insanity lies only in the change in attitude from split and alienation to the creative, immediate grasp of and response to the world. If psychoanalysis can help in this way, it can help to achieve true mental health; if it cannot, it will only help to improve compensatory mechanisms. To put it still differently: somebody may be "cured" of a symptom, but he can not be "cured" of a character neurosis. Man is not a thing, man is not a "case," and the analyst does not cure anybody by treating him as an object.* Rather, the analyst can only help a man to wake up, in a process in which the analyst is engaged with the "patient" in the process of their understanding each other, which means experiencing their oneness.

In stating all this, however, we must be prepared to be confronted with an objection. If, as I said above, the achievement of the full consciousness of the unconscious is as radical and difficult an aim as enlightenment, does it make any sense to discuss this radical aim as something which has any general application? Is it not purely speculative to raise seriously the question that only this radical aim can justify the hopes of psychoanalytic therapy?

If there were only the alternative between full enlightenment and nothing, then indeed this objection would be valid. But this is not so. In Zen there are many stages of enlightenment, of which *satori* is the ultimate and decisive step. But, as far as I understand, value is set on experiences which are steps in the direction of *satori*, although *satori* may never be reached. Dr Suzuki once illustrated this point in the following way: If one candle is brought into an absolutely dark room, the darkness disappears, and there is light. But if ten or a hundred or a thousand candles are added, the room will become brighter and brighter. Yet the decisive change was brought about by the first candle which penetrated the darkness.†

What happens in the analytic process? A person senses for the first time that he is vain, that he is frightened, that he hates, while consciously he had believed himself to be modest, brave and loving. The new insight may hurt him, but it opens a door; it permits him to stop projecting on others what he represses in himself. He proceeds; he experiences the infant, the child, the adolescent, the criminal, the insane, the saint, the artist, the male, *and* the female within himself; he

*Cf. my paper: "The Limitations and Dangers of Psychology," in *Religion and Culture*, ed., W. Leibrecht, (New York, Harper Brothers, 1959), p. 31 ff.

†In a personal communication, as I remember.

gets more deeply in touch with humanity, with the universal man; he represses less, is freer, has less need to project, to cerebrate; then he may experience for the first time how he sees colors, how he sees a ball roll, how his ears are suddenly fully opened to music, when up to now he only listened *to* it; in sensing his oneness and others, he may have a first glimpse of the illusion that his separate individual ego is some*thing* to hold onto, to cultivate, to save; he will experience the futility of seeking the answer to life by *having* himself, rather than by being and becoming himself. All these are sudden, unexpected experiences with no intellectual content; yet afterwards the person feels freer, stronger, less anxious than he ever felt before.

So far we have spoken about *aims,* and I have proposed that if one carries Freud's principle of the transformation of unconsciousness into consciousness to its ultimate consequences, one approaches the concept of enlightenment. But as to *methods* of achieving this aim, psychoanalysis and Zen are, indeed, entirely different. The method of Zen is, one might say, that of a frontal attack on the alienated way of perception by means of the "sitting," the koan, and the authority of the master. Of course, all this is not a "technique" which can be isolated from the premise of Buddhist thinking, of the behavior and ethical values which are embodied in the master and in the atmosphere of the monastery. It must also be remembered that it is not a "five hour a week" concern, and that by the very fact of coming for instruction in Zen the student has made a most important decision, a decision which is an important part of what goes on afterwards.

The psychoanalytic method is entirely different from the Zen method. It trains consciousness to get hold of the unconscious in a different way. It directs attention to that perception which is distorted; it leads to a recognition of the fiction within oneself; it widens the range of human experience by lifting repressedness. The analytic method is psychological-empirical. It examines the psychic development of a person from childhood on and tries to recover earlier experiences in order to assist the person in experiencing of what is now repressed. It proceeds by uncovering illusions within oneself about the world, step by step, so that parataxic distortions and alienated intellectualizations diminish. By becoming less of a stranger to himself, the person who goes through this process becomes less estranged to the world; because he has opened up communication with the universe within himself, he has opened up communication with the universe outside. False consciousness disappears, and with it the polarity conscious-unconscious. A new realism dawns in which "the mountains are mountains again.'' The psychoanalytic method is of course only a method, a preparation; but so is the Zen method. By the very fact that it is a method it never guarantees the achievement of the goal. The factors which permit this achievement are deeply rooted in the individual personality, and for all practical purposes we know little of them.

I have suggested that the method of uncovering the unconscious, if carried to its ultimate consequences, may be a step toward enlightenment, provided it is taken within the philosophical context which is most radically and realistically expressed in Zen. But only a great deal of further experience in applying this method will show how far it can lead. The view expressed here implies only a possibility and thus has the character of a hypothesis which is to be tested.

But what can be said with more certainty is that the knowledge of Zen, and a concern with it, can have a most fertile and clarifying influence on the theory and technique of psychoanalysis. Zen, different as it is in its method from psychoanalysis, can sharpen the focus, throw new light on the nature of insight, and heighten the sense of what it is to see, what it is to be creative, what it is to overcome the affective contaminations and false intellectualizations which are the necessary results of experience based on the subject-object split.

In its very radicalism with respect to intellectualization, authority, and the delusion of the ego, in its emphasis on the aim of well being, Zen thought will deepen and widen the horizon of the psychoanalyst and help him to arrive at a more radical concept of the grasp of reality as the ultimate aim of full, conscious awareness.

REFERENCES

References on psychoanalysis are too numerous to mention here, but the reader might find the following list of writings on Zen useful.

Ames, V. M. 1962. *Zen and American Thought.* Honolulu: University of Hawaii Press.

Herrigel, E. 1953. *Zen in the Art of Archery.* New York: Pantheon Books.

Hoffman, Y. *The Sound of the One Hand.* New York: Basic Books, 1975.

Lesh, T. V. Zen and psychotherapy: a partially annotated bibliography. *Journal of Humanistic Psychology,* vol. 10, no. 2, Spring 1970, 75–83.

Maupin, W. E. 1962. Zen Buddhism: A psychological review. *Journal of Consulting Psychology*, 26: 362–78.

Reps, P. *Zen Flesh, Zen Bones*. New York: Doubleday, 1961.

Ross, N. W. 1960. *The World of Zen*. New York: Random House.

Suzuki, D. T. 1964. *An Introduction to Zen Buddhism*, with forward by C. G. Jung. New York: Grove Press.

Watts, A. 1960. *This Is It*. New York: Pantheon Books.

9

The Psychology of Natural Childbirth

DEBORAH TANZER

Introduction*

Psychological aspects of childbirth have been insufficiently inves-
tigated, given the importance of childbirth to both the individual and
the species. This is especially true for natural childbirth, despite its
rapidly growing use. Natural childbirth has at its core the elimination
or reduction of analgesic and anesthetic agents in labor and delivery,
the resulting consciousness and participation of the mother during the
entire birth process, and various kinds of preparatory education and
activity during pregnancy; it also frequently includes active husband
participation.

Past investigations of natural childbirth, motivated by considerations of possible dangers from drugs, have concentrated on obstetrical
aspects, despite general acknowledgment by investigators that its
greatest value seemed in the psychological sphere.

Further motivation for the present investigation was a belief that
it could illuminate some broader areas. Psychological topics included
self concepts and self-actualization, growth and fulfillment, marital
interaction, mother-child relations, female psychology and male-fe-
male differences, and peak experiences. Psychophysiological topics included psychosomatic interrelations, particularly the relationship of

Source: From The Psychology of Pregnancy and Childbirth: An Investigation of
Natural Childbirth, Ph.D. dissertation, Brandeis University, 1967. Reprinted by permission of Deborah Tanzer.

*Dr. Tanzer's work is one of the few research reports dealing with the psychological
aspects of natural childbirth. A condensed version of it has appeared in *Psychology Today*, October 1968. [Ed.]

fear and anxiety to pain, the diminution of pain by psychological procedures, and cortico-visceral interaction.

The basic method was to compare two groups of women (41 altogether), one using the Psychoprophylactic Method of natural childbirth training and procedures and the other not using natural childbirth. Each subject was given extensive batteries of psychological and psychophysiological tests, twice during pregnancy and once post-partum; a narrative description of the entire labor and delivery experience was also obtained. Both quantitative and qualitative analyses were performed on the data.

The Experience of Childbirth

The overwhelming conclusion that emerges from examination of the descriptions of childbirth given by our subjects is that as a subjective experience, and in certain objective ways as well, childbirth is vastly different for women having natural childbirth and women not having it. With few exceptions, it was a very positive event for the former group, and a very negative one for the latter.

From our narrative material we shall see how, in their own words, the women described the various events of childbirth.

We will examine first some of the descriptions of the birth given by the natural childbirth subjects. How did they experience the "delivery" of their children into the world, and their first contacts with them?

> I was pushing all the way into the delivery room, and it was really the most wonderful thing in the world to watch the baby being born. It was just fantastic. And to push with all my might to get him out, and to see him, his little body.*
>
> . . .
>
> After that point I think the baby was born. There were a couple of more pushes, and there was a point where Dr. V. said "Don't push now." Right after the episiotomy, the baby's head was born, then the forearm and the shoulders, and it was marvelous. Everything else came so quickly. It was such a wonderful feeling, I can't tell you. Dr. V. said "Look, you have a son!" He was just as enthused as we were.

---

*Ellipses appear between statements of different subjects. To preserve confidentiality fictitious names and initials have been substituted in references to subjects, their husbands, their babies, and their doctors.

Everything happened very rapidly. I couldn't say how many pushes it was. All of a sudden he said "This is your baby's arm." I think I pushed another time, and he said "stop," and he said "You have a baby girl." It was that fast. And then I said "Don't I have to push out the placenta?" and they said "It's out." And I said "Well I didn't *feel* anything, did you give me anesthesia?" And they all laughed and said no.

We turn now to the statements given by the controls. How did they describe the events at the time of birth, or as close to it as they came? What were their recollections?

The next thing was about 8:20 A.M., and the doctor had my husband leave, and I remember being wheeled into the delivery room. The doctor just gave me a shot, and the next thing, he held up the baby, and put her on my stomach. And I remember yelling "Take her away!"
. . .

All I know is they gave me something that knocked me out, and I woke up, and I thought I was still in the labor room, but I was in the recovery room. And the same nurse who had been so mean was very nice. And I couldn't believe it. I didn't even feel my stomach the way they say you do, or say "is he healthy," or "isn't that nice." I just couldn't believe it.

The first difference that emerges, perhaps, is a difference of tone. The statements of natural childbirth women are largely positive, descriptions of feelings of happiness, excitement, joy. The statements of the control group do not describe a happy experience. They describe screaming, yelling, pain, moaning, fear and hostility.

The second difference that emerges is a tremendous sense of the *gap* in the experience of controls, and the continuous, whole nature of the experience for the natural childbirth women.

A third important difference, and one which may well contribute to the ultimate difference in the meaning and tone of the experience, is the fact that the control group women were anesthetized. That is, the experience of receiving and succumbing to anesthesia may be sufficiently unpleasant and frightening to contribute significantly, by conscious or unconscious association, to a negative memory of childbirth. The nature of the experience of being anesthetized is described graphically by some of our subjects:

Then he said "we're going to put you to sleep," and they immediately put the thing over my face. I don't know if you've ever had it, but I've talked to a lot of people, and it's a very scary feeling. You can hear them, but you feel you're going asleep. I felt like I was dying. Like I was between worlds. That this was permanent. That this was death.

The Role of the Husband

Our findings have shown strikingly the effects of a husband's presence at the birth of his child. In every case where the woman experienced rapturous or peak-experience feelings in childbirth, her husband had been present in the delivery room. The husband's presence would seem necessary for, almost an integral part of, the peak-experience in childbirth.

The outstanding thing that emerges at once is that there *are* vast differences in the way the husbands were perceived by the different groups of women.

The greatest general difference is in the overall tone of the statements about the husband, the direction of the "sign" given him. From the feelings and perceptions of the "natural childbirth" women, the husband emerges as a highly positive figure; from those of the "non-natural childbirth" women he emerges as negative or neutral. That is, almost all of the *statements* made by the natural childbirth group are positive, while most from the other group have a negative or neutral character. Let us now examine this in detail. We will consider first the statements of the "natural childbirth" women.

The husband is often described as a strong figure, to be praised explicitly, and whose presence and contribution were almost a necessity:

> There were moments, from the first phase of labor through delivery, that I could relive, that I wouldn't mind reliving again and again. Because people were so marvelous, and I can repeat this again and again, my husband and Dr. J.
>
> · · ·
>
> Roy was there, holding up my back. He was marvelous. He said a nurse was also doing it, but to me it was all Roy.

We see, then, that for the woman having natural childbirth, the husbands were viewed quite uniformly in highly positive terms. They were seen as important or indispensable in their presence, as strong and competent, as helpful in a variety of ways including active participation at the time of birth. They were described overall by very positive words. What, then, about the husbands of the controls, of the

women not having natural childbirth? How did they see their husbands? How did they describe them, and how did they feel toward
them?

The general tone that emerges from the statements by this group
of women about their husbands is a negative or neutral one. The husband is seen with substantial uniformity as an impotent or weak figure,
one who is in the way, or one who needs to be worried about and taken
care of.

Thus, one woman did not even want to tell her husband she was
in labor, for the following reason:

> I didn't want to tell my husband right away, because he's very
> nervous, he'd be hysterical all day.

Another woman stated:

> My husband was kind of tense. More so than I was at that point,
> and throughout.

The Effects on the Husband

Unfortunately, the study of the effects on a man of participating
in his wife's childbirth, like the questions of its other effects, has been
virtually ignored. This despite what would seem to be its obvious importance for theoretical questions in psychology, as well as its importance because the incidence of men "participating" in childbirth is
constantly increasing.

Our own examination did not study the husbands directly, and
hence we cannot categorically answer the questions posed above. We
can, however, learn something about the husbands' behavior and feelings indirectly, from the statements of their wives, as well as from
certain other sources we shall examine.

And his apparent reactions were in some cases a positive surprise
both to him and to his wife:

> I think till then I was worrying about the technique, all the drips,
> demerol, etc. . . . And about John, who was having to do so much. And
> I was worried he'd not be able to stand up to it all.
>
> Dr. N. came in and told me to push. I pushed for a half hour in the
> labor room. I remember John saying things like "Funny, I'm not at all
> squeamish." Because he's very fastidious. He was very helpful, includ-
> ing he kept lifting me up to get into position to push. And it was not very
> pretty at that point. Pushing was terrifically hard work, but it was okay.

The husband was described by one wife as feeling like a participant, to whom information was useful, *just as it was to her:*

> He explained all along everything that was going on, which was very good. It made me feel even more like a participant, and it was good for Ken too.
>
> . . .
>
> After everyone left, the nurse was cleaning up in there, and only John and I were there. And I felt terrifically proud of myself. Very replete. John was so vocal, more than usual. He kept running around like a maniac, really *manic.*
>
> . . .
>
> Bill was sitting on one side of me, and the baby was on the other . . . We sat there, the three of us, about forty minutes . . . and we sat there, and decided what to call him.

Many of the women spoke of how they and their husbands were *both,* or together, thrilled at the joint experience:

> Then they took the baby and me up to my room, and Ted was there. It was after one by this time. We were both absolutely exhausted, but exhilarated. So neither of us slept that night. Oh that night after you give birth is an endless, endless night. You can't wait for morning.

Contrary to many popular and academic notions about masculinity and femininity, the husbands of our study expressed interest in this area, wanted to and did *participate,* and had positive feelings about having done so.

This greater male "involvement" in childbirth by no means represents a de-masculinization of men. The husband who was involved in childbirth was not "feminized" or "sissified," as common thinking might expect, and which expectation may well lead many men *away* from involvement in childbirth. On the contrary, the "natural childbirth" husband emerged as strong, competent, important, and someone on whom in most cases his wife leaned and depended. These are attributes of traditional "maleness" or masculinity. In contrast, it was the uninvolved father, the non-natural childbirth" one, who emerged as weak, impotent, childlike, someone to be worried about rather than depended on at this time. And the corollary of this is that the nonnatural childbirth woman may become more dominant, controlling, contemptuous or, if one wishes, "castrating" toward her husband—the very charges that are frequently made against women having natural childbirth! It would seem then, that not having natural childbirth might result in greater polarization of the sexes, but hardly in a healthy direction!

Another major topic borne on by our findings about husband participation in childbirth is the question of growth, development, actualization in a woman. To these, it seems, a husband may contribute. Her conscious perceptions and attitudes may mature, even very rapidly, as we saw with one of our subjects, from her husband's presence with her in childbirth. By "non-conscious" mechanisms of operation, his presence may contribute to her experience of rapturous feelings and healthier perceptions of her self and the world. Thus in terms of growth and therapeutic development in a woman, a husband's presence at childbirth may be a significant contributing factor.

And most important of all, it may be that the husband-at-delivery is himself included in, *an integral part of the peak or rapturous experience* in the wife—not just necessary for its appearance, but an inextricable part of it. In support of this, one of the most graphic descriptions we obtained of childbirth contained a vivid depiction of the emotions and perceptions involved, and indeed, included the husband as part of the description:

> Rob . . . they had him all done up in the O.R. mask and shoes. And he was a sweetheart, a *sweetheart*. I think it was harder for him than for me, because at the end I was in so much pain I didn't care. But he said he felt so helpless. . . . And people said he kept going to the hall, asking couldn't someone do something for her.
>
> About forty minutes of pushing, then it was just all joy. It seems I was pushing for years. The joy at the end was such a knockout. I felt maybe there was a submarine in me, and the back pain was unbearable. And I thought maybe I would break my spine and it would be the first time in recorded history. And all of a sudden he said "Stop, don't push." And it was the first time I felt the urge to push. Edna directed my breathing to direct it.
>
> And then the head was born and he said "It's a boy!" It was one of the real wild experiences of my life. It became a baby for the first time . . . Then finally I felt the rest of the baby slide out, and that was heaven, just pure heaven. Then I heard the baby cry, and the feeling was a new one. It was real joy. Then he held him up, and I felt a big rush of fluid, and the backache was gone. And I felt every little bit of the baby. It was really something. . . . It was somewhat of an orgasm of a sort. . . . Oh my, that was really something.
>
> Like an orgasm . . . a different kind . . . the wonderful free feeling . . . the In-Space marvelous feeling. Joy, a wild joy. I had known it, but it was very special . . . seeing a real honest-to-goodness baby. He

looked like a porcelain eskimo, and all kinds of colors—blue, green, red, and shiny. And having Rob there . . . great.

Finally, it may well be that participation in childbirth can lead to a peak-experience for a man as well. We present now a document, not gathered as a part of our study directly, but presented to us as a personal communication from someone who knew of the research in progress.* It was written by a man who is a writer by profession, shortly after the birth of his son.

> I want especially to report on my own recent experience, becoming a father. You say that you have no knowledge of a father having a peak-experience associated with the birth of his child. I think this is probably because most fathers are not present nor intimately participating in the birth.
>
> I was lucky enough to be present (my wife Pat and I attended a series of classes, exercise and preparation, before the delivery; I was totally ready for the experience; it was amazing to me to realize how many "old wives' tales" I carried around inside my head, about birth, about fact and function of reproduction!) during the labor and delivery of our first child, Christopher, who is now twelve weeks and thriving.
>
> The first stage of my wife's labor was long (about fifteen hours) during which she used a variety of breathing-techniques and I coached her, rubbed her back, brought her magazines and tea, and generally made her as comfortable as possible. She was beginning to get too tired, so our doctor gave her a para-cervical block (novicane—my spelling is bad) and this was the only medication she had. She had some minor discomfort to this point, nothing she wasn't on top of. Then we went into the delivery room, where she pushed the baby out in fifteen minutes. We were both tired, but the experience in the delivery room was for me (and her too, but I am here talking about a father's reaction) a full fifteen minutes + of intense peak-experiences.
>
> I administered oxygen to her between contractions and coached her on pushing, holding her around the shoulders as support during each push. She was magnificent. Slowly I began to feel a kind of holiness about all of us there, performing an ageless human drama, a grand ritual of life. The trigger was probably the emergence of the baby's head—coughing, twisting, covered with blood, as purple as ever, so eager for life—that set me into such intensities of joy and excitement that I cannot possibly adequately describe them. It was all so powerful I felt as though my head might come off, that I might simply explode with joy and a sense

---

*Personal communication by William Mathes to Dr. Abraham H. Maslow. Presented here with permission of the author and the recipient.

of profound participation in a profound mystery. I did explode, was literally re-born myself, saw how my birth, all births, the idea of birth is profoundly right, good, joyous.

Christopher was placed in my wife's arms even before the umbilicus was cut; shortly after it was cut he was wrapped (still dripping and wonderfully new like a chick out of an egg) and given to me to hold while my wife got her strength back.

He was very alert, apparently able to focus his attention on me and on other objects in the room; as I held him he blossomed into pink, the various parts of his body turning from deep purple and almost blue, to pink, to rose. I was fascinated by the colors, time stopped; I thought my friends hooked on LSD should simply take a wife, have a baby, and watch it born!

Shortly, my wife sat up and nursed Christopher on the delivery table; our doctor and nurse left us alone; the three new people got acquainted.

The method of delivery (a modified Lamaze, Dick-Read method) in which the fathers participate and in which the medications are only a local, if that—it brings the child into the world quickly and almost easily, alert, able to feel alive and in the world as it is born. The mother has emotional and physical support from her husband; she experiences the birth as a grand effort; the couple are closer than ever at the supreme moment of their creation.

As you know, peak-experiences are difficult to describe; about all you can say is that when you have one, you know it. My first look at my son—and the days after his birth—are further experiences of the "peak" in my life. Even now as I write I am again caught up in the feeling, seem to expand and overflow as I recall.

The birth experience was so intense that my only regret—if you can call it that—was in not being able to adequately express the feeling. It called for a dance, or a physical-emotional expression of some kind. The irony in so much of being human is that one can feel (good and bad feelings) much more than one can "do anything out," express. There are probably a whole set of affective expressions potentially available to us that we were either not taught, or that have atrophied in the species . . . I know I wished I had a more refined nervous system in which to more completely experience and express what I felt. The peak-experience is fulfilling, but it often does not seem to apply to an expression; one is almost stuck with it like a pot boiling with tight lid.

REFERENCES

For the reader who is interested in gaining general knowledge of the natural childbirth method, the following list should prove useful.

Buxton, C. L. 1962. *A Study of Psychophysical Methods for the Relief of Childbirth.* Philadelphia: W. B. Saunders.

Chabon, I. 1966. *Awake and Aware: Participating in Childbirth Through Psychoprophylaxis.* New York: Delacorte Press.

Chertok, L. 1959. *Psychosomatic Methods in Painless Childbirth: History, Theory and Practice,* trans. Denis Leigh. New York: Pergamon Press.

Dick-Read, G. 1959. *Childbirth Without Fear: The Principles and Practice of Natural Childbirth,* 2nd edition revised. New York: Harper Brothers.

Karmel, M. 1959. *Thank You, Dr. Lamaze: A Mother's Experiences in Painless Childbirth.* Philadelphia: J. B. Lippincott.

Lamaze, F. 1958. *Painless Childbirth: Psychoprophylactic Method,* trans. L. R. Celestin. London: Burke Publishing.

Yahia, C., and Ulin, P. 1965. Preliminary experience with a psychophysical program of preparation for childbirth. *American Journal of Obstetrics and Gynecology,* vol. XCII, no. 7, Dec. 1: 942–49.

10

Dreams and Human Potential

STANLEY KRIPPNER and WILLIAM HUGHES

> Once Chuang Chou dreamed that he was a butterfly. He fluttered about happily, quite pleased with the state he was in, and knew nothing about Chuang Chou. Presently he awoke and found that he was very much Chuang Chou again. Now, did Chou dream that he was a butterfly or was the butterfly now dreaming that he was Chou? *Chuang Tzu,* Book II, c. 300 B.C.)

At the University of Chicago, in April, 1952, a graduate student noticed that periodically during the night the eyes of people who are asleep move rapidly for several minutes (Aserinsky & Kleitman, 1953). This discovery represents one of the rare instances of a scientific breakthrough that opens up an entirely new field of research. As early as 1892 a psychologist had speculated that the eyeballs might move during dreaming (Ladd, cited by Trillin, 1965) but his speculation was soon forgotten and most physiologists held that the eyes were in a position of rest during sleep. The 1952 discovery led to other psychophysiological findings that demonstrated that most of what had been believed about the dreaming process was not true.

Replacing the notion that dreams last only a few seconds was the finding that the EEG-monitored Rapid Eye Movement (REM) stages of sleep are rarely less than 10 minutes long and may last for an hour or more. In his doctoral dissertation, one investigator (Dement, 1958) demonstrated that the acting out, in waking life, of the content of the dream narrative takes about as long as the duration of the REM stages from which the dream was reported.

Source: Reprinted by permission from the Journal of Humanistic Psychology, *vol. 10, no. 1. (Spring 1970). The article as reprinted here contains recent revisions made by the authors (Ed.).*

Replacing the idea that one dreams only before waking was the discovery that there is an average of four or five REM stages in the course of a typical night's sleep. The average young adult subject spends about 20 percent of his sleep time in the REM state. During infancy and childhood the proportion is much higher, while during old age it is somewhat lower.

Replacing the assumption that many people dream rarely or never was the finding that virtually everyone dreams every night. It is true that some people *remember* their dreams more frequently than others, but this fact is related to situational and personality variables rather than to the actual amount of dream time. Foulkes (1966) has concluded, "Those who generally deny or ignore their world of private and subjective experience during wakefulness seem to recall fewer dreams than do those who accept and exploit this dimension of experience (pp. 59-60)."

The psychophysiological data refute not only the folklore on dreams but also many of the theoretical stances held by Freudian and Adlerian psychoanalysts (Foulkes, 1964). Both Freud and Adler felt that individuals dream in proportion to the number and intensity of their personal problems but the data demonstrate that the REM stages recur in a highly predictable cyclic pattern with few variations for each individual studied. Emotional problems often take advantage of the dreaming state and a skilled psychoanalyst can use dream content therapeutically. However, the recent research findings do not support the notion that one's emotional problems precipitate or "trigger" the REM state.

Evolutionary and Developmental Aspects of Dreaming

A clue as to the necessity of the dream state for human development may be found in studying the ontogenetic and phylogenetic data. The REM state has been observed in all higher mammalian species; considerable attention has been devoted to the cat, dog, monkey, and rat because of the similarity of many of their EEG patterns to those of humans (Foulkes, 1966). Some preliminary data suggest that the humanoid sleep-dream cycle does not occur among the lower mammals (Allison & Goff, 1968), amphibians (Rechtschaffen, Bassan, & Ledecky-Janereck, 1968), reptiles (Tauber, Roffwarg, & Weitzman, 1966), or fish (Tauber, Weitzman, & Korey, 1969). Nevertheless, enough similarities exist to point to an evolutionary development of the

REM state. For example, birds spend less than 1 percent of their total sleep time in the REM state (Jouvet, 1967) in comparison with the higher mammals' 20 percent (e.g., sheep) to 60 percent (e.g., cats). Furthermore, one species of fish has been identified which appears to engage in eye movement activity during gross overall inactivity (Tauber, Weitzman, & Korey, 1969).

The evolutionary evidence shows that the hunting species (e.g., cat, dog, humans) enjoy more REM sleep than the hunted (e.g., deer, rabbit). Furthermore, extensive REM sleep came as a rather late development in the evolution of the vertebrates (Jouvet, 1967). It may well be that the REM state (which is characterized by less sensitivity to external stimuli than are other sleep stages) was only able to develop to an appreciable extent among animals that were not in danger of extermination if their predators came upon them while they were dreaming—and while they were oblivious to external stimuli.

It is interesting to note that the larger animals with a longer lifespan and a lower metabolic rate tend to have longer sleep-dream cycles. The average length of time from the beginning of one REM stage to the next varies from four minutes in the mouse to 90 minutes in adult man (Hartmann, 1966). It has even been suggested that cyclical dreaming evolved because this arrangement gave the organism an opportunity to come to a state of near waking readiness and "sample" the environment for danger (Snyder, 1966). For example, when opossums are brought into a laboratory, they have a greater number of spontaneous REM state awakenings, just as their prehistoric brothers probably awoke more frequently when there were predators about.

Insofar as the proportion of the REM state is concerned, ontogeny does not neatly recapitulate phylogeny. Dewan (1968) explains this paradox by noting that REM sleep is basically a process for "programming" the brain; this programming system is homeostatic, organizing and storing memories [perceptual, cognitive, and behavioral programs]. Thus, lower or "fixed program" forms of life do not need much or any REM time while newborn higher life forms should have more REM time than adults to develop the central nervous system. Among the higher mammals (e.g., cat, man), slow wave sleep does not occur until the central nervous system has acquired a certain amount of maturity. In addition, REM time increases with phylogenetic development—although it decreases with ontogenetic development. The prematurely born infant spends about 80 percent of his sleeping time in the REM state. The full-term neonate spends about 50 percent of his sleep time dreaming, the 5-week-old infant about 40 percent, the 3-year-old child about 30 percent, the young adult about 20 percent, and the aged individual about 15 percent (Hartmann, 1966).

It is likely that the neonate—who sleeps three out of every four of his hours—spends more time in the REM state than in either the non-REM sleep state or the waking state. It is also possible that the fetus spends almost all of its time in the REM state.

An ancient Hindu tale describes man's three states of conscious-ness as *vaiswanara* (wakefulness), *prajna* (sleep in which dreams are absent), and *taijasa* (dreaming sleep). Why should *taijasa,* or at least its ontogenetic antecedent, assume such importance among the newly born as well as among developing fetuses?

Ullman (1969) has pointed out that the REM state is "a time when the sleeping brain most closely resembles the waking brain in its degree of electrical and physiological excitation" and notes the importance of the pons and the reticular activating system in REM sleep. Ephron and Carrington (1966) have suggested that the REM state serves the func-tion of promoting cortical efficiency. Therefore, the REM state may be needed to process the novel internal ane external perceptual data that impinge upon the fetus and the neonate. In addition, Roffwarg, Muzio, and Dement (1966) propose that the REM state itself is a source of stimulation:

> We have hypothesized that the REM mechanism serves as an endogenous source of stimulation, furnishing great quantities of func-tional excitation to higher centers. Such stimulation would be particu-larly crucial during the periods *in utero* and shortly after birth, before ap-preciable exogenous stimulation is available to the central nervous system. It might assist in structural maturation and differentiation of the sensory and motor areas within the central nervous system, partially pre-paring them to handle the enormous rush of stimulation provided by the postnatal milieu, as well as contributing to their further growth after birth.

If the REM state serves a developmental function, one might be able to detect a disturbed or atypical sleep-dream cycle among indi-viduals with central nervous system dysfunction. If this dysfunction responds to therapy, one might expect to see a reflection of this change in the sleep-dream cycle.

Some data now exist to support both of these suppositions. Fein-berg (1968) studied 27 mentally retarded adults diagnosed as mon-golian, phenylketonuric, brain-damaged, etc. A significant positive relationship was found between their scores on an individually administered intelligence test and their amount of REM activity, with those subjects having the lowest test scores showing the least REM activity during their REM stages. Feinberg concluded, "These results further support the view that during sleep the brain carries out processes required for cognition" and that "the EEG of sleep is a more sensitive index of the integrity of brain function than any other physiological measure."

Greenberg and Dewan (1969) proposed that dreaming serves to integrate new information into existing past information stores and hypothesized that the improvement of speech production and comprehension (i.e., "reprogramming") would alter the sleep-dream cycle of aphasics. They studied six aphasic patients who were responding to speech therapy and compared them with nine aphasic patients who were not responding. The improving group had a greater proportion of REM stage sleep than the nonimproving group and it was concluded that the data were "evidence of a relationship between a clearly existing reprogramming situation (improvement in aphasia) and higher levels of REM sleep."

Thus, it appears that the REM state serves an evolutionary as well as a developmental function. Because the developmental function (i.e., stimulating the maturation and differentiation of the central nervous system) must exist within the evolutionary framework (i.e., assuring the organism's survival), ontogeny does not recapitulate phylogeny insofar as the proportion of sleep time spent in the REM state is concerned.

Nevertheless, the association between the REM state and cortical efficiency may make it a useful diagnostic tool in cases of central nervous system dysfunction as well as a prognostic instrument to predict and measure the effectiveness of therapeutic techniques in cases of cognitive disorder related to brain injury.

Psychological and Sociological Aspects of Dreaming

Because REM time is of such critical importance, it is essential that further research be done on the chemical agents which reduce or increase the proportion of time the sleeper spends in the REM state. Table 1 summarizes this work; it will be noted that barbiturates—often taken to induce sleep—decrease one's amount of REM time. The terrifying dreams that often occur when barbiturate use is suspended often motivate the individual to resume usage of the drug—an important factor in barbiturate addiction. Alcohol reduces the amount of time spenc in the REM state and the vivil hallucinations experienced by the heavy drinker when he temporarily stops imbibing alcohol may represent an effort of his central nervous system to "catch up" on REM time (Hartmann, 1965).

TABLE 1   EFFECTS OF SELECTED DRUGS ON RAPID EYE MOVEMENT (REM) SLEEP

Drug (partial list)	Effect on REM Sleep
Alcohol	Decrease
Amphetamines	Decrease
Barbiturates	Decrease
Caffeine	None
Chloral hydrate	None
Chlorpromazine	Decrease with small doses; Increase with larger doses
LSD	Slight increase
Marijuana	Unknown
Reserpine	Increase with small doses; Decrease with larger doses
Typtophane	Increase

The available data suggest that the basic necessity of the REM state is developmental in nature, and serves a programming function that enhances binocular vision and promotes cortical efficiency. However, the individual superimposes a number of additional elements on the dream process—elements which reflect instinctoid pressures (e.g., hunger, power, security, sex) as well as elements from one's unresolved traumatic experiences, current problems, and hopes for the future. It is this material which serves as the basis of dream interpretation, especially as undertaken by psychoanalysts.

Plato (1937) anticipated Freud's position on dreams when he spoke of man's ability, while dreaming, to commit any "conceivable folly or crime—not excepting incest or any other unnatural union, or parricide, or the eating of forbidden food. . . ." In addition, Freud's notion of "wish fulfillment" was foreshadowed by Lucretius (1924) in *De rerum natura*. The Freudian point of view (1955) holds that unconscious strivings, feelings, and wishes are expressed in dreams, often in a disguised fashion. Through free association and other psychoanalytic techniques, the Freudian analyst attempts to help the patient recall, interpret, and work through the dream material.

Artemidorous (1644), in the second century A.D., produced the first systematic interpretation of dreams. He asserted that truth exists within dream symbols—as when Joseph interpreted Pharoah's dream of the seven fat and seven lean cattle as seven years of plenty followed by seven years of famine. Rather than serving as evidence of communication with God, Artemidorous looked upon Pharoah's dream as an indication of human intuition.

Contemporary writers have also utilized the concept of dream symbols, some of them departing from Freud's stress on psychosexual symbolism (1955). Jung (1938), felt that dream symbols are often "archetypal"—reflecting the religious and mythic concerns of the patient as well as the sexual ones. Furthermore, Jung saw the life style of the dream as often different from the patient's waking style (or "typology"), thus pointing out ways in which the patient might grow and develop. Adler (1958) proposed that the dream was always consonant with one's waking life style and that the dream makes use of those images and incidents which best express the patient's present problem. This emphasis on the symbol that expresses rather than on the symbol that disguises is consistent with Adler's notion of a continuity between waking and dreaming style and is also the keystone of Fromm's (1951) and Hall's (1966) theories of dream symbolism.

Bonime (1962) has stressed the learning experience by which a psychoanalyst passes on the skill of dream interpretation to the patient. Feeling that dream content is basically a derivative of social experience, Bonime helps the patient relate dream symbols to his daily life. A similar point of view is taken by Ullman (1960) who states, "The elements in the dream are symbolic, not in the sense of disguising impulses, but because they represent the best approximation in personal terms that the individual can construct for himself of the real forces operating upon him and impinging upon the area of vulnerability with which the dream is concerned and which are not objectively known to the individual."

Ullman (1960) has also concerned himself with the roles that dreams play in a particular culture. He notes that dreams of preliterate people reflect the prevailing mythology and that dreams often act as a channel for a person's idiosyncratic modes of viewing the cultural myths. Ullman cites the case of a patient who dreamed that her sexual organs were separate from her functioning self and that they were bought and sold. He suggests that the patient may have been overly conditioned by those aspects of the American society which emphasize the buying and selling of various personal capacities which are divorced from the person and treated as objects. Ullman concludes:

> The view presented differs essentially from the classical Freudian position insofar as it considers the source of unconscious motivating influences as linked to specific experiences in a given social and cultural milieu and not as originating in the biological nature of man, or as due to man's inherent vulnerability because of his extreme dependence on symbolic processes. . . . When functional alterations in consciousness occur, as in states of dreaming, the key to their understanding lies not in such dualistic concepts as . . . wish-fulfillment and disguise, but in the basic notion that an individual in a state of partial arousal is striving to express in a very concrete way the totality of factors, some known, some unknown, governing his reactions to a specific life experience.

A provocative example of dream sociology involves the 12,000-member Senoi tribe of the Malay Peninsula who claim an absence from their society of violent crime or mental illness (Stewart, 1969). Dreams play a major role in the cultural life pattern of the Senoi; at breakfast, the individual's dreams are discussed with members of the family who aid his interpretation of the content.

The Senoi assume that the dreamer creates mental images of the outside world as part of an adaptive process. As some of these images are negative, they will produce mental illness and/or hostility if allowed to become internalized. Therefore, the tribe assists in the individual's expression, neutralization, and utilization of dream imagery. Positive dreams are acted out socially while negative dreams are interpreted and discharged.

The social acceptance of the dream implies, to tribe members, a full acceptance of the individual. From an early age, the Senoi tribesman finds that the feelings and thoughts of his inner life are accepted by others. He also learns that by expressing his internal imagery, he can integrate his own personality at the same time that he is coordinating his behavior with the social pattern of the tribe. American culture, by emulating this aspect of personal development, may reduce the nation's growing rate of crime and violence. Stewart (1969) has noted that Westerners "do not respond to dreams as socially important" nor are dreams included in the educational process. He concludes, "This social neglect of the side of man's reflective thinking when the creative process is most free, seems poor education."

A few American institutions and groups (e.g., The Association for Research and Enlightenment, Virginia Beach, Va.) have sponsored ongoing seminars in dream interpretation for individuals interested in self-development. In addition, many individuals keep dream diaries and attempt to gain knowledge about the self in this manner.

In either instance, a number of specific suggestions are available to assist dream recall (Kettlekamp, 1968; Krippner, in Steiger, 1969; Progoff, 1963):

1. When you first awaken in the morning, lie quietly before jumping out of bed. Let your mind dwell on the first thing that comes up. Do not allow day-time interests to interrupt. Your first waking thoughts may remind you of the contents of your last dream before awakening and allow you, with further practice, to remember more and more details of the dream. You may need to try this technique several mornings in a row in order to get results.

2. Keep a notebook of the dreams you do remember for a month. Look for important ideas or themes running through the dreams. You may discover that you have been working on a problem at night without being aware of it. You may even find instances in which your dreams suggested actions which you were actually able to carry out later.

3. Look for items in your dreams that might be symbolic of something. Avoid making hard and fast judgments. Get the opinion of your family and friends. Remember, however, that it is more important that you enjoy your dream than that you correctly analyze it. It is more important that you learn to appreciate your inner life than that you become an amateur psychoanalyst.

4. Look for puns in your dreams (e.g., a play on words, a play on numbers). These puns are common and can often be discovered. This may further aid you in finding the meaning in some of your dream images.

5. Before you go to sleep at night, review the work you have done on a problem or on a question that has frustrated you. Concentrate for several evenings in a row, if necessary. If you have given the problem enough pre-sleep attention, you may find upon awakening in the morning that you can remember a dream in which the possible solution appeared. This is one way of encouraging creative dreams.

6. Try directing your dream thoughts as you might direct your waking consciousness. If a negative image seems to be following a negative course, try to reverse it, either in that dream or in a continuation of the dream. If your dream is a positive one, extend it as long as you can and try to derive some use or valuable product from it.

7. Keep dream diaries. Record your dream for six months or a year. Try to get other members of your family or your circle of friends to do the same. Determine, as best as you can, which dreams reflected per-

sonal problems, which dreams involved national or international events, which dreams were creative, and which dreams were highly symbolic.

8. Avoid books which present non-scientific approaches to dreams—or read them with a skeptical attitude. Select books that present varied viewpoints on dreams but which lean heavily on scientific data and/or clinical experience (Bonime, 1962; Foulkes, 1966; Freud, 1955; MacKenzie, 1965).

As an individual begins to remember his dreams, he will notice that there are qualitative differences among some of the nighttime memories. He may be recalling non-REM thoughts, hypnagogic images, and hypnopompic images as well as dreams.

Non-REM awakenings of sleeping subjects indicate that considerably from person to person (Bertini, Lewis, & Witkin, 1969). 1966, pp. 99–120). The non-REM reports differ qualitatively from REM reports in that they contain a greater proportion of conceptual thinking, less perceptual material, and content that is less vivid, emotional, or distorted. Non-REM sleep mentation seems to be populated by fewer people but the events bear a greater correspondence to the sleeper's daily life than during REM sleep. Basically, non-REM mentation seems to involve more direct and simplified thought processes that are less concerned with a manifestation of the inner life.

The hypnagogic state occurs between waking and going to sleep while the hypnopompic state occurs between sleep and awakening. Various images often occur in these borderline states but vary considerably from person to person (Bertini, Lewis, [7] Witkin, 1969). For some people, however, there is no recollection of any experience during these times. For others, however, the hypnagogic and hypnopompic states may contain striking visualizations, majestic music, and/or personal insights.

The contents of the non-REM, hypnagogic, hypnopompic, and REM states are in large measure influenced by psychological and sociological factors. As more data are obtained on the sleep-dream cycle, researchers may find ways in which the integration of dream material and the utilization of its recall (both for therapeutic and self-development purposes) will assist in the actualization of human potential.

Creative Aspects of Dreaming

Many writers have seen little possibility that the dream in any way could perform a creative function. The Nobel Prize-winning zoologist, J. P. Medawar (in MacKenzie, 1965, p. 11) has stated that most dreams are totally devoid of meaning and "convey no information whatsoever." Mercutio, in Shakespeare's *Romeo and Juliet,* foreshadowed this assertion when he declaimed:

> I talk of dreams,
> Which are the children of an idle brain,
> Begot of nothing but vain fantasy,
> Which is as thin of substance as the air,
> And more inconstant than the wind.

An opposing point of view has been put forward by Ullman (1964) who noted four creative aspects of dreaming: the element of originality, the joining together of disparate elements into new patterns, the concern of the dreamer with essence, and the felt reaction of participating in an involuntary experience—a reaction that also characterizes other creative experiences. Ullman conceded that the end-product could be banal or ecstatic but noted "it is an act of creation to have the dream in the first place."

Adelson (1957) has reported that his less creative patients generally described simple and conventional dreams while his more creative patients reported dreams that were highly imaginative. One patient who was decidedly insensitive to artistic work "could not allow himself fancy, metaphor, or reverie"; he was "on guard against any mode of experience which was not logical, rational, and coherent." Another patient, highly creative, reported complex and fanciful dreams. Stimulated by these examples, Adelson made a formal study of 15 college girls who were students in a creative writing course. The eight "highly imaginative" subjects had more dreams in exotic settings—an African jungle, an Arabian mosque, a Parisian bistro—than the seven "uninventive" subjects whose dreams characteristically took place in their immediate environments. The imaginative subjects also had a greater proportion of dreams that were transformed in identity, in which humorous incidents occurred, and in which color played a significant part.

In a similar study (Schechter, Schmeidler, & Staal, 1965), creativity tests were administered to 105 college students who had kept dream diaries. It was found that art students remembered their dreams significantly more frequently than science and engineering students. In addition, there was a statistically significant relationship between dream imaginativeness and creativity test scores.

Several distinguished scientists and artists have utilized their dreams for creative purposes. Robert Louis Stevenson, early in his life, discovered that he could dream complete stories and even go back to them on succeeding nights if the end was unsatisfactory. He once described his dreaming consciousness as filled with "little people" who every evening provided him with "truncheons of tales upon their lighted theater." Perhaps his greatest dream achievement came one night when he pictured a criminal, pursued by the police, who imbibed a potion and changed his appearance. This dream eventually appeared as the classic story of Dr. Jekyll and Mr. Hyde. Goethe, Blake, Cowper, Poe, Voltaire, Dante, Shelley, Heine, La Fontaine, Tolstoy, and Coleridge also found dream material useful for their poetry and prose.

A number of composers reportedly were inspired by melodies heard during the REM state. Tartini heard in a dream a sonata from which he drew inspiration for his famous "Devil's Trill." Mozart, Schumann, Saint-Saëns, and d'Indy claimed that some of their music was first heard by them in dreams (De Becker, 1968).

A number of instances exist in which dreams have served a problemsolving function. When he was a student, the physicist Niels Bohr had a vivid dream. He saw himself on a sun consisting of burning gas while planets seemed to whistle as they passed by. The planets appeared to be attached to the sun by thin filaments and revolved around it. Suddenly the burning gas cooled and solidified; the sun and planets crumbled away. Bohr awakened realizing he had conceptualized the model of an atom, the sun being the fixed center around which electrons revolved. Much of the basic theory upon which atomic physics is based came out of this dream.

Otto Loewi, a pharmacologist, won a Nobel Prize for the discovery that control of the heartbeat is not through direct nerve influence. When he accepted the Nobel Prize in 1936, he said, "The story of this discovery shows that an idea may sleep for decades in the unconscious mind and then suddenly return to the consciousness." Loewi had first disagreed with the prevailing theory in 1903, but it was not until 1920 that his ruminations on the problem congealed in the dream state. In fact, he wrote down this dream on paper and went back to sleep. The following morning, Loewi looked at his writing and was unable to decipher it. That night he had an identical dream, awakened, and went directly to his laboratory. He prepared two frogs for an experiment which demonstrated that nerves affect heart function through a mediating chemical rather than through a direct connection.

Louis Agassiz, the naturalist, once attempted to transfer the image of a fossil fish from a stone but found the image blurred. A few nights after he abandoned the project, he had a dream in which he saw the entire fossilized fish. The following morning, he hurried to his laboratory—but found the fossil to be as obscure as ever. The next night, the dream returned; he examined the slab the next morning but found the vague image unchanged. Hoping he might have the dream a third time, Agassiz placed pencil and paper by his bedside. When the dream returned, he took the paper and drew his image upon it with the pencil. On the following morning, he was surprised at the details he had produced in total darkness. Returning to his laboratory, he used the drawing as a guide and slowly began to chisel the slab. As a layer of stone fell loose, he found the fossil in excellent condition—the identical fossil which had occurred in his dreams. Other scientific discoveries emerged in dreams reported by Cannon (a neurologist) and Galen (a physician).

Elias Howe had been frustrated in his early attempts to perfect the sewing machine; for years, everything he tried had failed. One night, he dreamed he had been captured by savages who dragged him before their king. The king issued a royal ultimatum: if within 24 hours Howe had not produced a machine that would sew, he would die by the spear. Howe failed to meet the deadline and saw the savages approaching; he saw the spears slowly raise, then start to descend. Suddenly, Howe forgot his fear as he noticed that the spears all had eye-shaped holes in their tips. Howe awakened, realizing that, for his sewing machine, the eye of the needle should be near the point, not at the top or in the middle. Rushing to his laboratory, he filed a needle to the proper size, drilled a hole near its tip, and inserted it into the machine. It worked well and the problem was solved.

Another inventor, James Watt, had been working on lead shot for shotguns. The standard process involved cutting or chopping metal and was quite costly. About this time, Watt had a recurring dream. He seemed to be walking through a heavy storm; instead of rain, he was showered with tiny lead pellets. Awakening, he surmised that the dream might indicate that molten lead, falling through air, would harden into small spheres. Obtaining permission to experiment in a church which had a water-filled moat at its base, Watt melted several pounds of lead and flung it from the bell tower. Hastening down the stairs, he scooped from the bottom of the moat the tiny leaden pellets— inaugurating a process that revolutionized the lead shot industry.

While in the army, René Descartes spent a winter of inactive duty in a hotel room. Discontent with army life, ideas spun through his brain in a disconnected, contradictory fashion. One night he had a dream in which all his previous thoughts fell into harmony. That illumination was the beginning of the philosophical and mathematical formulations that were to change the course of Western thought.

Such philosophers as Al-Mamun and Synesius and the mathematicians Condorcet and Carden acknowledged their dependence on dream recall for some of their insights. Carden claimed that one of his books on mathematics was virtually composed in his dreams.

Fehr (in Wells, 1968) studied the working habits of his colleagues in mathematics. Of those who responded to his survey, the majority said that they had solved problems in their dreams or thought it was a likely possibility. Whether one solves his problems in the dream symbolically (e.g., Howe, Watt) or directly (e.g., Loewi, Agassiz), he has utilized an altered state of consciousness for creative, productive purposes.

Murphy (1958) has described the four phases in the creative process as immersion, consolidation, illumination, and evaluation. In the first phase, the sensitive mind is immersed in some medium which gives delight and fulfillment—color, tone, movement, space, time, words, images, social relationships, contemplation, etc. In the second phase this sensitivity leads to the acquisition of "storehouses full of experiences" and consolidation into ordered, structured patterns. From these storehouses, the illumination—whether it be sudden or gradual—emerges. This is followed up by the fourth phase in which the creative product is perfected, sifted, tested, and evaluated.

When the dream plays a role in an artistic development or a scientific breakthrough, it typically enters into the third stage of creative thinking. In the waking state, Archimedes leaped from the bathtub shouting, "I have it!" as he discovered the principle of displacement. In the daydreaming state, Kekulé saw the components of the benzene ring arrange themselves. In the dream state, Bohr conceptualized the structure of the atom and later worked out (in the fourth phase) the ramifications and implications of his insight.

It would make sense for creative people to pay close attention to their dreams and to use them for problem-solving whenever possible. Because the REM state plays an important role in storing perceptual, cognitive, and behavioral memories (thus helping to build up one's "storehouses full of experiences"), it is a natural arena in which a creative inspiration may occur.

Paranormal Aspects of Dreaming

In primitive and ancient societies, dreams were typically thought to be the work of supernatural entities, appearing to mortals with messages of hope or despair. Some peoples believed that the soul left the physical body in sleep and wandered in a spirit world. It was generally believed that dreams could provide a glimpse of the future, reveal events happening at a distance, or indicate the thoughts of another person (MacKenzie, 1965).

The development of psychoanalysis caused the observation of the paranormal dream to move from the anecdotal to the clinical level. Ever since the early conjectures of Freud (1933) regarding the possibility of telpathic influence on dream content, reports have appeared in the psychiatric literture describing presumptively paranormal dreams occurring in the context of the psychotherapeutic situation (e.g., Ehrenwald, 1948). Tribbe (1969) speculates as to the connection between paranormal dream content and the dreamer's typical material:

> . . . An individual's basic dream pattern runs continuously during REM periods much like a hyper-sensitive videotape that is being simultaneously produced and projected in the "closed circuit" of the mind. . . . This basic videotape, like photographic paper, is so very sensitive that it will pick up a wide variety of materials, some wholly extraneous. . . . The juxtaposition of images may frequently seem a meaningless hodge-podge—and some of the items have no meaning of value for the dreamer. . . . The discomfort of the sleeper, his biological pressures of the moment, his sex drive, all may force the creation of "added" dream material. Also there are the sensory and the extrasensory items that are seemingly forced, unwanted, upon the dreamer; then, there are extrasensory items which the "self" seemingly wants and has gone questing for. . . .

With the development of psychophysiological techniques for the monitoring of dreams, it became possible to move from a clinical level of discussion and observation to an experimental level involving the investigation of paranormal dreams. In 1962, a dream laboratory was established at the Maimonides Medical Center, Brooklyn, New York, for the study of telepathy and dreams. Most of these experiments have yielded statistically significant results. (Ullman, Krippner, and Vaughan, 1973).

For the typical study, volunteer subjects spent one night at the Dream Laboratory. A staff member spent the night attempting to influence the subjects' dreams by means of telepathy. Target pictures were famous art prints, randomly selected from a large number of prints once the subjects had gone to bed. When the subject was in bed, the agent selected a number from a book which contained thousands of numerals. Usually the agent opened the book randomly, pointed to a line of numerals, added each digit in the line, and kept adding the digits until he obtained a one-digit number. Each art print was in an opaque envelope. The agent counted down the stack of envelopes until he reached the number arrived at through the random selection procedure. The envelope was taken to the agent's room (usually about 100 feet from the room in which the subject was sleeping) and opened it. The agent attempted, during the course of the night, to influence the subject's dreams by concentrating on the art print. The agent never knew what the art print for the night would be until the subject was in bed. Random procedures of this type were necessary to eliminate any possible sensory communication between the agent and the subject.

On the following morning, the subjects were asked to match their dream recall against the entire collection of target pictures, selecting that art print which most closely resembled their dreams. Three outside judges did the same type of matching using copies of the art prints and typed transcripts of the subjects' dreams. For example, one night the art print ''Animals'' by Rufino Tamayo was randomly selected. The subject dreamed about eating meat at a banquet with a friend who behaved in a very gluttonous manner. The art print depicts bones from the animals' repast, thus demonstrating a correspondence with the dream.

Several attempts to replicate the Maimonides studies (e.g., Hall, 1967; Globus *et al.*, 1968) have been published. In addition, a successful attempt to influence the waking hours of sleeping subjects by extrasensory means has been reported (Bleksley, 1963).

Conclusion

The importance of altered states of consciousness and their relation to human potential was stressed by William James, America's first psychologist of eminence. James (1902) wrote that

> our normal waking consciousness . . . is but one special type of consciousness, whilst all about it, parted from it by the filmiest of screens, there lie potential forms of consciousness entirely different. We may go

> through life without suspecting their existence; but apply the requisite stimulus, and at a touch they are there in all their completeness. . . . No account of the universe in its totality can be final which leaves these other forms of consciousness quite disregarded.

The psychophysiological study of the sleep-dream cycle has confirmed James' speculations because the importance of the REM state (a profound alteration in "normal" consciousness) has been frequently demonstrated during the last decade.

Dreaming appears to be an active, creative, integrating process rather than a reactive or compensatory event (Weiss, 1964). It is true that dreams may reflect instinctoid pressures as well as elements from a traumatic past, a disturbing present, or a wished-for-future. In doing so, however, these elements lose their isolated nature and combine with the evolutionary, developmental, programming, data processing, problem-solving, and even paranormal aspects of an event which becomes an integrated whole. Dreaming, to use Maslow's terms (1962), is a "growth phenomenon" rather than a "deficiency phenomenon."

Contemporary interest in the dreaming process appears to be part of a larger movement affecting a growing proportion of the population. For most of its history, the American nation has been absorbed in externals. Americans have devoted their energies to the settling of the continent, the fight for independence, the winning of the West, the utilization of natural resources, the development of technology, the manufacture of consumer goods, the establishment of the country as a world power, and the exploration of outer space. In recent years, these external events have failed to stimulate many Americans—especially a sizable portion of the country's youth—whose attention has started to turn inward. Large numbers of college students, high school students, members of intentional communities, and adults in various professional fields have taken a keen interest in the altered states of consciousness which accompany sensory overload, sensory deprivation, hypnosis, meditation, spiritual discipline, feedback training, psychedelic chemical experience, reverie, and dreaming.

Most of the tradition-directed institutions of American society have little use for introspection, internal events, and the inner life. The pursuit of these interests is often regarded as "unproductive," "nonachieving," and "narcissistic." On the other hand, those individuals who make a persistent, conscientious, disciplined attempt to cope with internal events typically report that the quest has assisted their capacity to perceive and understand the various levels of reality, to accept and enjoy the self, to behave spontaneously, to appreciate art and nature, to develop close interpersonal relationships, to work creatively—in other words, to become a more fully realized human being (Maslow, 1962).

The current interest in dreams and other forms of altered consciousness is a promising development for humanistically oriented psychology, psychiatry, religion, education, and other fields of endeavor which seek to produce what Aldous Huxley (1962) has called "full-blown human beings." As a larger number of professionals and nonprofessionals become involved in the inner life, the possibility grows that there is a new consciousness emerging in our time—a consciousness geared toward self-actualization and the full development of the human potential.

REFERENCES

Adelson, J. 1957. Creativity and the dream. Paper read at the annual convention of the American Psychological Association.

Adler, A. 1958. *What Life Should Mean to You*. New York: Capricorn Books.

Allison, T., and Goff, W. R. 1968. Sleep in a primitive mammal, the spiny anteater (Abstract). *Psychophysiology,* 5: 200.

Artemidorous. 1644. *Oneiroctitica*. London: Wood.

Aserinsky, E., Kleitman, N. 1953. Regularly occurring periods of eye motility and concomitant phenomena during sleep. *Science,* 118: 273–74.

Bertini, M., Lewis, H. B. and Witkin, H. A. 1969. Some preliminary observations with an experimental procedure for the study of hypnagogic and related phenomena. In C. Tart, ed., *Altered States of Consciousness*. New York: John Wiley & Sons.

Bleksley, A. 1963. An experiment on long-distance ESP during sleep. *Journal of Parapsychology,* 27: 1–15.

Bonime, W. 1962. *The Clinical Use of Dreams*. New York: Basic Books.

Caillois, R., ed. 1963. *The Dream Adventure*. New York: Orion Press.

De Becker, R. 1968. *The Understanding of Dreams and Their Influence on the History of Man*. New York: Hawthorn Books.

Dement, W. 1958. The physiology of dreaming. Ph.D. dissertation, University of Chicago.

Dewan, E. M. 1968. The P (programming) hypothesis for REMS (Abstract). *Psychophysiology,* 4: 365.

Ehrenwald, J. 1948. *Telepathy and Medical Psychology.* New York: W. W. Norton.

Ephron, H. S., and Carrington, P. 1966. Rapid eye movement sleep and cortical homeostasis. *Psychological Review,* 73: 500–26.

Feinberg, I. 1968. Eye movement activity during sleep and intellectual function in mental retardation. *Science,* 159: 1256.

Foulkes, D. 1964. Theories of dream formation and recent studies of sleep consciousness. *Psychological Bulletin,* 62: 236–42.

———. 1966. *The Psychology of Sleep.* New York: Charles Scribner's Sons. Freud, S. 1955. *The Interpretation of Dreams.* New York: Basic Books.

———. 1933. *New Introductory Lectures on Psychoanalysis.* New York: W. W. Norton.

Fromm, E. 1951. *The Forgotten Language.* New York: Grove Press.

Globus, G., et al. 1968. An appraisal of telepathic communication in dreams (Abstract). *Psychophysiology,* 4: 365.

Greenberg, R., and Dewan, E. M. 1969. Aphasia and rapid eye movement sleep. *Nature,* 223: 183–84.

Hall, C. 1966. *The Meaning of Dreams,* 2nd edition. New York: McGraw-Hill.

———. 1967. Experimente zur telepathischen beeinflussing von träumen. *Zeitschrift für Parapsychologie und Grenzgebiete der Psychologie,* 10: 18–47.

———, and Van de Castle, R. 1966. *The Content Analysis of Dreams.*

Hartmann, E. L. 1966. The D-state: a review and discussion of studies on the physiological state concomitant with dreaming. *International Journal of Psychiatry,* 2: 11–31.

———. 1965. The D-state: a review and discussion of studies on the physiological state concomitant with dreaming. *New England Journal of Medicine,* 273: 30–5, 87–92.

Huxley, A. 1962. *Island.* New York: Harper & Row.

James, W. 1902. *The Varieties of Religious Experience.* New York: Longmans.

Jouvet, M. 1967. The states of sleep. *Scientific American,* 216: 62–72.

Jung, C. G. 1938. *Psychology and Religion.* New Haven: Yale University Press.

Kettelkamp, L. 1968. *Dreams.* New York: William Morrow.

Krippner, S. 1969. The paranormal dream and man's pliable future. *Psychoanalytic Review,* 56: 28–43.

Lucretius. 1924. *De Rerum Natura.* Cambridge: Harvard University Press.

MacKenzie, N. 1965. *Dreams and Dreaming.* New York: Vanguard.

Maslow, A. H. 1962. *Toward a Psychology of Being.* New York: Van Nostrand.

Plato. 1937. *The Republic.* New York: Random House.

Progoff, I. 1963. *The Symbolic and the Real.* New York: Julian Press.

Rechtschaffen, A., Bassan, M., and Ledecky-Janecek, S. 1968. Activity patterns in Caiman Sclerops (Crocodilia) (Abstract). *Psychophysiology,* 5: 201.

———, and Verdone, P. 1964. Amount of dreaming; effect of incentive, adaptation to laboratory, and individual differences. *Perceptual and Motor Skills,* 19: 947–58.

Roffwarg, H. P., Munzio, J. N., and Dement, W. C. 1966. Ontogenetic development of the human sleep-dream cycle. *Science,* 152: 604–19.

Schechter, N., Schmeidler, G. R., and Staal, M. 1965. Dream reports and creative tendencies in students of the arts, sciences, and engineering. *Journal of Consulting Psychology,* 29: 415–21.

Snyder, F. 1966. Toward an evolutionary theory of dreaming. *American Journal of Psychiatry,* 123: 123–36.

Steiger, B. 1969. New discoveries about dreaming. *Saga,* June.

Stewart, K. 1969. Dream theory in Malaya. In C. Tart, ed., *Altered States of Consciousness.* New York: John Wiley & Sons.

Tauber, E. S., Roffwarg, H. P., and Weitzman, E. D. 1966. Eye movements and electroencephalogram activity during sleep in diurnal lizards. *Nature,* 212: 1612–13.

———, Weitzman, E. D., and Korey, S. R. 1969. Eye movements during behavioral inactivity in certain Bermuda reef fish. *Communications in Behavioral Biology,* 3: 131–35.

Tribbe, F. C. 1969. Personal communication, August.

Trillin, C. 1965. A third state of existence. *New Yorker,* 18 September.

Ullman, M. 1964. Discussion (of F. A. Weiss' Dreaming—a creative process). *American Journal of Psychoanalysis,* 24: 10–12.

———. 1960. The social roots of the dream. *American Journal of Psychoanalysis,* 20: 180–96.

———. 1969. The dream scene. *Journal of the American Society of Psychosomatic Dentistry and Medicine,* 16: 4–6.

———., Krippner, S., and Vaughan, A. 1973. *Dream Telepathy.* New · York: Macmillan.

Weiss, F. A. 1964. Dreaming—a creative process. *American Journal of Psychoanalysis,* 24: 1–10.

Wells, E. F. 1968. Your dreams: important—or nonsense? *Success Unlimited,* April.

11

Dream Exploration among the Senoi

KILTON STEWART

If you should hear that a flying saucer from another planet had landed on Gualangra, a lonely mountain peak in the Central Mountain Range of the Malay Peninsula a hundred years ago, you would want to know how the space ship was constructed and what kind of power propelled it, but most of all you would want to know about the people who navigated it and the society from which they came. If they lived in a world without crime and war and destructive conflict, and if they were comparatively free from chronic mental and physical ailments, you would want to know about their methods of healing and education, and whether these methods would work as well with the inhabitants of the earth. If you heard further that the navigators of the ship had found a group of 12,000 people living as an isolated community among the mountains, and had demonstrated that these preliterate people would utilize their methods of healing and education, and reproduce the society from which the celestial navigators came, you would probably be more curious about these psychological and social methods that conquered space inside the individual, than you would about the mechanics of the ship which conquered outside space.

As a member of a scientific expedition traveling through the unexplored equatorial rain forest of the Central Range of the Malay Peninsula in 1935, I was introduced to an isolated tribe of jungle folk, who employed methods of psychology and interpersonal relations so astonishing that they might have come from another planet. These people, the Senoi, lived in long community houses, skillfully

Source: From Creative Psychology and Dream Education (New York: Stewart Foundation for Creative Psychology), pp. 23–36. Reprinted by permission of Mrs. Clara Stewart Flagg, widow.

constructed of bamboo, rattan and thatch, and held away from the ground on poles. They maintained themselves by practicing dry-land, shifting agriculture, and by hunting and fishing. Their language, partly Indonesian and partly Mon-Kamian, related them to the peoples of Indonesia to the south and west, and to the Highlanders of Indo-China and Burma, as do their physical characteristics.

Study of their political and social organization indicates that the political authority in their communities was originally in the hands of the oldest members of patrilineal clans, somewhat as in the social structure of China and other parts of the world. But the major authority in all their communities is now held by their primitive psychologists whom they call *halaks*. The only honorary title in the society is that of *Tohat*, which is equivalent to a doctor who is both a healer and an educator, in our terms.

The Senoi claim there has not been a violent crime, or an intercommunal conflict for a space of two or three hundred years because of the insight and inventiveness of the *Tohats* of their various communities. The foothill tribes which surround the Central Mountain Range have such a firm belief in the magical powers of this Highland group that they give the territory a wide berth. From all we could learn, this attitude of the Lowlanders is a very ancient one. Because of their psychological knowledge of strangers in their territory, the Senoi said they could very easily devise means of scaring them off. They did not practice black magic, but allowed the nomadic hill-folk surrounding them to think that they did if strangers invaded their territory.

This fear of Senoi magic accounts for the fact that they have not, over a long period, had to fight with outsiders. But the absence of violent crime, armed conflict, and mental and physical diseases in their own society can only be explained on the basis of institutions which produce a high state of psychological integration and emotional maturity, along with social skills and attitudes which promote creative, rather than destructive, interpersonal relations. They are, perhaps, the most democratic group reported in anthropological literature. In the realms of family, economics, and politics, their society operates smoothly on the principle of contract, agreement and democratic consensus, with no need of police force, jail or psychiatric hospital to reinforce the agreements or to confine those who are not willing or able to reach consensus.

Study of their society seems to indicate that they have arrived at this high state of social and physical cooperation and integration through the system of psychology which they have discovered, invented and developed, and that the principles of this system of psychology are understandable in terms of Western scientific thinking.

It was the late H. D. Noone, the Government Ethnologist of the Federated Malay States who introduced me to this astonishing group. He agreed with me that they have built a system of interpersonal relations which, in the field of psychology, is perhaps on a level with our attainments in such areas as television and nuclear physics. From a year's experience with these people working as a research psychologist, and another year with Noone in England integrating his seven years of anthropological research with my own findings, I am able to make the following formulations of the principles of Senoi psychology.

Being a pre-literate group, the principles of their psychology are simple and easy to learn, understand, and even employ. Fifteen years of experimentation with these Senoi principles have convinced me that all men, regardless of their cultural development, might profit by studying them.

Senoi psychology falls into two categories. The first deals with dream interpretation; the second with dream expression in the agreement trance or cooperative reverie. The cooperative reverie is not participated in until adolescence and serves to initiate the child into the status of adulthood. After adolescence, if he spends a great deal of time in the trance state, a Senoi is considered a specialist in healing or in the use of extra-sensory powers.

Dream interpretation, however, is a feature of child education and is the common knowledge of all Senoi adults. The average Senoi layman practices the psychotherapy of dream interpretation on his family and his associates as a regular feature of education and daily social intercourse. Breakfast in the Senoi house is like a dream clinic, with the father and older brothers listening to and analyzing the dreams of all the children. At the end of the family clinic the male population gathers in the council, at which the dreams of the older children and all the men in the community are reported, discussed, and analyzed.

While the Senoi do not of course employ our system of terminology, their psychology of dream interpretation might be summed up as follows: Man creates features or images of the outside world in his own mind as part of the adaptive process. Some of these features are in conflict with him and with each other. Once internalized, these hostile images turn man against himself and against his fellows. In dreams man has the power to see these facets of his psyche, which have been disguised in external forms, associated with his own fearful emotions, and turned against him and the internal images of other people. If the individual does not receive social aid through education and therapy, these hostile images, built up by man's normal receptiveness to the outside world, get tied together and associated with one another in a way which makes him physically, socially and psychologically abnormal.

Unaided, these dream beings, which man creates to reproduce inside himself the external sociophysical environment, tend to remain against him the way the environment was against him, or to become disassociated from his major personality and tied up in wasteful psychic, organic, and muscular tensions. With the help of dream interpretation, these psychological replicas of the socio-physical environment can be redirected and reorganized and again become useful to the major personality.

The Senoi believes that any human being, with the aid of his fellows, can outface, master, and actually utilize all beings and forces in the dream universe. His experience leads him to believe that, if you cooperate with your fellows or oppose them with good will in the day time, their images will eventually help you in your dreams, and that every person sould and can become the supreme ruler and master of his own dream or spiritual universe, and can demand and receive the help and cooperation of all the forces there.

In order to evaluate these principles of dream interpretation and social action, I made a collection of the dreams of younger and older Senoi children, adolescents, and adults, and compared them with similar collections made in other societies where they had different social attitudes toward the dream and different methods of dream interpretation. I found through this larger study that the dream process evolved differently in the various societies, and that the evolution of the dream process seemed to be related to the adaptability and individual creative output of the various societies. It may be of interest to the reader to examine in detail the methods of Senoi dream interpretation:

The simplest anxiety or terror dream I found among the Senoi was the falling dream. When the Senoi child reports a falling dream, the adult answers with enthusiasm, "That is a wonderful dream, one of the best dreams a man can have. Where did you fall to, and what did you discover?" He makes the same comment when the child reports a climbing, traveling, flying or soaring dream. The child at first answers, as he would in our society, that it did not seem so wonderful, and that he was so frightened that he awoke before he had fallen anywhere.

"That was a mistake," answers the adult-authority. "Everything you do in a dream has a purpose, beyond your understanding while you are asleep. You must relax and enjoy yourself when you fall in a dream. Falling is the quickest way to get in contact with the powers of the spirit world, the powers laid open to you through your dreams. Soon, when you have a falling dream, you will remember what I am saying, and as you do, you will fell that you are traveling to the source of the power which has caused you to fall.

"The falling spirits love you. They are attracting you to their land, and you have but to relax and remain asleep in order to come to grips with them. When you meet them, you may be frightened of their terrific power, but go on. When you think you are dying in a dream, you are only receiving the powers of the other world, your own spiritual power which has been turned against you, and which now wishes to become one with you if you will accept it."

The astonishing thing is that over a period of time, with this type of social interaction, praise, or criticism, imperatives, and advice, the dream which starts out with fear of falling changes into the joy of flying. This happens to everyone in the Senoi society. That which was an indwelling fear of anxiety, becomes an indwelling joy or act of will; that which was ill esteem toward the forces which caused the child to fall in his dream, becomes good will toward the denizens of the dream world, because he relaxes in his dream and finds pleasurable adventures, rather than waking up with a clammy skin and a crawling scalp.

The Senoi believe and teach that the dreamer—the "I" of the dream—should always advance and attack in the teeth of danger, calling on the dream images of his fellows if necessary, but fighting by himself until they arrive. In bad dreams the Senoi believe real friends will never attack the dreamer or refuse help. If any dream character who looks like a friend is hostile or uncooperative in a dream, he is only wearing the mask of a friend.

If the dreamer attacks and kills the hostile dream character, the spirit or essence of this dream character will always emerge as a servant or ally. Dream characters are bad only as long as one is afraid and retreating from them, and will continue to seem bad and fearful as long as one refuses to come to grips with them.

According to the Senoi, pleasurable dreams, such as of flying or sexual love, should be continued until they arrive at a resolution which, on awakening, leaves one with something of beauty or use to the group. For example, one should arrive somewhere when he flies, meet the beings there, hear their music, see their designs, their dances, and learn their useful knowledge.

Dreams of sexual love should always move through orgasm, and the dreamer should then demand from his dream lover the poem, the song, the dance, the useful knowledge which will express the beauty of his spiritual lover to the group. If this is done, no dream man or woman can take the love which belongs to human beings. If the dream character demanding love looks like a brother or a sister, with whom love would be abnormal or incestuous in reality, one need have no fear of expressing love in the dream, since these dream beings are not, in fact, brother or sister, but have only chosen these taboo images as a disguise. Such dream beings are only facets of one's own spirtual or psychic make-up, disguised as brother or sister, and useless until they are reclaimed or possessed through the free expression of love in the dream universe.

If the dreamer demands and receives from his love partner a contribution which he can express to the group on awakening, he cannot express or receive too much love in dreams. A rich love life in dreams indicates the favor of the beings of the spiritual or emotional universe. If the dreamer injures the dream images of his fellows or refuses to cooperate with them in dreams, he should go out of his way to express friendship and cooperation on awakening, since hostile dream characters can only use the image of people for whom his good will is running low. If the image of a friend hurts him in a dream, the friend should be advised of the fact, so he can repair his damaged or negative dream image by friendly social intercourse.

Let us examine some of the elements of the social and psychological processes involved in this type of dream interpretation:

First, the child receives social recognition and esteem for discovering and relating what might be called an anxiety-motivated psychic reaction. This is the first step among the Senoi toward convincing the child that he is acceptable to authority even when he reveals how he is inside.

Second, it describes the working of his mind as rational, even when he is asleep. To the Senoi it is just as reasonable for the child to adjust his inner tension states for himself as it is for a Western child to do his homework for the teacher.

Third, the interpretation characterizes the force which the child feels in the dream as a power which he can control through a process of relaxation and mental set, a force which is his as soon as he can reclaim it and learn to direct it.

Fourth, the Senoi education indicates that anxiety is not only important in itself, but that it blocks the free play of imaginative thinking and creative activity to which dreams could otherwise give rise.

Fifth, it establishes the principle that the child should make decisions and arrive at resolutions in his night-time thinking as well as in that of the day, and should assume a responsible attitude toward all his psychic reactions and forces.

Sixth, it acquaints the child with the fact that he can better control his psychic reactions by expressing them and taking thought upon them, than by concealing and expressing them.

Seventh, it initiates the Senoi child into a way of thinking, which will be strengthened and developed throughout the rest of his life, and which assumes that a human being who retains good will for his fellows and communicates his psychic reactions to them for approval and criticism, is the supreme ruler of all the individual forces of the spirit— subjective—world whatsoever.

Man discovers his deepest self and reveals his greatest creative power at times when his psychic processes are most free from immediate involvement with the environment and most under the control of his indwelling balancing or homeostatic power. The freest type of psychic play occurs in sleep, and the social acceptance of the dream world would, therefore, constitute the deepest possible acceptance of the individual.

Among the Senoi the child accumulates good will for people because they encourage on every hand the free exercise and expression of that which is most basically himself, either directly or indirectly, through the acceptance of the dream process. At the same time, the child is told that he must refuse to settle with the denizens of the dream world unless they make some contribution which is socially meaningful and constructive as determined by social consensus on awakening. Thus his dream reorganization is guided in a way which makes his adult aggressive action socially constructive.

Among the Senoi where the authority tells the child that every dream force and character is real and important, and in essence permanent, that it can and must be outfaced, subdued, and forced to make a socially meaningful contribution, the wisdom of the body operating in sleep, seems in fact to reorganize the accumulating experience of the child in such a way that the natural tendency of the higher nervous system to perpetuate unpleasant experiences is first neutralized and then reversed.

We could call this simple type of interpretation dream analysis. It says to the child that there is a manifest content of the dream, the root he stubbed his toe on, or the fire that burned him, or the composite individual that disciplined him. But there is also a latent content of the dream, a force which is potentially useful, but which will plague him until he outfaces the manifest content in a future dream, and either persuades or forces it to make a contribution which will be judged useful or beautiful by the group, after he awakes.

We could call this type of interpretation suggestion. The tendency to perpetuate in sleep the negative image of a personified evil is neutralized in the dream by a similar tendency to perpetuate the positive image of a sympathetic social authority. Thus, accumulating social experience supports the organizing wisdom of the body in the dream, making the dreamer first unafraid of the negative image and its accompanying painful tension state, and later enabling him to break up that tension state and transmute the accumulated energy from anxiety into a poem, a song, a dance, a new type of trap, or some other creative product, to which an individual or the whole group will react with approval (or criticize) the following day.

The following further examples from the Senoi will show how this process operates:

A child dreams that he is attacked by a friend, and, on awakening, is advised by his father to inform his friend of this fact. The friend's father tells his child that it is possible that he has offended the dreamer without wishing to do so, and allowed a malignant character to use his image as a disguise in the dream. Therefore, he should give a present to the dreamer and go out of his way to be friendly toward him, to prevent such an occurrence in the future.

The aggression building up around the image of the friend in the dreamer's mind thereby becomes the basis of a friendly exchange. The dreamer is also told to fight back in future dreams, and to conquer any dream character using the friend's image as a disguise.

Another example of what is probably a less direct tension state in the dreamer toward another person is dealt with in an equally skillful manner. The dreamer reports seeing a tiger attack another boy of the long house. Again, he is advised to tell the boy about the dream, to describe the place where the attack occurred and, if possible, to show it to him so he can be on his guard, and in future dreams kill the tiger before it has a chance to attack him. The parents of the boy in the dream again tell the child to give the dreamer a present, and to consider him a special friend.

Even a tendency toward unproductive fantasy is effectively dealt with in the Senoi dream education. If the child reports floating dreams, or a dream of finding food, he is told that he must float somewhere in his next dream and find something of value to his fellows, or that he must share the food he is eating; and if he has a dream of attacking someone he must apologize to them, share a delicacy with them, or make them some sort of toy. Thus, before aggression and jealousy can influence social behavior, the tensions expressed in the permissive dream state become the hub of social action in which they are discharged without being destructive.

My data on the dream life of the various Senoi age groups would indicate that dreaming can and does become the deepest type of creative thought. Observing the lives of the Senoi it occurred to me that modern civilization may be sick because people have sloughed off, or failed to develop, half their power to think. Perhaps the most important half. Certainly, the Senoi suffer little by intellectual comparison with outselves. They have equal power for logical thinking while awake, considering their environmental data, whereas our capacity to solve problems in dreams is infantile compared to theirs.

In the adult Senoi a dream may start with a waking problem which has failed solution, with an accident, or a social debacle. A young man brings in some wild gourd seeds and shares them with his group. They have a purgative effect and give everyone diarrhea. The young man feels guilty and ashamed and suspects that they are poisonous. That night he has a dream, and the spirit of the gourd seeds appears, makes him vomit up the seeds, and explains that they have value only as a medicine, when a person is ill. Then the gourd spirit gives him a song and teaches him a dance which he can show his group on awakening, thereby gaining recognition and winning back his self-esteem.

Or, a falling tree which wounds a man appears in his dreams to take away the pain, and explains that it wishes to make friends with him. Then the tree spirit gives him a new and unknown rhythm which he can play on his drums. Or, the jilted lover is visited in his dreams by the woman who rejected him, who explains that she is sick when she is awake and not good enough for him. As a token of her true feeling she gives him a poem.

The Senoi does not exhaust the power to think while asleep with these simple social and environmental situations. The bearers who carried out our equipment under very trying conditions became dissatisfied and were ready to desert. Their leader, a Senoi shaman, had a dream in which he was visited by the spirit of the empty boxes. The song and music this dream character gave him so inspired the bearers, and the dance he directed so relaxed and rested them, that they claimed the boxes had lost their weight and finished the expedition in the best of spirits.

Even this solution of a difficult social situation, involving people who were not all members of the dreamer's group, is trivial compared with the dream solutions which occur now that the Senoi territory has been opened up to alien culture contacts.

Datu Bintung at Jelong had a dream which succeeded in breaking down the major social barriers in clothing and food habits between his group and the surrounding Chinese and Mohammedan colonies. This was accomplished chiefly through a dance which is dream prescribed. Only those who did his dance were required to change their food habits and wear the new clothing, but the dance was so good that nearly all the Senoi along the border chose to do it. In this way, the dream created social change in a democratic manner.

Another feature of Datu Dintung's dream involved the ceremonial status of women, making them more nearly equals of the men, although equality is not a feature of either Chinese or Mohammedan societies. So far as could be determined this was a pure creative action which introduced greater equality in the culture, just as reflective thought has produced more equality in our society.

In the West the thinking we do while asleep usually remains on a muddled, childish, or psychotic level because we do not respond to dreams as socially important and include dreaming in the educative process. This social neglect of the side of man's reflective thinking, when the creative process is most free, seems poor education.

Among the Senoi, the terror dream, the anxiety dream, and the simple pleasure dream, as well as muddled dreams of vague inconsequential happenings, such as a meaningless repetition of the day's activities, largely disappear before puberty. From puberty on, the dream life becomes less and less fantastic and irrational, and more and more like reflective thinking, problem solving, exploration of unknown things or people, emotionally satisfying social intercourse, and the acquiring of knowledge from a dream teacher or spirit guide. However dull or unimportant an individual may be, he can always count on receiving a hearing from his family members and from the larger group through his dreams.

There would seem to be a rational basis for the Senoi ideology and practice if we accept the view that man's psycho-physical structure is not merely altered as experience accumulates, but must be reorganized in line with some principle of inner homeostatic balance.

The internalized social order, which largely makes up the intellectual structure of the individual, does not integrate well with man's power to reorganize and unify his accumulating experience, unless the individual maintains a feeling of good will toward the members of his society, whose images are being internalized as the process of socialization takes place.

If the social authorities, who have a counterpart in the psychic structure of the individual, listen to his dreams with appreciation and respond with criticism, praise and imperatives or directives, the homeostatic processes have the power to reorganize the elements of the mind, as well as those of the body, in a way which keeps both the body and the mind healthy, and permits of a type of social interaction which does not obtain in societies where man is not encouraged and directed to reorganize his accumulating experience in dreams.

Civilized man pays little attention to the thinking he has the power to do in his sleep through dreams. Western society is rife with war, crime and wasteful economic conflict, insanity, neurosis and chronic psychogenic physical ills. The Senoi make their dreams the major focus of their intellectual and social interest, and have solved the problem of violent crime and destructive economic conflict, and largely eliminated insanity, neurosis and psychogenic illness. They have done this without the help of a written language, or of the scientific method as we think of it.

REFERENCE

An interesting, modern application of the Senoi approach has been described by Patricia Garfield in her book *Creative Dreaming,* Chapter 5: "Learn from Senoi dreamers," pp. 80–117. New York: Ballantine, 1974.

12

Education on the Non-Verbal Level

ALDOUS HUXLEY

Early in the mid-Victorian period the Reverend Thomas Binney, a Congregationalist divine, published a book with the alluring title, *Is It Possible to Make the Best of Both Worlds?* His conclusion was that perhaps it might be possible. In spite of its unorthodox message, or perhaps because of it, the book was a best seller, which only showed, said the more evangelical of Mr. Binney's Nonconformist colleagues and Anglican opponents, how inexpressibly wicked Victorian England Really was.

What Mr. Binney's critics had done (and their mistake is repeated by all those who use the old phrase disapprovingly) was to equate "making the best of both worlds" with "serving two masters." It is most certainly very difficult, perhaps quite impossible, to serve Mammon and God simultaneously—to pursue the most sordid interests while aspiring to realize the highest ideals. This is obvious. Only a little less obvious, however, is the fact that it is very hard, perhaps quite impossible, to serve God while failing to make the best of both worlds—of *all* the worlds of which, as human beings, we are the inhabitants.

Man is a multiple amphibian and exists at one and the same time in a number of universes, dissimilar to the point, very nearly, of complete incompatibility. He is at once an animal and a rational intellect; a product of evolution closely related to the apes and a spirit capable of self-transcendence; a sentient being in contact with the brute data of his own nervous system and the physical environment and at the same time the creator of a home-made universe of words and other symbols,

Source: Reprinted from "Science and Technology in Contemporary Society," by permission of Daedalus, Journal of the American Academy of Arts and Sciences, *Boston, Massachusetts (Spring 1962).*

in which he lives and moves and has anything from thirty to eighty percent of his being. He is a self-conscious and self-centered ego who is also a member of a moderately gregarious species, an individualist compelled by the population explosion to live at ever closer quarters, and in ever tighter organizations, with millions of other egos as self centered and as poorly socialized as himself. Neurologically, he is a lately evolved Jekyll-cortex associated with an immensely ancient brainstem-Hyde. Physiologically, he is a creature whose endocrine system is perfectly adapted to the conditions prevailing in the lower Paleolithic, but living in a metropolis and spending eight hours a day sitting at a desk in an air-conditioned office. Psychologically, he is a highly educated product of twentieth-century civilization, chained, in a state of uneasy and hostile symbiosis, to a disturbingly dynamic unconsious, a wild phantasy and an unpredictable id—and yet capable of falling in love, writing string quartets, and having mystical experiences.

Living amphibiously in all these incommensurable worlds at once, human beings (it is hardly surprising) find themselves painfully confused, uncertain where they stand or who they really are. To provide themselves with a recognizable identity, a niche in the scheme of things that they can call "home," they will give assent to the unlikeliest dogmas, conform to the most absurd and even harmful rules of thought, feeling, and conduct, put on the most extravagant fancy dress and identify themselves with masks that bear almost no resemblance to the faces they cover. "Bovarism (as Jules de Gaultier calls it) is the urge to pretend that one is something that in fact one is not. It is an urge that manifests itself, sometimes weakly, sometimes with overpowering strength, in all human beings, and one of the conditions of its manifestation is precisely our uncertainty about where we stand or who we are. To explore our multiple amphilbiousness with a view to doing something constructive about it is a most laborious process. Our minds are congenitally lazy, and the original sin of the intellect is oversimplification. Dogmatism and boveristic identification with a stereotype are closely related manifestations of the same kind of intellectual delinquency. "Know thyself." From time immemorial this has been the advice of all the seers and philosophers. The self that they urge us to know is not, of course, the stylized persona with which, bovaristically, we try to become identified; it is the multiple amphibian, the inhabitant of all those incompatible worlds that we must somehow learn to make the best of.

A good education may be defined as one which helps the boys and girls subjected to it to make the best of all the worlds in which, as human beings, they are compelled, willy-nilly, to live. An education that prepares them to make the best of only one of their worlds, or of only a few of them, is inadequate. This is a point on which, in principle, all educators have always agreed. *Mens sana in corpore sano* is an ancient educational ideal and a very good one. Unfortunately, good ideals are never enough. Unless they are accompanied by full instructions regarding the methods by which they may be realized, they are almost useless. Hell is paved with good intentions, and whole periods of history have been made hideous or grotesque by enthusiastic idealists who failed to elaborate the means whereby their lofty aspirations might be effectively, and above all harmlessly, implemented.

Just how good is modern education? How successful is it in helping young people to make the best of all the worlds which, as multiple amphibians, they have to live in? In a center of advanced scientific and technical study this question gets asked inevitably in terms of what may be called the paradox of specialization. In science and technology specilization is unavoidable and indeed absolutely necessary. But training for this unavoidable and necessary specilization does nothing to help young amphibians to make the best of their many worlds. Indeed, it pretty obviously prevents them from doing anything of the kind. What then is to be done? At the Massachusetts Institute of Technology and in other schools where similar problems have arisen, the answer to this question has found expression in a renewed interest in the humanities. Excessive scientific specialization is tempered by courses in philosophy, history, literature, and social studies. All this is excellent so far as it goes. But does it go far enough? Do courses in the humanities provide a sufficient antidote for excessive scientific and technical specialization? Do they, in the terminology we have been using, help young multiple amphibians to make the best of a substantially greater number of their worlds?

Science is the reduction of the bewildering diversity of unique events to manageable uniformity within one of a number of symbol systems, and technology is the art of using these symbol systems so as to control and organize unique events. Scientific observation is always a viewing of things through the refracting medium of a symbol system, and technological praxis is always the handling of things in ways that some symbol system has dictated. Education in science and technology is essentially education on the symbolic level.

Turning to the humanities, what do we find? Courses in philosophy, literature, history, and social studies are exclusively verbal. Observation of and experimentation with nonverbal events have no place in these fields. Training in the sciences is largely on the symbolic level, training in the liberal arts is wholly and all the time on that level. When courses in the humanities are used as the only antidote to too much science and technology, excessive specialization in one kind of symbolic education is being tempered by excessive specialization in another kind of symbolic education. The young amphibians are taught to make the best, not of all their worlds, but only of two varieties of the same world—the world of symbols. But this world of symbols is only one of the worlds in which human beings do their living and their learning. They also inhabit the nonsymbolic world of unconceptualized or only slightly conceptualized experience. However effective it may be on the conceptual level, an education that fails to help young amphibians to make the best of the inner and outer universes on the hither side of symbols is an inadequate education. And however much we may delight in Homer or Gibbon, however illuminating in their different ways Pareto and William Law, Hui-neng and Bertrand Russell may strike us as being, the fact remains that the reading of their works will not be of much help to us in our efforts to make the best of our worlds of unconceptualized, nonverbal experience.

And here, before I embark on a discussion of these nonverbal worlds, let me add parenthetically that even on the verbal level, where they are most at home, educators have done a good deal less than they might reasonably have been expected to do in explaining to young people the nature, the limitations, the huge potentialities for evil as well as for good, of that greatest of all human inventions, language. Children should be taught that words are indispensable but also can be fatal—the only begetters of all civilization, all science, all consistency of high purpose, all angelic goodness, and the only begetters at the same time of all superstition, all collective madness and stupidity, all worse-than-bestial diabolism, all the dismal historical succession of crimes in the name of God, King, Nation, Party, Dogma. Never before, thanks to the techniques of mass communication, have so many listeners been so completely at the mercy of so few speakers. Never have misused words—those hideously efficient tools of all the tyrants, war-mongers, persecutors, and heresy-hunters—been so widely and so disastrously influential as they are today. Generals, clergymen, advertisers, and the rulers of totalitarian states—all have good reasons for disliking the idea of universal education in the rational use of language. To the military, clerical, propagandist, and authoritarian mind such training seems (and rightly seems) profoundly subversive. To those who think that liberty is a good thing, and who hope that it may some day become possible for more people to realize more of their desirable potentialities in a society fit for free, fully human individuals to live in, a thorough education in the nature of language, in its uses and abuses, seems indispensable. Whether in fact the mounting pressures of overpopulation and overorganization in a world still enthusiastically dedicated to nationalistic idolatry will permit this kind of subversive linguistic education to be adopted by even the more democratic nations remains to be seen.

And now, after this brief digression, let us return to our main theme, the education of multiple amphibians on levels other than the verbal and the symbolic. "Make the body capable of doing many things," wrote Spinoza. "This will help you to perfect the mind and come to the intellectual love of God." Substitute "psychophysical organism" for "body," and you have here the summary of a program for universal education on the nonsymbolic level, supplemented by a statement of the reasons why such an education is desirable and indeed, if the child is to grow into a fully human being, absolutely necessary. The detailed curriculum for an education in what may be called the nonverbal humanities has still to be worked out. All I can do at this time is to drop a few fragmentary hints.

Two points, to begin with, must be emphatically stressed. First, education in the nonverbal humanities is not just a matter of gymnastics and football, of lessons in singing and folk dancing. All these, of course, are good, but by themselves not good enough. Such traditional methods of training young people in nonverbal skills need to be supplemented, if they are to yield their best results, by other kinds of training, beginning with a thorough training in elementary awareness. And the second point to be remembered is that education in the nonverbal humanities is a process that should be started in the kindergarten and continued through all the years of school and college—and thereafter, as self-education, throughout the rest of life.

At the end of a delightful anthology entitled *Zen Flesh, Zen Bones,* its editor, Mr. Paul Reps, has printed an English version of an ancient Tantrik text in which Shiva, in response to Parvati's questions about the nature of enlightened consciousness, gives a list of one hundred and twelve exercises in the art of being aware of inner and outer reality on its nonsymbolic levels. *Gnosce Teipsum.* But how? From the vast majority of our pastors and masters no answer is forthcoming. Here, for a blessed change, is a philosophical treatise that speaks of means as well as of ends, of concrete experience as well as of high abstractions. The intelligent and systematic practice of any half-dozen of these hundred and twelve exercises will take one further towards the realization of the ancient ideal of self-knowledge than all the roaring or pathetic eloquence of generations of philosophers, theologians, and moralists. (Let me add, in passing, that whereas Western philosophy tends to be concerned with the manipulation of abstract symbols for the benefit of the speculative and moralizing intellect, oriental philosophy is almost always essentially operational. "Perform such and such psychophysical operations," the exponents of this philosophy say, "and you will probably find yourself in a state of mind which, like all those who have achieved it in the past, you will regard as selfevidently and supremely valuable. In the context of this state of mind, speculation about man and the universe leads us, as it led earlier thinkers, to the metaphysical doctrine of *Tat tvam asi* [thou art That], and to its ethical corollary—universal compassion. In this philosophy it is the experiential element that is important. Its speculative superstructure is a thing of words, and words, though useful and necessary, should never be taken too seriously.")

Education in elementary awareness will have to include techniques for improving awareness of internal events and techniques for improving awareness of external events as these are revealed by our organs of sense. In his introductions to several of F. M. Alexander's books, John Dewey insisted upon the importance of a properly directed training in the awareness of internal events. It was Dewey's opinion that the training methods developed by Alexander were to education what education is to life in general—an indispensable condition for any kind of improvement. Dewey had himself undergone this training and so knew what he was talking about. And yet in spite of this high praise bestowed by one of the most influential of modern philosophers and educational reformers, Alexander's methods have been ignored, and schoolchildren still receive no training in the kind of internal awareness that can lead to what Alexander described as "creative conscious control."

The educational and therapeutic values of training aimed at heightening awareness of internal events was empirically demonstrated during the first quarter of the present century by the eminently successful Swiss psychiatrist, Dr. Roger Vittoz. And in recent years methods similar to those of Vittoz and to the Tantrik exercises attributed many centuries ago to Shiva have been developed and successfully used both in the treatment of neurotics and for the enrichment of the lives of the normal by the authors of *Gestalt Therapy,* Drs. Frederick F. Perls, Ralph F. Hefferline, and Paul Goodman.

All our mental processes depend upon perception. Inadequate perceiving results in poor thinking, inappropriate feeling, diminished interest in and enjoyment of life. Systematic training of perception should be an essential element in all education.

Our amphibiousness is clearly illustrated in the two modes of our awareness of external events. There is a receptive, more or less unconceptualized, aesthetic and "spiritual" mode of perceiving; and there is also a highly conceptualized, stereotyped, utilitarian, and even scientific mode. In his *Expostulation and Reply* and *The Tables Turned,* Wordsworth has perfectly described these two modes of awareness and has assigned to each its special significance and value for the human being who aspires to make the best of both worlds and so, by teaching his psychophysical organism to "do many things," to "perfect the mind and come to the intellectual love of God."

> "Why, William, on that old grey stone,
> Thus for the length of half a day,
> Why William, sit you thus alone,
> And dream your time away?
>
> Where are your books?—that light bequeathed
> To being else forlorn and blind?
> Up! Up! and drink the spirit breathed
> From dead men to their kind.
>
> You look round on your Mother Earth,
> As if she for no purpose bore you;
> As if you were her first-born birth,
> And none had lived before you."
>
> One morning thus, by Esthwaite lake,
> When life was sweet, I knew not why,
> To me my good friend Matthew spake,
> And thus I made reply.
>
> "The eye it cannot choose but see;
> We cannot bid the ear be still;
> Our bodies feel, where'er they be,
> Against or with our will.
>
> Nor less I deem that there are Powers
> Which of themselves our minds impress;
> That we can feed this mind of ours
> In a wise passiveness.

Think you, 'mid all this mighty sum
Of things for ever speaking,
That nothing of itself will come,
But we must still be seeking?

Then ask not wherefore, here, alone,
Conversing as I may,
I sit upon this old grey stone
And dream my time away."

In *The Tables Turned* it is the poet who takes the offensive against his studious friend. "Up! up! my Friend," he calls, "and quit your books." And then, "Books!" he continues impatiently.

"Books! 'tis a dull and endless strife;
Come, hear the woodland linnet;
How sweet his music! on my life,
There's more of wisdom in it.

And hark how blithe the throstle sings!
He too is no mean preacher.
Come forth into the light of things,
Let Nature be your teacher.

One impulse from a vernal wood
May teach you more of man,
Of moral evil and of good
Than all the sages can.

Sweet is the lore which Nature brings;
Our meddling intellect
Mis-shapes the beauteous forms of things—
We murder to dissect.

Enough of Science and of Art;
Close up those barren leaves;
Come forth and bring with you a heart
That watches and receives.

Mathew and William—two aspects of the multiple amphibian that was Wordsworth, that is each one of us. To be fully human, we must learn to make the best of William's world as well as of Matthew's. Matthew's is the world of books, of the social heredity of steadily accumulating knowledge, of science and technics and business, of words and the stock of second-hand notions which we project upon external reality as a frame of reference, in terms of which we may explain, to our own satisfaction, the enigma, moment by moment, of ongoing existence. Over against it stands William's world—the world of sheer mystery, the world as an endless succession of unique events, the world as we perceive it in a state of alert receptiveness with no thought of explaining it, using it exploiting it for our biological or cultural purposes. As things now stand, we teach young people to make the best only of Matthew's world of familiar words, accepted notions, and useful techniques. We temper a too exclusive concentration on scientific symbols, not with a training in the art of what William calls "wise passiveness," not with lessons in watching and receiving, but with the injunction to concentrate on philosophical and sociological symbols, to read the books that are reputed to contain a high concentration of "the spirit breathed from dead men to their kind." (Alas, dead men do not always breathe a spirit; quite often they merely emit a bad smell.)

It is related in one of the Sutras that on a certain occasion the Buddha preached a wordless sermon to his disciples. Instead of saying anything, he picked a flower and held it up for them to look at. The disciples gaped uncomprehendingly. Only Mahakasyapa understood what the Tathagata was driving at, and all that he did was to smile. Gautama smiled back at him, and when the wordless sermon was over, he made a little speech for the benefit of those who had failed to comprehend his silence. "This treasure of the unquestionable teaching, this Mind of Nirvana, this true form that is without forms, this most subtle Dharma beyond words, this instruction that is to be given and received outside the pale of all doctrines—this I have now handed on to Mahakasyapa." Perceived not as a botanical specimen, not as the analyzed and labeled illustration of a pre-existent symbol system, but as a nameless, unique event, in which all the beauty and the mystery of existence are manifest, a flower can become the means to enlightenment. And what is true of a flower is true, needless to say, of any other event in the inner or outer world—from a toothache to Mount Everest, from a tapeworm to The Well-Tempered Clavichord—to which we choose to pay attention in a state of wise passiveness. And wise passiveness is the condition not only of spiritual insight. ("In prayer," wrote St. Jeanne Chantal, "I always want to *do* something, wherein I do very wrong. . . . By wishing to accomplish something myself, I spoil it all.") In another context, wise passiveness, followed in due course by wise hard work, is the condition of creativity. We do not fabricate our best ideas; they "occur to us," they "come into our heads." Colloquial speech reminds us that, unless we give our subliminal mind a chance, we shall get nowhere. And it is by allowing ourselves at frequent intervals to be wisely passive that we can most effectively help the subliminal mind to do its work. The *cogito* of Descartes should be emended, said Von Baader, to *cogitor*. In order to actualize our potentialities, in order to become fully human and completely ourselves, we must not merely think; we must also permit ourselves to be thought. In Gardner Murphy's words, "Both the historical record of creative thought and the laboratory report of its appearance today, indicate clearly that creative intelligence can spring from the mind that is not strained to its highest pitch, but is utterly at ease." Watching and receiving in a state of perfect ease or wise passiveness is an art which can be cultivated and should be taught on every educational level from the most elementary to the most advanced.

Creativity and spiritual insight—these are the highest rewards of wise passiveness. But those who know how to watch and receive are rewarded in other and hardly less important ways. Receptivity can be a source of innocent and completely harmless happiness. A man or woman who knows how to make the best of both worlds—the world revealed by wise passiveness and the world created by wise activity— tends to find life enjoyable and interesting. Ours is a civilization in which vast numbers of children and adults are so chronically bored that they have to resort during their leisure hours to a regimen of non-stop distractions. Any method which promises to make life seem enjoyable and the commonplaces of everyday experience more interesting should be welcomed as a major contribution to culture and morality.

In *Modern Painters* there is a remarkable chapter on "the Open Sky"—a chapter which even by those who find Ruskin's theology absurd and his aesthetics frequently perverse may still be read with profit and admiring pleasure. "It is a strange thing," Ruskin writes, "how little in general people know about the sky. It is the part of creation in which nature has done more for the sake of pleasing man, more for the sake and evident purpose of talking to him and teaching him, than in any of her works, and it is just the part in which we least attend to her. . . . There is not a moment in any day of our lives in which nature is not producing (in the sky) scene after scene, picture after picture, glory after glory, and working always upon such exquisite and constant principles of the most perfect beauty, that it is quite certain it is all done for us and intended for our perpetual pleasure." But, in point of fact, does the sky produce in most people the perpetual pleasure which its beauty is so eminently capable of giving? The answer, of course, is No. "We never attend to it, we never make it a subject of thought. . . . We look upon it . . . only as a succession of monotonous and meaningless ac-

cidents, too common or too vain to be worthy of a moment of watchful-
ness or a glance of admiration. . . . Who, among the chattering
crowd, can tell me of the forms and the precipices of the chain of tall
white mountains that girded the horizon at noon yesterday? Who saw
the narrow sunbeam that came out of the south and smote their sum-
mits until they melted and mouldered away in a dust of blue rain?
. . . . All has passed unregretted as unseen; or if the apathy be ever
shaken off, if even for an instant, it is only by what is gross or what is
extraordinary." A habit of wise passiveness in relation to the everyday
drama of the clouds and mist and sunshine can become a source, as
Ruskin insists, of endless pleasure. But most of the products of our
educational system prefer Westerns and alcohol.

In the art of watching and receiving Ruskin was self-educated.
But there seems to be no reason why children should not be taught that
wise passiveness which gave this victim of a traumatic childhood so
much pleasure and kept him, in spite of everything, reasonably sane for
the greater part of a long and productive life. A training in watching and
receiving will not turn every child into a great stylist but, within the
limits imposed by constitution, temperament, and the circumambient
culture, it will make him more sensitive, more intelligent, more capable
of innocent enjoyment and, in consequence, more virtuous and more
useful to society.

In the United States life, liberty, and the pursuit of happiness are
constitutionally guaranteed. But if life hardly seems worth living, if
liberty is used for subhuman purposes, if the pursuers of happiness
know nothing about the nature of their quarry or the elementary techniques of hunting, these constitutional rights will not be very meaningful. An education in that wise passiveness recommended by the saints
and the poets, by all who have lived fully and worked creatively, might
help us to transform the paper promises of a democratic constitution
into concrete contemporary fact.

Let us now consider very briefly two other areas in which an
education in the art of making the best of all our seemingly incommensurable worlds would certainly be helpful and might also turn out
to be practicable within the system now prevailing in our schools and
colleges. It is a matter of observable fact that all of us inhabit a world of
phantasy as well as a world of first-order experience and a world of
words and concepts. In most children and in some adults this world of
phantasy is astonishingly vivid. These people are the visualizers of
Galton's classical dichotomy. For them the world presented to their
consciousness by their story-telling, image-making phantasy is as real

as, sometimes more real than, the given world of sense impressions and the projected world of words and explanatory concepts. Even in nonvisualizers the world of phantasy, though somewhat shadowy, is still real enough to be retreated into or shrunk from, tormented by or voluptuously enjoyed. The mentally ill are the victims of their phantasy, and even more or less normal people find themselves tempted into folly, or inhibited from behaving as they know they ought to behave, by what goes on in the superreal but unrealistic world of their imagination. How can we make the best of this odd, alien, almost autonomous universe that we carry about with us inside our skulls?

The question has been partially answered by the apostles of those numerous religious movements stemming from "New Thought." Using a vaguely theological language and interpreting the Bible to suit themselves, they have given a religious form to a number of useful and practical methods for harnessing imagination and its suggestive power in the service of individual well-being and social stability. For about a quarter or perhaps a third of the population their methods work remarkably well. This is an important fact, of which professional educators should take notice and from whose implications they should not be ashamed to learn. Unfortunately, men and women in high academic positions tend to be intellectually snobbish. They turn up their noses at the nonscientific, distressingly "inspirational" but still astute and experienced psychologists of the modern heretical churches. This is deplorable. Truth lives, proverbially, at the bottom of a well, and wells are often muddy. No genuinely scientific investigator has any right to be squeamish about anything.

And here is another truth-containing well abhorred by academic scientists of the stricter sort. Excellent techniques for teaching children and adults to make the best of the chaotic world of their phantasy have been worked out by the Dianeticists and their successors, the Scientologists. Their Imagination Games deserve to be incorporated into every curriculum. Boys and girls, and even grown men and women, find these games amusing and, what is more important, helpful. Made the worst of, our imagination will destroy us; made the best of, it can be used to break up long-established habits of undesirable feeling, to dissipate obsessive fears, to provide symbolic outlets for anger and fictional amends for real frustrations.

In the course of the last three thousand years how many sermons have been preached, how many homilies delivered and commands roared out, how many promises of heaven and threats of hell-fire solemnly pronounced, how many good-conduct prizes awarded and how many childish buttocks lacerated with whips and canes? And what has been the result of all this incalculable sum of moralistic words, and of the rewards and savage punishments by which the verbiage has been accompanied? The result has been history—the successive generations of human beings comporting themselves virtuously and rationally enough for the race to survive, but badly enough and madly enough for it to be unceasingly in trouble. Can we do better in the future than we are doing today, or than our fathers did in the past? Can we develop methods more effective than pious talk and Pavlovian conditioning?

For an answer to these questions—or at least for some hints as to the nature of a possible answer—we must turn to history and anthropology. Like many primitive societies today, many highly civilized societies of the past provided their members with realistically amphibious methods for dealing with negative emotions and the instinctive drives that are incompatible with communal living. In these societies morality and rational behavior were not merely preached and rewarded; they were made easier by the provision of religiously sanctioned safety valves, through which the angry, the frustrated, and the anxiously neurotic could release their aggressive or self-destructive tendencies in a satisfyingly violent and yet harmless and socially acceptable way. In Ancient Greece, for example, the orgies of Dionysus and, at a somewhat later date, the Corybantic dances, sacred to the Great Mother, were safety valves through which rage and resentment found an innocuous outlet, while the paralyzing inhibitions of anxiety were swept away in a wild rush of nervous, muscular, and hormonal activity. In this ethical and therapeutic context Dionysus was known as Lusios, the Liberator. His orgies delivered the participants from the dismal necessity of running amok, or retreating into catatonia, or stoically bottling up their feelings and so giving themselves a psychosomatic illness. Corybantic dancing was regarded as a form of medical treatment and at the same time as a religious rite, cathartic to the soul no less than to the adrenalin-charged body. Which did most for morality and rational behavior—the dialogues of Plato or the orgies of Dionysus, Aristotle's *Ethics* or the Corybantic dances? My guess is that, in this competition, Lusios and the Great Mother would be found to have won hands down.

In a society like ours it would doubtless be impracticable to revive Maenadism or the congregational antics of the Dionysian orgies. But the problem of what multiple amphibians should do about their frustrations and their tendencies to aggression remains acute and still unsolved. Sixty years ago William James wrote an essay entitled *The*

Moral Equivalent of War. It is an excellent essay as far as it goes; but it does not, unfortunately, so far enough. Moral equivalents must be found not only for war but also for delinquency, family squabbles, bullying, puritanical censoriousness, and all the assorted beastliness of daily life. Preaching and conditioning will never of themselves solve these problems. It is obvious that we must take a hint from the Greeks and provide ourselves with physical safety valves for reducing the pressure of our negative emotions. No ethical system which fails to provide such physical safety valves, and which fails to teach children and their elders how to use them, is likely to be effective. It will be the business of psychologists, physiologists, and sociologists to devise acceptable safety valves, of moralists and clergymen to provide rationalizations in terms of the local value systems and theologies, and for educators to find a place in the curriculum for courses in the indispensable art of letting off steam.

And there is another art that merits the educator's closest attention—the art of controlling physical pain. Pain, as recent studies have made abundantly clear, is not simply a mechanical affair of peripheral receptors and special centers in the brain, and its intensity is not directly proportional to the extent of the injury which is its cause. Pain may be aggravated or inhibited by numerous psychological and even cultural factors. Which means, of course, that to some extent at least pain is controllable. This fact, needless to say, has been known from time immemorial, and for the last century and a half (from the days of Elliotson and Esdaile) has been systematically exploited in hypnotic anesthesia. Neurological research is now discovering the organic and functional reasons for these old observations and empirical practices; a somewhat disreputable "wild" phenomenon is in process of being turned into a domesticated scientific fact, consonant with other well-known facts and safely caged within a familiar symbol-system. Taking advantage of the new-found respectability of hypnosis and suggestion, educators should now include elementary pain control in the curriculum of physical training. Control of pain through suggestion and autosuggestion is an art which, as every good dentist knows, can be learned by most children with the greatest of ease. Along with singing and calisthenics, it should be taught to every little boy and little girl who can learn it.

Training in a closely similar art may prove to be very useful as a part of ethical education. In his book *Auto-Conditioning* Professor Hornell Hart has outlined simple and thoroughly practical methods for changing moods, intensifying motivations, and implementing good intentions. There are no educational panaceas, no teachniques that work perfectly in every case. But if autoconditioning produces good results in only twenty or thirty percent of those who have been instructed in the art, it deserves to take its place in every educator's armamentarium.

That we are multiple amphibians is self-evident, and the corollary of this self-evident truth is that we must attack our problems on every front where they arise—on the mental front and on the physiological front, on the front of concepts and symbols and on the front of word-less experience, on the rational front and on the irrational front, the individual front and the social front. But what should be our strategy? How are we to learn and successfully practice the art of attacking on all the fronts simultaneously? Many valuable discoveries were made by the amphibians of earlier times and alien cultures, and many dis-coveries are being made within our own culture today. These empirical findings of the past and the present should be studied, tested, related to the best scientific knowledge now available, and finally adapted for practical use within our educational systems. Ten million dollars from the coffers of one of the great foundations would pay for the necessary research and large-scale experimentation. Out of such research and ex-perimentation might come, within a few years, a radical improvement in the methods currently used to prepare young people to meet the challenges of their manifold amphibiousness and to make the best of all the strangely assorted worlds in which, as human beings, they are predestined to live.

13

Two Kinds of Teaching

HUSTON SMITH

When I think back over the memorable teachers I had or have known, the fact that stands out most is the diversity of their styles. Bill Levi at Roosevelt College would sit cross-legged on the desk, moving nothing during the entire class hour save his lips and his mind. Meanwhile, at nearby University of Chicago, David Greene was a pacer. Fresh from his farm at eight on wintry mornings, manure still clinging to his boots as Greek poured from his mouth, he strode with a vigor that made the advancing wall seem adversary. We felt sure that sooner or later he would slam his face into it, but he never did; invariably in the nick of time he would swirl and bounce off the wall not his head but his behind thereby gaining momentum for the return journey. Gustav Bergmann, logical positivist at the State University of Iowa, was so authoritarian that when a student dared to question something he had said he thundered, "Let's get one thing straight: from 10:00 to 11:00 A.M. on Mondays, Wednesdays, and Fridays, there is but one God, and his name is Bergmann!" His opposite was a teacher so nondirective on principle that students used to say he not only didn't believe anything, he didn't even suspect anything. I had teachers who wrestled with me socratically as evangelists wrestled with the village drunkard, and teachers who simply dished it out — very well indeed!

The surprising thing is that learning occurred in all these contexts. I conclude that there is no one way to teach; in writing here of two ways I write only of ways that have taken shape in me. Who knows who learns and under what conditions? The act remains

Source: From "Two Kinds of Teaching," Journal of Humanistic Psychology, *vol. 15, no. 4 (Fall 1975), pp. 3–12. Reprinted by permission of Huston Smith and the publisher.*

essentially mysterious, like love, or sex, or life itself; more strange than familiar, less science than art, a word to which I shall return.

Method I

During its first 20 years, my teaching followed a single pattern. Questions and discussion were encouraged and were fun, but lectures were the focus.

Today, lecturers are on the defensive. Almost everything we would like students to know we can place in their hands via paperback. They can read faster than they can listen to us, and print is durable; they can go back if they miss something or forget.

All this is true, but the points don't add up to the conclusion that lectures are passé. One of my most memorable learning experiences was a course Thornton Wilder offered, once only, at the University of Chicago. The classroom was in fact an auditorium, and it was invariably packed. If there was a single question or comment from the floor I don't remember it, yet the exhilaration of those hours I shall never forget. I would leave the auditorium walking on air. In those early afternoons of autumn even Chicago was beautiful.

Plays, too, can be read faster than we can sit through an evening at the theater, but reading doesn't take the place of the performance. Moreover, lectures provide the opportunity for trying out ideas while they are in process of formation and are thus part of the teacher's laboratory. The advantage to the listener is that he or she is not presented with a finished treatise but is watching a living mind at work and being given an insight into its strategies.

Just as there is no one way to teach, so too there is no one way to lecture. John Dewey's lectures are said to have been rambling and dull—until the student awoke to the fact that he was witness to a powerful mind's direct involvement in the act of thinking. Minds have their own dispositions: some, like Wittgenstein's, are splitters; mine happens to be a lumper. This fact, so apparent that I suspect that it is grounded in my brain structure, makes metaphysical reticence impossible for me. And, as it affects my approach to lecturing in other ways as well, before saying more about lecturing proper I propose to indicate why a wholistic approach to my field is, in my case, the only approach possible.

Gestalt psychology has made its mark, and gestalt therapy is bidding to do so. In this age of analysis, this heyday of analytic philosophy, is there a place for wholistic, gestalt philosophy as well?

If this discipline takes its cues from the sciences, the answer seems clearly "yes." Gestalt psychology I have already mentioned; psychology abandoned atomism with its discovery that there is no area of experience, perceptual or otherwise, that is free from what positivists used to call noncognitive factors. In biology, the attempts of molecular genetics "to reach the beautiful simplicity of biological principles through concepts derived from experimental systems in which the ordered structure that is the source of this simplicity has been destroyed [are proving to be] increasingly futile," and physics, in its complete experience, "does not support the precept that all complex systems are explicable in terms of properties observable in their isolated parts [Commoner, 1969]."

Turning to philosophy itself, epistemology has found element analysis ineffectual. Whether we approach knowing analytically or phenomenologically, reports agree: there is no datum unpatterned, no figure without ground, no fact without theory. Instead of a one-way process whereby through perceptual archeology irrefrangible primitive elements—Hume's impressions, Russell and Moore's sense data—are first spotted and *then* built into wholes, knowing (we now see) is polar. Part and whole are in dialogue from the start. No man looks at the world with pristine eyes; he sees it edited, and editorial policy is always forged in the widest field of vision available.

The same holds true for ethics, for doing is vectored by overview as much as knowing is. "Deeper and more fundamental than sexuality, deeper than the craving for social power, deeper even than the desire for possessions, there is a still more generalized and more universal craving in the human make-up. It is the craving for knowledge of the right direction—for orientation [Shelton, 1936]."

In playing the game of life-orientation, the first rule is to capture everything in sight, for the elusive might prove to be crucial; if it is and it escapes your net, you may get rich, but you won't win. The second rule is to set what has been captured in order, to array it in pattern or design. Thus the twin principles of gestalt philosophy are: *(a)* attention to the whole, taking care to see that nothing of importance has been omitted; and *(b)* attention to the pattern of the whole's parts. Complementing clarity and consistency which are the virtues of analytic philosophy, the virtues of gestalt philosophy are scope and design.

Now back to lecturing. As a gestalt philosopher both these principles of scope and design figure in the way I approach my task. Scope enters to position the topic to be discussed within the panoply of human interests generally. Why among the myriad of things we could talk about during this hour or this semester are we giving time to this?

The answer needn't take much time; indeed, no time at all if it is self-evident and acceptable. But it must be evident and acceptable to students, not just to me; that's crucial. Answers which, however evident, are *not* acceptable to students are: "because the professor happens to be working on a paper of the subject," "because this is what the instructor was taught in graduate school, so knows most about—read, is most invulnerable with respect to' " "because having avoided math the student needs a course in philosophy to graduate" or "because it will help those who intend to continue in philosophy to get into graduate school."

Once the topic has been positioned in the sense of linked to an acknowledged human interest or need, the elements bearing on the topic must be positioned. Enter pattern or design.

Paintings begin with a discovery, a new and exhilarating perception. Immediately the painter faces enormous difficulties; he must force shapes and static colors to embody what he has felt and seen. The lecturer's task is analogous. He, too, must fix, articulate, and objectify what on first discovery was nebulous, fluid, and private. How, within the artifice of a class hour, can he make a subtle aspect of life or being evident? Every sentence calls for knowledge of his materials and their limitations and an unswerving eye on the effect intended. It is an old problem: how anything of the real can pass the gap between intuition and expression. The passage can be effected only by translation, not from one language into another but from one mode of being into another, from reception into creation. Everything at the instructor's disposal—facts, concepts, anecdotes, analogies, arguments, humor—must work to enforce the intended impression to the end that at the hour's close the student feels, "that's true and important, or at least interesting." It's no good if he stops with "that's true." As Whitehead noted, "It is more important that a proposition be interesting than that it be true. The importance of truth is that it adds to interest." As irrelevancies deaden the effect, omission is of the essence.

What constitutes a masterpiece here, or (to drop hyperbole) at least an authentic work of art? When a person for whom the topic in question is vital, who as consequence has lived with it and pondered it, summons everything he or she has discerned on the proglem, distills it, compresses it, pounds it into a form that makes sense! Thoughts emerge, not in mere succession but architecturally, in meaningful pattern—possibly, in addition, they emerge as incarnated in a life that is being lived, his or her own. That's what sent me walking out of Mandel Hall on air those Chicago afternoons. And that, now that I think of it, is the way subliminally I have sensed myself as a lecturer: traveller, pilgrim, archeologist of space and time, trying with the help of a parcel here and a fragment there to piece together the largest possible meaning for life and the world. Such meaning, though it is intelligible, exceeds the merely rational. Or if one prefers, is the highest category of the rational.

In characterizing lecturing as art, my model has been the painter rather than the actor. Not that lectures can't be dramatic performances too; they can be, as the adage that every good teacher is part ham attests. But the comparison means little to me—again, the variety in teaching styles. Writing is as different from speaking as reading is from listening, but the feelings that infuse me while writing and lecturing are much the same. Attention is fixed on content; issues of delivery and audience contact work themselves out unconsciously.

Method II

It will be apparent from what I have said that I haven't lost faith in the mix of lecture and discussion that is higher education's abiding rubric. I continue to teach one course each term by this format; it involves me and, given the averages, students show symptoms of satisfaction. But there has been a change. For the last eight years I have also taught a course by almost opposite canons.

This second course roots back to the summer of 1965, when I was invited to Bethel, Maine, to observe for two weeks the work of the National Training Laboratories with small groups: T (for Training-) groups, encounter groups, or human interaction laboratories as they have come to be called. By pleasant coincidence, I was to bring back from Bethel what Bethel had originally drawn from my own home base, for it was from Kurt Lewin's pioneering work at M.I.T. that the National Training Laboratories evolved. Something happened to me at Bethel, but it is also the case that I was ready for it to happen. It wasn't that I had grown disillusioned with higher education, but the question of whether it might not be better had become insistent. For however one assessed its virtues, university learning struck me—and still strikes me—as:

1. *Insufficiently experimental.* It scans less than does industry for improved ways of doing things.
2. *Too authoritarian.* Persons aged 17 to 25 years would at

other times have been launched in the world. Here they continue to be subjected overwhelmingly to directives that flow down to them instead of rising from their own volitions.

3. *Too passive* in the role in which it places students. On this point clean proof is at hand. Take a word count in almost any class: who talks most, even in discussion classes and seminars? As learning requires doing, the arrangement is ideal for teachers, but one hears that it's the students who pay tuition.

4. *Too detached* from students' on-going lives, their hopes and involvements, the points where their psychic energy is most invested. It is as if the curriculum's cerebral thrust connects with the top 6 inches of the student's frame while leaving the other 60 inches idling. "It is by living, by dying, by being damned that one becomes a theologian," Luther advises us, "not by understanding, reading, and speculating." Or perhaps by both? What is clear is that academic reading, speculating, and understanding is joined very little to students' living, dying, and damnation. The most substantial recent study of American education, Charles Silberman's (1970) *Crisis in the Classroom,* concludes that reformers and innovators have an obligation to lobby for more emphasis on the education of feelings and the imagination and for a slow-down in cognitive rat-racing.

5. *Too impersonal.* Colleges used to be communities. Universities have in our time become almost the opposite: huge anticommunities like virtually every other institution in our mass, mobile, agglomerate society where rules and regulations take precedence over persons and seasoned relationships.

What encounter groups showed me first and above all else was a way to generate involvement. I hadn't been at Bethel 48 hours before my entire life seemed to sink or swim in terms of my group—my 15 strangers, none of whom I had laid eyes on two days before nor was I likely to see again 10 days thereafter. Swiftly, almost instantly, the criss-cross of human interactions—words, feelings, glances, gestures—had enmeshed me. Thought was emphatically involved, for apart from the therapeutic hour each afternoon when I deliberately turned my mind off and flung myself into the blissfully uncritical arms

of impersonal nature (a lake), every waking moment was given to trying to make sense of what was happening. But not thought only; perception, too, as I tried to see what was transpiring in nuances of
gesture, tone, and silence, and to feel what was happening in me at
subliminal levels. My will, too, was engaged as I wrestled with whether
to speak, risk, act.

New possibilities demanded consideration. How, precisely, encounter groups might ameliorate education's weaknesses, I had no
idea; but it was inconceivable to me that, operating powerfully in
precisely the areas of those weaknesses, they would have nothing to
offer. For encounter groups are:

1. *Experimental.* This remains the case even though they have
   been with us in various forms since World War II. The extent
   to which they have caught on suggests that they tend to be
   useful, but they are no panacea. Their utility is neither
   unvarying nor established by objective criteria.

2. *Nonauthoritarian.* It is part of their definition that leaders
   leave them largely unstructured, let them develop in their
   own ways, and use whatever transpires for leaving vehicles.
   Part of the fascination of such groups derives from seeing
   what does develop when 8 to 16 lives are closeted for appreciable time while deprived of task, agenda, and assigned
   hierarchy.

3. *Activating.* Where nothing happens save by the group's
   initiative, boredom, or anxiety, the will to power and the will
   to play see to it that initiative is taken.

4. *Involving.*

5. *Personal.* Attention is focused on the here and now, and in
   encounter groups, this mean people. Again, remove tasks, to
   which lives tend to get subordinated, and lives change from
   means to ends.

I shall not try here to say what encounter groups are. Let me say
only that since 1965, half of my pedagogical interest has been devoted
to trying to discern the potential for higher education latent in what
Rogers himself considers this "most rapidly spreading social invention
of the century, and probably the most potent." To the end of augment-
ing my understanding of group processes, and effectiveness in facilitating them, I have participated in training programs conducted by the

National Training Laboratory, Tavistock Institute, and the Washington School of Psychiatry; and have led seminars and workshops each summer at Esalen Institute and other growth centers. To explore their relevance for formal education, I have in each of the past 12 semesters taught courses ranging in subject matter from "Introduction to Philosophy" to "Philosophical Anthropology" which combine encounter techniques with cognitive learning. Students are apprised of the intended mix during preregistration screening interviews; registration is closed at 16 students; and a balance of men and women is desirable. The course opens with an encounter weekend, which means that we spend 13 hours together before we open a book. My object is to get the Waring Blender of human interaction churning, then fed into it eyedropper drips of cognitive content. After the opening weekend the class meets for a three-hour stretch each week. Typically, the first hour goes to student-directed discussion of the week's reading assignment; the second hour is mine to either lecture or continue the first hour's discussion under my direction, and the third hour continues the weekend encounter group. In mid-semester, we have a second weekend encounter, if possible off-campus and out of the city. When I can secure budget or prevail upon the good offices of my wife who works professionally with groups, I have an outside trainer conduct the weekends. This helps to reduce student-teacher distance and to get authority issues more openly onto the floor.

How has it gone? Roughly 85% of the 160 students who have been in these courses report on anonymous, postcourse checksheets that they were glad we used this approach and would recommend that it be continued. They report that compared with other humanities courses they enjoyed it more, were more interested in it, and learned more from it. I have no illusion that these statistics are clean, particularly the last one. If one esteems not only "learning that" but also "learning how" (i.e., learning how effectively to occupy a place in life as contrasted with merely knowing about life), Kierkegaard's truth as subjective transformation of oneself, and education as "the curriculum one had to run through in order to catch up with oneself," even the last statistic could be valid. I doubt, however, that students have acquired as much cerebral knowledge of subject matter in these courses as they do in others. Encounter aspects of the courses seem to fill such a vacuum in students' lives and become thereby so seductive that I find I must constantly throw the weight of my office on the side of cognitive learning to keep the course from developing into encounter group only. Being unsettled in my mind as to how cognitive learning does fare in such courses, I do not recommend casting all education in their mold. I should think it might be ideal for each university undergraduate to carry one encounter course each term, but not more. As a side benefit, a college that instituted the policy of having them do so might, I suspect, find itself reducing its psychiatric and counselling staff appreciably.

With regard to the specifics of ways in which I have tried to link group process to cognitive learning, I would happily say nothing, for I am far from satisfied with my formulae and keep devising new ones constantly. But this is the nub of the matter, so lest my statement on T-group teaching, or peer-group learning as it might better be called, end up looking like a Taoist composition around the void, I list some samples of things I have tried.

1.   Have students pair with partners they know least, look into one another's eyes for two minutes without speaking, then express nonverbally how they feel toward each other. For their next reading assign Martin Buber's (1970) *I and Thou*. Did the pairing exercise illumine experimentally what Buber means by an I-Thou relation?

2.   Ask students to take 10 minutes to recall and write down their earliest childhood memory. Place the statements in the middle of the circle. Ask a student to select and read one of the statements at random. Can the group guess who wrote it? Does the discussion corroborate ontogenetic emphasis on the formative influence of early experiences as argued, say, in Erik Erikson's (1964) *Childhood and Society?*

3.   Read Konrad Lorenz' (1966) *On Aggression*. Do its theses shed light on the competition and hostility that have come to light within the group's own experience?

4.   Read Nietzsche's (1968) *Will to Power*. How much of the group's life—most obviously the struggles for leadership within it, but not these only—support its central thesis?

5.   The greatest anxiety I, personally, have felt in a group setting was in the initial meeting of 65 persons who were closeted for two and one-half hours with no agenda whatever. Watching every attempt to structure that chaos come to naught was an unnerving experience, but it was insightful too, for it showed me directly the way formlessness without produces formlessness within. Not knowing my place in the group, I didn't know where I stood in *any* context: who I was, how I should act, anything. Compare Heidegger's (1962) notion of *angst* in *Being and Time* as symptom of the collapse of "the worldhood of the world;" also Harry Stack-Sullivan's (1950) famous essay on "The Illusion of Personal Individuality."

6.   Read the first essay in Leonard Nelson's (1949) *Socratic*

Method and Critical Philosophy and ask if the goal of encounter education is to complete Nelson's approach to philosophy with two emenda-
tions: the Socratic method becomes the *group* Socratic method with
the total group replacing a single individual as midwife, and feelings as
well as thoughts are intentionally brought into the picture.

7. A "low" tends to settle in on groups the last few sessions
before they terminate. The impending death of the group seems to
awaken presentiments of individual, personal death. The experience
provides concrete, shareable data relating to Heidegger's notion of
being-unto-death as a critérion of authentic living.

I stress that I have not listed these projects in order to recommend them to others. I cite them only as instances of the kinds of
bridges that can be thrown from group experience to cognitive learning. It appears to be of the essence of encounter teaching that no
canned rubric will work for long. I wish I could report that I feèl like a
veteran architect of bridges of the kind described, but the fact is the opposite. I have come to suspect that how and where to throw such
bridges will be my pedagogical *koan* (Zen meditational problem
resolvable in life only, not in words or formulae) till I retire.

If I have neither solved the problem of relating group process to
cognitive learning nor believe that it admits of standardized solutions,
why do I make of it more than a marginal issue? Others who have ven-
tured into these waters and stayed long enough to ask questions will
probably answer as I do. A new panorama has opened before me. With
it has come every variety of self-doubt, fear, and suspicion: Am I
simply giving students what they like, afraid to demand of them hard
work and drudgery; am I playing group therapist; am I merely hungry
for intimacy? But in the end I have been forced to listen to a new claim.
Let me articulate that claim. *We need wisdom. To this end we need
knowledge, but knowledge that is established in life—that connects
with feelings, illumines choices, and is in touch with wills.* Such
knowledge today's academy is not structured to elicit.

REFERENCES

Buber, M. 1970. *I and Thou.* New York: Charles Scribners' Sons.

Commoner, B. 1969. In M. Grene, ed., *Approaches to a Philosophical
    Biology.* New York: Basic Books.

Erikson, E. 1964. *Childhood and Society.* New York: W. W. Norton.

Heidegger, M. 1962. *Being and Time*. New York: Harper & Row.

Lorenz, K. 1966. *On Aggression*. New York: Harcourt, Brace & World.

Nelson, L. 1949. *The Illusion of Personal Individuality*. New York: Dover Publications.

Nietzsche, F. 1967. *Will to Power*. New York: Random House.

Shelton, W. 1936. *Psychology and the Promethean Will*. New York: Harper Brothers.

Silberman, C. 1970. *Crisis in the Classroom*. New York: Random House.

Sullivan, H. S. 1950. *Psychiatry, XIII.*

14

The Forgotten Man of Education

LAWRENCE KUBIE

Every discipline has its tools, and each such tool has its own inherent errors. The finest microscope produces an image not of facts alone but of facts embedded in a setting of obscuring artifacts which the microscope itself creates. The first thing that the young microscopist is taught is how to distinguish the one from the other. A discipline comes of age and a student of that discipline reaches maturity when it becomes possible to recognize, estimate, and allow for the errors of their tools. This is true for physics, chemistry, physiology, the social sciences, the humanities, history, literature, and the arts. Within its own field each of these disciplines is meticulously self-critical about the sources of error which reside in its special instruments.

Yet there is one instrument which every discipline uses without checking its errors, tacitly assuming that the instrument is error-free. This, of course, is the human psychological apparatus. As a result of the failure to consider the sources of error in the human being himself, when our academic disciplines assemble together in our great educational institutions they reenforce the tacit, fallacious assumption that man can understand the world that lies outside of himself without concurrently understanding himself. Actually, each man is his own microscope with his own idiosyncrasies, to which he alone can penetrate. Therefore we cannot perceive the outside world without distorting our very perceptions unless we search out individually the sources of error which lie hidden within. This is precisely what every mature discipline does in its own field: yet it is what no discipline does for the broad concept of education as a whole.

Source: Reprinted by permission of the Harvard Alumni Bulletin, LVI (1954), pp. 349–53. © 1954 by the Harvard Alumni Bulletin, Inc.

As we view the world around us, and as we look and listen and think and feel and interact with our fellow man and his works and his history, we view all such external realities through a cloud of distorting projections of our own unconscious problems. It is a scene observed as through the wavering convection currents over a hot fire. This is why it is impossible to reduce scholars who in the true sense of the word are wise men, if they know nothing about themselves. Without self-knowledge in depth, the master of any field will be a child in human wisdom and human culture. Even the seemingly objective data of his own field at the same time represent projections of his own unresolved problems in dreamlike symbolic disguises: and as long as he knows nothing of his own inner nature, his apparent knowledge merely disguises his spiritual confusion.

What I am saying is nothing that has not been said many times since Socrates: namely, that man must know himself. When modern psychiatry adds to this ancient adage is that self-knowledge if it is to be useful and effective must comprise more than superficial self-description. It must include an understanding of unconscious as well as conscious levels of psychological processes. Yet such self-knowledge, which requires the mastery of intricate new tools of psychological exploration, is wholly overlooked throughout the entire scheme of "modern" education, from the kindergarten to the highest levels of academic training.

This deepening of our self-knowledge is in turn intimately dependent on the nature of symbolic thinking. Learning depends upon a progressive mastery of the many processes of symbolic thought. Symbols, however, are not all alike. They fall into three groups. There is the realistic form of symbolic thinking in which we are fully aware of the relationship of the symbols of language to that which they represent. Here the function of the symbol is to communicate the hard core, the bare bones, of thoughts and purposes. Secondly there is the symbol whose relationship to its root is figurative and allegorical. The purpose of this second form of symbolic thinking is to communicate by inference all of the nuances of thought and feeling, all of the collateral references which cluster around the central core of meaning. This is the symbolic language of creative thinking whether in art or science. In technical jargon, the first is called *conscious,* and the second *preconscious.* Third, there is the symbolic process in which the relationship between the symbol and what it represents has been buried or distorted, so that the symbol becomes a disguised and disguising representative of unconscious levels of psychological processes. Here the function of the symbolic process is not to communicate but to hide. This is the unconscious symbolic process of the dream and of psychological illness.

Yet all three already operate together, with the consequence that every single thing we ever do or say or think or feel is a composite product of them all. Consequently when a scientist is studying atomic energy or a biological process or the chemical properties of some isotope, when a sociologist studies the structure of government and society, when a historian studies the development of events, or an economist the play of economic forces, when a classicist studies an ancient tongue, or a musicologist the intricacies of musical composition, when a theologian studies theology, each deals with his subject on all three of these levels at once. On the *conscious* level the deals with them as realities. On the *preconscious* level he deals with their allegorical and emotional import, direct and indirect. On the *unconscious* level, without realizing it, he uses his special competence and knowledge as an opportunity to express the unconscious, conflict-laden, and confused levels of his own spirit, using the language of his specialty as a vehicle for the projection outward of his internal struggles. Since this happens without his knowledge, it is a process which can take over his creative thinking in his own field, distorting and perverting it to save his unconscious needs and purposes.

The result is a structure of unconscious compromises which may render great intellectual brilliance as futile and as impotent as are any other symptomatic products of the neurotic process. It is for this reason that we can no longer tolerate with complacency the fact that art and science and every other cultural activity are hybrids, born of an unhealthy fusion of that which is finest and that which is sickest in human nature. It is a further consequence that the greater the role played by the unconscious components of symbolic thought, the wider must become the gap between erudition and wisdom. A scholar may be erudite on conscious and preconscious levels, yet so obtuse about the play of unconscious forces in his own life, that he cannot tell when he is using realistically and creatively the subject of which he is a master, or when he is using it like the inkblot on a Rorschach card. Education for wisdom must close this gap, by providing insight which penetrates into those areas of human life in which unconscious forces have always hitherto played the preponderant role.

This is the challenge which psychoanalytic psychiatry brings to the goals and techniques of education. At first thought the suggestion seems simple, a mere extension of the ancient Socratic admonition to

"Know Thyself," making it read "Know Thyself in Depth." Yet these two added words, "in depth," will demand one of the most difficult cultural steps which civilized man has ever taken: a step which is essential if the man of the future is to be saved from man's present fate. And what has been that fate? It has been that in spite of a growing knowledge of the world around him he has repeated like an automaton the errors of his past; and that furthermore he has repeated these old errors in forms which become increasingly destructive and cata- strophic as he becomes more educated. Whether his erudition has been in history, art, literature, the sciences, religion, or the total para- phernalia of modern culture, this has been the limiting factor in our Culture of Doom.

This automaticity of conduct which is governed predominantly by our unconscious psychological mechanisms is dependent directly upon their remaining inaccessible. Therefore, if "self-knowledge in depth" ever becomes the goal of a new concept of education, and if it becomes a part of the equipment which education brings to the cultured man, it will make it possible for man to attain freedom from his ancient slavery to those repetitive psychological processes over which at present he has no control. In his *Personal Record* Joseph Conrad describes himself as a knight in shining armor, mounted on a magnificent horse. The picture was quite flattering until on looking more closely, he noticed that little knaves were running by the head of the horse and holding onto the bridle. Thereupon he realized that he did not know who was guiding that horse; the knight on the horse's back, or the knaves running by its head. This is the image of the educated man of to- day. He is a noble figure on a noble charger, magnificently armed. But the knaves who trot unheeded by the horse's head, with their hands on the reins, are guiding that horse far more than is the pretentious figure of culture astride the horse's back.

Like infinity, self-knowledge is an ideal which can be approached but never reached. Therefore like education it is a process which is never finished, a point on a continuous and never-ending journey. It is relative and not absolute. Consequently, the achievement of self- knowledge is a process which goes on throughout life, demanding constant vigilance; and because it requires a continuous struggle, true self-knowledge never becomes an occasion for smug complacency.

The man who knows himself in depth does not look down his nose at the rest of the world from a perch on Mt. Olympus. Rather will he acknowledge with proper humility the impossibility of knowing himself fully, and the importance of struggling constantly against the lure of insidious, seductive illusions about himself. Nor on the other hand will he be incessantly preoccupied with his own conscious and unconscious motivations. Instead the more fully he approaches self-awareness, the more coherent and integrated become the various levels of his personality.

As a result, self-knowledge brings with it the right to trust his impulses and his intuitions. He may continue to watch himself out of the corner of his eye with vigilant self-scepticism, but he will give the center of his attention to his job and to the world around him. Thus, self-knowledge brings freedom and spontaneity to the most creative alliance of the human spirit, the alliance between conscious and preconscious processes: and it brings this spiritual liberation by freeing us from the internal blocking and distortion which occur when conscious and preconscious processes are opposed by an irreconcilable unconscious. Thus my vision of the educated man of the future is not an unreal fantasy of an individual out of whom all of the salty seasoning of preconscious and unconscious processes will have been dissolved, like a smoked ham which has soaked too long. It is rather of a man whose creative processes are relatively freed of the burden of unconscious internal conflicts.

In turn, however, this does not mean that to become educated a man must be psychoanalyzed. It means rather that new procedures must be introduced into the pattern of education which will make therapeutic analyses necessary only for those in whom the educational process has failed. The positive goal of this vital aspect of education is to shrink the dark empire in which unconscious forces have in the past played the preponderant role, and to broaden those areas of life in which conscious and preconscious processes will play the dominant role.

It is one thing, however, to describe self-knowledge in depth as the ultimate goal for culture and education. To achieve it is another. I will not presume here to write out a prescription on how this can be done. In dealing with any individual patient we know that without too much difficulty the psychiatrist can trace the interweaving patterns of complex, conscious, preconscious, and unconscious forces which have shaped an entire life. Yet many weeks, months, and even years of additional work may be required to communicate the analyst's insight to the patient himself. If the communication of insight to a single individual presents such formidable problems, we should not be surprised that the communication of insight to successive generations will require the development of basically new techniques of education, techniques which will have to start in the nursery and continue into old age, techniques which will have to circumvent adroitly the unconscious opposition of the oldsters among us who lack these insights and who feel personally threatened by them. Thus a new and critical version of the ancient battle between the generations is surely in the making.

Yet I believe that the whole future of human culture depends upon our solving this problem of how to introduce into education processes which will in essence be both preventive and curative. They will be preventive in the sense that they will limit and guide the fateful dichotomy which occurs early in life between conscious and preconscious processes on the one hand, and the inaccessible unconscious on the other. It will have to be curative as well, because we cannot expect prevention ever to work perfectly. Consequently we shall always have to build into the concepts and techniques of education certain types of therapeutic experiences, both for groups and for individuals, which will be designed to reintegrate unconscious with conscious and preconscious processes. Even to attempt this will require that we overcome not only the individual resistances and prejudices to which I have just referred, but also the entrenched opposition of many existing social, cultural, religious, and educational institutions. This is no small order: and I would hesitate to offer the challenge, if I did not have so deep a conviction that all of our vaunted culture and education, as we have known them in the past, have failed mankind completely.

Some may feel these views to be unduly pessimistic. Yet I believe that these criticisms of our educational processes are rooted in optimism, and pursue an optimistic ideal. It is not pessimism to face the fact of past failure, if our purpose in studying our failures is to learn how not to fail in the future. It was neither pessimism nor a morbid fascination with death which led medicine to the autopsy table, but rather courage, optimism, spiritual humility, and a determination to avoid the endless repetition of past error. Mankind's reward is scientific medicine; and we must now face the failure of education with the same combination of humility and determination. Because education has failed mankind in the past, it does not follow that it must necessarily continue to fail, unless we cling obstinately and defensively to methods which have already been tried without success.

Yet the tendency to prescribe more of the old medicines is deep in us. For instance, when I read that a new college president declares that what we need in education is a greater emphasis on religion, I confess that my heart sinks. This is not because he singled out religion. I have the same sinking feeling when someone says that what we need is more of the humanities, or when Hutchins and Adler call for more of the "great" books by "great" thinkers out of the past, or when a classicist calls for more of the classics, or a mathematician for more mathematics, or a chemist for more chemistry.

It is not a pretty spectacle, nor a reassuring measure of the maturity of educators, when in the face of our general cultural failure each cultural specialist cries out for larger doses of his own specific remedy. Such spiritual arrogance and obstinacy, whether from the pulpit or from the laboratory, should have no place in the deliberations of educated men. Indeed, it is a symptom of the very illness I am stressing, namely, that our educational system produces men of erudition with little wisdom or maturity; with the consequence that every cultural discipline is led by human beings who spend their time defending their vested interests in their own special fields. In this respect, the great washed have little on the great unwashed.

It is important to understand that scientists, including psychiatrists, are not immune to these frailties; and that they are equally true for all of those who carry the banners of culture. It is an old story of youthful idealism, of young confidence that *the* way to the good life is in their hands, then of a gradual disillusionment which usually is masked by a paradoxical defensiveness and a refusal to face the limitations of existing methods, turning instead in anger against anyone who is honest and sceptical enough to challenge his particular road to salvation.

All of us want to go on educating as we have in the past, making at the most only trivial curricular changes. But what mankind actually needs is a cultural stride of far grander dimensions. A little more or less of science, or of history, or of sociology, or of the classics, or of languages whether ancient or modern (for man can be as foolish in five languages as in one), or of philosophy or theology, or in the history of any of these: None of these gives to man the power to change and grow. Having devoted a lifetime to mastering some erudite discipline, and having thereby become a pew-holder in a towering cathedral with a limited seating capacity (to plagiarize Robert Nathan and *The Bishop's Wife*), it is indeed difficult for any of us to say, "This technique of mine which I have mastered at such great cost is just not enough." Instead we say, "Give the patient more of my medicine. More of the same is what he needs. Pour it down his throat. It may not have worked in the past: but more of it will surely cure him in the future."

These words are an expression of the human frailties which the artist, writer, historian, scientist, and theologian share equally with the least "cultured" man in the community. Every one of us is guilty of this—the scientists, the technologists, the classicists, the romanticists, the humanists, the musicians, the writers, the sculptors, and the dramatists. And especially is it true of the theologians of every sect and variety, because they give to this arrogance a divine sanction, in which I am sure that the Divinity would have no part. All say "Believe in me," "Believe in my way," "Believe in my special field." Few among us have the courage to say: "Do not *believe* at all. What I advocate is at best a working hypothesis to be rigorously and sceptically tested, but never believed. I ask for no credulity or faith. My challenge is to the courage and dignity of doubting, and to the duty of testing and experimenting. Man id Man not by virtue of believing, but by virtue of challenging belief. Let believing be the starting point for an investigation, but never its end." Just once in my life have I been privileged to hear a great religious teacher say from his pulpit, "It is the search for truth which is religion: and as soon as any religion believes that it has found the truth, it ceases to be religious."

Those who represent the world of the mind and of the spirit must acquire the humility which led medicine to study its defeats at the autopsy table. This was a unique moment in human culture. We need now to apply the same self-scrutiny to all of culture. And as we do this, let us stop to remind ourselves that when a patient dies, the doctor does not blame the patient: he blames himself. But when humanity fails, the artists and the writers scold, and the theologian thunders angry denunciations of human deficiencies, when they should be turning a pitiless scrutiny on themselves, their beliefs, and their techniques.

What then must education achieve? It must make it possible for human beings themselves to change. That is the next necessary goal of education. Wewould find it hard to prove that even the greatest works of art, of literature, of music, of philosophy, of religion have freed the hearts of men. Yet until we have found out how to make it possible for man himself to change, we have no right to revere our culture as though it were a creative and moving force in the Divine Comedy. Until what we call culture, whether with a small "c" or a capital "K," can free man from the domination of his own unconscious, it is not culture. An education which gives man only sophistication, taste, historical perspective, manners, erudite parlor conversation, and knowledge of how to use and control the forces of nature is a fraud on the human spirit, no matter what inflated pretensions and claims it makes.

It is we, the educated and the educators, who have failed mankind, not mankind which has failed us. Science and art and philosophy and religion and learning have failed; just as it is medicine which has failed when a patient dies, not the corpse. This charge is not made lightly; not is it to be brushed aside in facile self-defense. The next goal of education is nothing less than a progressive freeing of man—not merely from external tyrannies of nature and of other men, but from internal enslavement by his own unconscious automatic mechanisms. Therefore, all of education and all of art and culture must contribute to this. It has long been recognized that in spite of technological progress, and in spite of art, literature, religion, and scholarly learning, the heart of man has not changed. This is both a challenge and a rebuke to our complacent acceptance of this bitter and devastating commentary on culture. My answer is based on the conviction that it is possible to break through the sonic barrier between conscious and unconscious processes, and thereby to bring to man for the first time in human history the opportunity to evolve beyond his enslaved past. That is why this thesis can claim for itself a realistic spiritual optimism.

Toward this goal a first step will be a deeper study of those early crisis in human development, when the symbolic process begins to splinter into conscious, preconscious, and unconscious systems. The purpose of such a study of infancy would be to illuminate the origins of the repressive processes which produce these cleavages, since it is these which must be guided and controlled. As its second goal such a study would aim at the reintegration of unconscious with preconscious and conscious processes: something which has to be done not merely once, but repeatedly throughout the entire process of growth, from infancy through childhood, puberty, adolescence, and on into adult years. Just as the battle for political freedom must be won over and over again, so too in every life the battle for internal psychological freedom must be fought and won again and again, if men are to achieve and retain freedom from the tyranny of their own unconscious processes, the freedom to understand the forces which determine their thoughts, feelings, purposes, goals, and behavior. This freedom is the fifth and ultimate human freedom; and like every other freedom, it demands eternal vigilance.

At present, except in a few experiments (like those which are made in a few pioneering institutions, such as Goddard College) education is making no effort to meet this challenge. At present a farmer is given more training for raising stock than all of our institutions of lower or higher learning offer to men and women for raising the children whose lives they will make and break.

I would not give the impression that I believe that this is all there is to education. But what I do believe is that without this at its heart education, culture, literature, art, science, and religion are all hollow frauds. Without this, education has sold humanity down the river— back into slavery. And I believe that this will continue to be true until we rescue from his present oblivion this forgotten man of education.

I want to repeat that self-knowledge in depth is not all there is to wisdom, but that it makes maturity and wisdom possible; and what is even more important, it frees us from the tyranny of those rigid compulsive mechanisms which have made impossible our psychological evolution. Without self-knowledge in depth, we can have dreams but not art, we can have the neurotic raw material of literature, but not mature literature. Without it we have no adults, but only aging children armed with words, paints, clay, and atomic weapons, none of which they understand. It is this which makes a mockery of the pretentious claims of education, of religion, of the arts, and of science. Self-knowledge is the Forgotten Man of our entire educational system and indeed of human culture in general. Without self-knowledge it is possible to be erudite, but never wise. My challenge to all of us is to have the humility to face this failure, and the determination to do something effective about it before it is too late.

15

Student-Centered Teaching as Experienced by a Participant

SAMUEL TENENBAUM and CARL R. ROGERS

INTRODUCTION, by Carl R. Rogers

In the summer of 1958 I was invited to teach a four-week course at Brandeis University. My recollection is that the title was "The Process of Personality Change." I had no great expectations for the course. It was to be one of several courses which the students were taking, meeting for three two-hour sessions per week, rather than the concentrated workshop pattern which I prefer. I learned in advance that the group was to be unusually heterogeneous—teachers, doctoral candidates in psychology, counselors, several priests, at least one from a foreign country, psychotherapists in private practice, school psychologists. The group was, on the average, more mature and experienced than would ordinarily be found in a university course. I felt very relaxed about the whole thing. I would do what I could to help make this a meaningful experience for us all, but I doubted that it could have the impact of, for example, the workshops on counseling which I had conducted.

Perhaps it was because I had very modest expectations of the group and of myself, that it went so well. I would without doubt class it as among the most satisfying of my attempts to facilitate learning in

Source: From On Becoming a Person, *by Carl R. Rogers, pp. 297–313.* © *1961 by Carl R. Rogers. Reprinted by permission of the author and Houghton Mifflin.*

For Dr. Rogers' earlier and lengthy discussion on the subject, see Chapter 9, "Student-Centered Teaching" in his *Client-Centered Therapy* (Houghton-Mifflin, 1951). [Ed.].

courses or workshops. This should be borne in mind in reading Dr. Tenenbaum's material.

I would like to digress for a moment here to say that I feel far more assurance in confronting a new client in therapy than I do in confronting a new group. I feel I have a sufficient grasp of the conditions of therapy so that I have a reasonable confidence as to the process which will ensue. But with groups I have much less confidence. Sometimes when I have had every reason to suppose a course would go well, the vital, self-initiated, self-directed learning has simply not occurred to any great degree. At other times when I have been dubious, it has gone extremely well. To me this means that our formulation of the process of facilitating learning in education is not nearly as accurate or complete as our formulations regarding the therapeutic process.

But to return to the Brandeis summer course. It was clearly a highly significant experience for almost all of the participants, as evident in their reports on the course. I was particularly interested in the report by Dr. Tenenbaum, written as much for his colleagues as for me. Here was a mature scholar, not an impressionable young student. Here was a sophisticated educator, who already had to his credit a published biography of William H. Kilpatrick, the philosopher of education. Hence his perceptions of the experience seemed unusually valuable.

I would not want it to be understood that I shared all of Dr. Tenenbaum's perceptions. Portions of the experience I perceived quite differently, but this is what made his observations so helpful. I felt particularly concerned that it seemed to him so much a "Rogers" approach, that it was simply my person and idiosyncrasies which made the experience what it was.

For this reason I was delighted to get a long letter from him a year later, reporting his own experience in teaching. This confirmed what I have learned from a wide variety of individuals, that it is not simply the personality of a specific teacher which makes this a dynamic learning experience, but the operation of certain principles which may be utilized by any "facilitator" who holds the appropriate attitudes.

I believe the two accounts by Dr. Tenenbaum will make it clear why teachers who have experienced the kind of group learning which is described can never return to more stereotyped ways of education. In spite of frustration and occasional failure, one keeps trying to discover, with each new group, the conditions which will unleash this vital learning experience.

CARL R. ROGERS AND NON-DIRECTIVE TEACHING
by Samuel Tenenbaum

As one interested in education, I have participated in a classroom methodology that is so unique and so special that I feel impelled to share the experience. The technique, it seems to me, is so radically different from the customary and the accepted, so undermining of the old, that it should be known more widely. As good a description of the process as any—I suppose the one that Carl R. Rogers, the instructor, himself would be inclined to use—would be "non-directive" teaching.

I had some notion what that term meant, but frankly I was not prepared for anything that proved so overwhelming. It is not that I am convention-bound. My strongest educational influences stem from William Heard Kilpatrick and John Dewey, and anyone who has even the slightest acquaintance with their thinking would know that it does not smack of the narrow or the provincial. But this method which I saw Dr. Rogers carry out in a course which he gave at Brandeis University was so unusual, something I could not believe possible, unless I was part of the experience. I hope I shall manage to describe the method in a way to give you some inkling of the feelings, the emotions, the warmth and the enthusiasms that the method engendered.

The course was altogether unstructured; and it was exactly that. At no moment did anyone know, not even the instructor, what the next moment would bring forth in the classroom, what subject would come up for discussion, what questions would be raised, what personal needs, feelings and emotions aired. This atmosphere of non-structured freedom—as free as human beings could allow each other to be—was set by Dr. Rogers himself. In a friendly, relaxed way, he sat down with the students (about 25 in number) around a large table and said it would be nice if we stated our purpose and introduced ourselves. There ensued a strained silence; no one spoke up. Finally, to break it, one student timidly raised his hand and spoke his piece. another uncomfortable silence, and then another upraised hand. Thereafter, the hands rose more rapidly. At no time did the instructor urge any student to speak.

Unstructured Approach

Afterwards, he informed the class that he had brought with him quantities of materials—reprints, brochures, articles, books; he handed out a bibliography of recommended reading. At no time did he indicate that he expected students to read or do anything else. As I recall, he made only one request. Would some student volunteer to set up this material in a special room which had been reserved for students of the course? Two students promptly volunteered. He also said he had with him recorded tapes of therapeutic sessions and also reels of motion pictures. This created a flurry of excitement, and students asked whether they could be heard and seen and Dr. Rogers answered yes. The class then decided how it could be done best. Students volunteered to run tape recorders, find a movie projector; for the most part this too was student initiated and arranged.

Thereafter followed four hard, frustrating sessions. During this period, the class didn't seem to get anywhere. Students spoke at random, saying whatever came into their heads. It all seemed chaotic, aimless, a waste of time. A student would bring up some aspect of Rogers' philosophy; and the next student, completely disregarding the first, would take the group away in another direction; and a third, completely disregarding the first two, would start fresh on something else altogether. At times there were some faint efforts at a cohesive discussion, but for the most part the classroom proceedings seemed to lack continuity and direction. The instructor received every contribution with attention and regard. He did not find any student's contribution in order or out of order.

The class was not prepared for such a totally unstructured approach. they did not know how to proceed. In their perplexity and frustration, they demanded that the teacher play the role assigned to him by custom and tradition; that he set forth for us in authoritative language what was right and wrong, what was good and bad. Had they not come from far distances to learn from the oracle himself? Were they not fortunate? Were they not about to be initiated in the right rituals and practices by the great man himself, the founder of the movement that bears his name? The notebooks were poised for the climactic moment when the oracle would give forth, but mostly they remained untouched.

Queerly enough, from the outset, even in their anger, the members of the group felt joined together, and outside the classroom, there was an excitement and a ferment, for even in their frustration, they had communicated as never before in any classroom, and probably never before in quite the way they had. The class was bound together by a common, unique experience. In the Rogers class, they had spoken their minds; the words did not come from a book, nor were they the reflection of the instructor's thinking, nor that of any other authority. The ideas, emotions and feelings came from themselves; and this was the releasing and the exciting process.

In this atmosphere of freedom, something for which they had not bargained and for which they were not prepared, the students spoke up as students seldom do. During this period, the instructor took many blows; and it seemed to me that many times he appeared to be shaken; and although he was the source of our irritation, we had, strange as it may seem, a great affection for him, for it did not seem right to be angry with a man who was so sympathetic, so sensitive to the feelings and ideas of others. We all felt that what was involved was some slight misunderstanding, which once understood and remedied would make everything right again. But our instructor, gentle enough on the surface, had a "whim of steel." He didn't seem to understand; and if he did, he was obstinate and obdurate; he refused to come around. Thus did this tug-of-war continue. We all looked to Rogers and Rogers looked to us. One student, amid general approbation, observed: "We are Rogers-centered, not student-centered. We have come to learn from Rogers."

Encouraging Thinking

Another student had discovered that Rogers had been influenced by Kilpatrick and Dewey, and using this idea as a springboard, he said he thought he perceived what Rogers was trying to get at. He thought Rogers wanted students to think independently, creatively; he wanted students to become deeply involved with their very persons, their very selves, hoping that this might lead to the "reconstruction" of the person—in the Dewey sense of the term—the person's outlook, attitudes, values, behavior. This would be a true reconstruction of experience; it would be learning in a real sense. Certainly, he didn't want the course to end in an examination based on textbooks and lectures, followed by the traditional end-term grade, which generally means completion and forgetting.* Rogers had expressed the belief almost from the outset of the course that no one can teach anyone else anything. But thinking, this student insisted, begins at the fork in the

---

*It should be noted that Dr. Rogers neither agreed nor disagreed. It was not his habit to respond to students' contributions unless a remark was directed specifically to him; and even then he might choose not to answer. His main object, it seemed to me, was to follow students' contributions intelligently and sympathetically.

road, the famed dilemma set up by Dewey. As we reach the fork in the road, we do not know which road to take if we are to reach our destination; and then we begin to examine the situation. Thinking starts at that point.

Kilpatrick also sought original thinking from his students and also rejected a regurgitant textbook kind of learning, but he presented crucial problems for discussion, and these problems aroused a great deal of interest, and they also created vast changes in the person. Why can't committees of students or individual students get up such problems for discussion?* Rogers listened sympathetically and said, "I see you feel strongly about this?" That disposed of that. If I recall correctly, the next student who spoke completely disregarded what had been suggested and started afresh on another topic, quite in comformity with the custom set by the class.

Spasmodically, through the session, students referred favorably to the foregoing suggestions, and they began to demand more insistently that Rogers assume the traditional role of a teacher. At this point, the blows were coming Rogers' way rather frequently and strongly and I thought I saw him bend somewhat before them. (Privately, he denied he was so affected.) During one session, a student made the suggestion that he lecture one hour and that we have a class discussion the next. This one suggestion seemed to fit into his plans. He said he had with him an unpublished paper. He warned us that it was available and we could read it by ourselves. But the student said it would not be the same. The person, the author, would be out of it, the stress, the inflection, the emotion, those nuances which give value and meaning to words. Rogers then asked the students if that was what they wanted. They said yes. He read for over an hour. After the vivid and acrimonious exchanges to which we had become accustomed, this was certainly a letdown, dull and soporific to the extreme. This experience squelched all further demands for lecturing. In one of the

---

*One student compiled such a list, had it mimeographed, distributed it, and for practical purposes that was the end of that.

In this connection, another illustration may be in order. At the first session, Rogers brought to class tape recordings of therapeutic sessions. He explained that he was not comfortable in a teacher's role and he came "loaded," and the recordings served as a sort of security. One student continually insisted that he play the recordings, and after considerable pressure from the class, he did so, but he complied reluctantly; and all told despite the pressure, he did not play them for more than an hour in all the sessions. Apparently, Rogers preferred the students to make real live recordings rather than listen to those which could only interest them in an academic way.

moments when he apologized for this episode ("It's better, more excusable, when students demand it."), he said: "You asked me to lecture. It is true I am a resource, but what sense would there be in my lecturing? I have brought a great quantity of material, reprints of any number of lectures, articles, books, tape recordings, movies."

By the fifth session, something definite had happened; there was no mistaking that. Students spoke to one another; they by-passed Rogers. Students asked to be heard and wanted to be heard, and what before was a halting, stammering, self-conscious group became an interacting group, a brand new cohesive unit, carrying on in a unique way; and from them came discussion and thinking such as no other group but this could repeat or duplicate. The instructor also joined in, but his role, more important than any in the group, somehow became merged with the group; the group was important, the center, the base of operation, not the instructor.

What caused it? I can only conjecture as to the reason. I believe that what happened was this: For four sessions students refused to believe that the instructor would refuse to play the traditional role. They still believed that he would set the tasks; that he would be the center of whatever happened and that he would manipulate the group. It took the class four sessions to realize that they were wrong; that he came to them with nothing outside of himself, outside of his own person; that if they really wanted something to happen, it was they who had to provide the content—an uncomfortable, challenging situation indeed. It was they who had to speak up, with all the risks that that entailed. As part of the process, they shared, they took exception, they agreed, they disagreed. At any rate, their persons, their deepest selves were involved; and from this situation, this special, unique group, this new creation was born.

Importance of Acceptance

As you may know, Rogers believes that if a person is accepted, fully accepted, and in this acceptance there is no judgment, only compassion and sympathy, the individual is able to come to grips with himself, to develop the courage to give up his defenses and face his true self. I saw this process work. Amid the early efforts to communicate, to find a *modus vivendi,* there had been in the group tentative exchanges of feelings, emotions and ideas; but after the fourth session, and progressively thereafter, this group, haphazardly thrown together, became close to one another and their true selves appeared. As they interacted, there were moments of insight and revelation and understanding that were almost awesome in nature; they were what, I believe, Rogers would describe as "moments of therapy," those pregnant moments when you see a human soul revealed before you, in all its breathless wonder; and then a silence, almost like reverence, would overtake the class. And each member of the class became enveloped with a warmth and a loveliness that border on the mystic. I for one, and I am quite sure the others also, never had an experience quite like this. It was learning and therapy; and by therapy I do not mean illness, but what might be characterized by a healthy change in the person, an increase in his flexibility, his openness, his willingness to listen. In the process, we all felt elevated, freer, more accepting of ourselves and others, more open to new ideas, trying hard to understand and accept.

This is not a perfect world, and there was evidence of hostility as members differed. Somehow in this setting every blow was softened, as if the sharp edges had been removed; if undeserved, students would go off to something else; and the blow was somehow lost. In my own case, even those students who originally irritated me, with further acquaintance I began to accept and respect; and the thought occurred to me as I tried to understand what was happening: Once you come close to a person, perceive his thoughts, his emotions, his feelings, he becomes not only understandable but good and desirable. Some of the more aggressive ones spoke more than they should, more than their right share, but the group itself, by its own being, not by setting rules, eventually made its authority felt; and unless a person was very sick or insensitive, members more or less, in this respect, conformed to what was expected of them. The problem—the hostile, the dominant, the neurotic—was not too acute; and yet if measured in a formal way, with a stop watch, at no time was a session free of aimless talk and waste of time. But yet as I watched the process, the idea persisted that perhaps this waste of time may be necessary; it may very well be that that is the way man learns best; for certainly, as I look back at the whole experience, I am fairly certain that it would have been impossible to learn as much or as well or as thoroughly in the traditional classroom setting. If we accept Dewey's definition of education as the reconstruction of experience, what better way can a person learn than by becoming involved with his whole self, his very person, his root drives, emotions, attitudes and values? No series of facts or arguments, no matter how logically or brilliantly arranged, can even faintly compare with that sort of thing.

In the course of this process, I saw hard, inflexible, dogmatic persons, in the brief period of several weeks, change in front of my eyes and become sympathetic, understanding and to a marked degree nonjudgmental. I saw neurotic, compulsive persons ease up and become more accepting or themselves and others. In one instance, a student who particularly impressed me by his change, told me when I mentioned this: "It is true. I feel less rigid, more open to the world. And I like myself better for it. I don't believe I ever learned so much anywhere." I saw shy persons become less shy and aggressive persons more sensitive and moderate.

One might say that this appears to be essentially an emotional process. But that I believe would be altogether inaccurate in describing it. There was a great deal of intellectual content, but the intellectual content was meaningful and crucial to the person, in a sense that it meant a great deal to him as a person. In fact, one student brought up this very question. "Should we be concerned," he asked, "only with the emotions? Has the intellect no play?" It was my turn to ask, "Is there any student who has read as much or thought as much for any other course?"

The answer was obvious. We had spent hours and hours reading; the room reserved for us had occupants until 10 o'clock at night, and then many left only because the university guards wanted to close the building. Students listened to recordings; they saw motion pictures; but best of all, they talked and talked and talked. In the traditional course, the instructor lectures and indicates what is to be read and learned; students dutifully record all this in their notebooks, take an examination and feel good or bad, depending on the outcome; but in nearly all cases it is a complete experience, with a sense of finality; the laws of forgetting begin to operate rapidly and inexorably. In the Rogers course, students read and thought inside and outside the class; it was they who chose from this reading and thinking what was meaningful to them, not the instructor.

This non-directive kind of teaching, I should point out, was not 100 per cent successful. There were three or four students who found the whole idea distasteful. Even at the end of the course, although nearly all became enthusiastic, one student to my knowledge, was intensely negative in his feelings; another was highly critical. These wanted the instructor to provide them with a rounded-out intellectual piece of merchandise which they could commit to memory and then give back on an examination. They would then have the assurance that they had learned what they should. As one said, "If I had to make a report as to what I learned in this course, what could I say?" Admittedly, it would be much more difficult than in a traditional course, if not impossible.

The Rogers method was free and flowing and open and permissive. A student would start an interesting discussion; it would be taken up by a second; but a third student might take us away in another direction, bringing up a personal matter of no interest to the class; and we would all feel frustrated. But this was like life, flowing on like a river, seemingly futile, with never the same water there, flowing on, with no one knowing what would happen the next moment. But in this there was an expectancy, an alertness, an aliveness; it seemed to me as near a smear of life as one could get in a classroom. For the authoritarian person, who puts his faith in neatly piled up facts, this method I believe can be threatening, for here he gets no reassurance, only an openness, a flowing, no closure.

A New Methodology

I believe that a great deal of the stir and the ferment that characterized the class was due to this lack of closure. In the lunch room, one could recognize Rogers' students by their animated discussions, by their desire to be together; and sometimes, since there was no table large enough, they would sit two and three tiers deep; and they would eat with plates on their laps. As Rogers himself points out, there is no finality in the process. He himself never summarizes (against every conventional law of teaching). The issues are left unsolved; the problems raised in class are always in a state of flux, ongoing. In their need to know, to come to some agreement, students gather together, wanting understanding, seeking closure. Even in the matter of grades, there is no closure. A grade means an end; but Dr. Rogers does not give the grade; it is the student who suggests the grade; and since he does so, even this sign of completion is left unsolved, without an end, unclosed. Also, since the course is unstructured, each has staked his person in the course; he has spoken, not with the textbook as the guage, but with his person, and thus as a self he has communicated with others, and because of this, in contradistinction to the impersonal subject matter that comprises the normal course, there develops this closeness and warmth.

To describe the many gracious acts that occurred might convey some idea of this feeling of closeness. One student invited the class to her home for a cookout. Another student, a priest from Spain, was so taken with the group that he talked of starting a publication to keep track of what was happening to the group members after they disbanded. A group interested in student counseling met on its own. A member arranged for the class to visit a mental hospital for children and adults; also he arranged for us to see the experimental work being done with psychotic patients by Dr. Lindsley. Class members brought in tape recordings and printed matter to add to the library material set aside for our use. In every way the spirit of good-will and friendliness was manifest to an extent that happens only in rare and isolated instances. In the many, many courses I have taken I have not seen the like. In this connection, it should be pointed out that the members comprised a group that had been haphazardly thrown together; they had come from many backgrounds and they included a wide age range.

I believe that what has been described above is truly a creative addition to classroom methodology; it is radically different from the old. That it has the capacity to move people, to make them freer, more open-minded, more flexible, I have no doubt. I myself witnessed the power of this method. I believe that non-directive teaching has profound implications which even those who accept this point of view cannot at present fully fathom. Its importance, I believe, goes beyond the classroom and extends to every area where human beings communicate and try to live with one another.

More specifically, as a classroom methodology, it warrants the widest discussion, inquiry and experimentation. It has the possibility of opening up a whole new dimension of thinking, fresh and original, for in its approach, in its practice, in its philosophy it differs so fundamentally from the old. It seems to me this approach ought to be tried out in every area of learning—elementary, high school, college, wherever human beings gather to learn and improve on the old. At this stage we should not be overly concerned about its limitations and inadequacies, since the method has not been refined and we do not know as much about it as we ought. As a new technique, it starts off with a handicap. We are loath to give up the old. The old is bolstered by tradition, authority and respectability; and we ourselves are its product. If we view education, however, as the reconstruction of experience, does not this presume that the individual must do his own reconstructing? He must do it himself, through the reorganization of his deepest self, his values, his attitudes, his very person. What better method is there to engross the individual; to bring him, his ideas, his feelings into communication with others; to break down the barriers that create isolation in a world where for his own mental safety and health, man has to learn to be part of mankind?

A PERSONAL TEACHING EXPERIENCE
by Samuel Tennenbaum*

I feel impelled to write to you about my first experience in teaching after being exposed to your thinking and influence. You may or may not know I had a phobia about teaching. Since my work with you, I began to perceive more clearly where the difficulty lay. It was mostly in my concept of the role I had to play as a teacher—the motivator, director and the production chief of a performance. I always feared being "hung up" in the classroom—I believe it's your expression and I have come to like it—the class listless, uninterested, not responding, and my yammering and yammering, until I lost poise, the sentences not forming, coming out artificially, and the time moving slowly, slowly, ever more slowly. This was the horror I imagined. I suppose pieces of this happen to every teacher, but I would put them all together, and I would approach the class with foreboding, not at ease, not truly myself.

And now comes my experience. I was asked to give two summer courses for the Graduate School of Education of Yeshiva University, but I had a perfect alibi. I was going to Europe and I couldn't. Wouldn't I give an interim course, a concentrated course of 14 sessions during the month of June; and this would not interfere with the trip? I had no excuse and I accepted—because I no longer wanted to dodge the situation and more, also, because I was determined once and for all to face it. If I didn't like to teach (I haven't taught for nearly ten years), I would learn something. And if I did, I would also learn something. And if I had to suffer, it was best this way, since the course was concentrated and the time element was short.

You know that I have been strongly influenced in my thinking about education by Kilpatrick and Dewey. But now I had another powerful ingredient—you. When I first met my class, I did something I never did before. I was frank about my feelings. Instead of feeling that a teacher should know and students were there to be taught, I admitted weakness, doubts, dilemmas, and NOT KNOWING. Since I sort of dethroned my role as a teacher to the class and myself, my more natural self came out more freely and I found myself talking easily and even creatively. By "creatively" I mean ideas came to me as I spoke, brand new ideas which I felt were good.

Another important difference: It is true that since I was influenced by the Kilpatrick methodology I always welcomed the

*As reported to Dr. Rogers one year later.

widest discussion, but I now know, I still wanted and expected my students to know the text and the lecture material set out for them. Even worse, I now know that although I welcomed discussion, I wanted, above all things, that, after all was said and done, the final conclusions of the class to come out according to my way of thinking. Hence none of the discussions were real discussions, in the sense that it was open and free and inquiring; none of the questions were real questions, in the sense that they sought to evoke thinking; all of them were loaded, in the sense that I had pretty definite convictions about what I thought were good answers and at times right answers. Hence, I came to the class with subject matter and my students were really instruments by which situations were manipulated to produce the inclusion of what I regarded as desirable subject matter.

In this last course, I didn't have the courage to discard all subject matter, but this time I really listened to my students; I gave them understanding and sympathy. Although I would spend hours and hours preparing for each session, I found that not once did I refer to a note from the voluminous material with which I entered the room. I allowed students free rein, not holding anyone down to any set course, and I permitted the widest diversion; and I followed wherever the students led.

I remember discussing this with a prominent educator and he said, in what I thought was a disappointed and disapproving tone: "You insist, of course, on good thinking." I quoted William James, who in effect said that man is a speck of reason in an ocean of emotion. I told him that I was more interested in what I would call a "third dimension," the feeling part of the students.

I cannot say I followed you all the way, Dr. Rogers, since I would express opinions and at times, unfortunately, lecture; and that I believe is bad, since students, once authoritative opinions are expressed, tend not to think, but to try to guess what is in the instructor's head and provide him with what he might like, so as to find favor in his eyes. If I had to do it over again, I would have less of that. But I did try and I believe I succeeded in large measure to give to each student a sense of dignity, respect and acceptance; farthest from my mind was to check on them or evaluate and mark them.

And the result—and this is why I am writing you—was for me an unparalleled experience, inexplicable in ordinary terms. I myself cannot fully account for it, except to be grateful that it happened to me. Some of the very qualities which I experienced in your course I found in this which I gave. I found myself liking these particular students as I have never liked any other group of persons, and I found—and they expressed this in their final report—that they themselves began to feel warm and kindly and accepting of one another. Orally and in their papers, they told of how moved they were, how much they learned, how well they felt. For me this was a brand new experience, and I was overwhelmed and humbled by it. I have had students who, I believe, respected and admired me, but I never had a classroom experience from which came such warmth and closeness. Incidentally, following your example, I avoided setting any fixed requirements in terms of reading or classroom preparation.

That the foregoing was not "biased perception" was evidenced from reports I got outside the classroom. The students had said such nice things about me that faculty members wanted to sit in the class. Best of all, the students at the end of the course wrote Dean Banjamin Fine a letter in which they said the nicest things about me. And the Dean in turn wrote me to the same effect.

To say that I am overwhelmed by what happened only faintly reflects my feelings. I have taught for many years but I have never experienced anything remotely resembling what occurred. I, for my part, never have found in the classroom so much of the whole person coming forth, so deeply involved, so deeply stirred. Further, I question if in the traditional set-up, with its emphasis on subject matter, examinations, grades, there is, or there can be a place for the "becoming" person, with his deep and manifold needs, as he struggles to fulfill himself. But this is going far afield. I can only report to you what happened and to say that I am grateful and that I am also humbled by the experience. I would like you to know this, for again you have added to and enriched my life and being.

Editor's Note

That this was not an isolated experience for Dr. Tenenbaum is indicated by a quotation from still another personal communication, many months later. He says: "With another group I taught, following the first one, similar attitudes developed, only they were more accentuated, because, I believe, I was more comfortable with the technique and, I hope, more expert. In this second group there was the same release of the person, the same exhilaration and excitement, the same warmth, the same mystery that attaches to a person as he succeeds in shedding portions of his skin. Students from my group told me that while attending other classes, their eyes would meet, drawn to one another, as if they were unique and apart, as if they were bound together by a special experience. In this second group, also, I found that the students had developed a personal closeness, so that at the end of the semester they talked of having annual reunions. They said that somehow or other they wanted to keep this experience alive and not lose one another. They also spoke of radical and fundamental changes in their person—in outlook, in values, in feelings, in attitudes both toward themselves and toward others.''

16

A Life of One's Own

MARION MILNER

The Coming and Going of Delight

Having discovered that the acts of my experience were an ever-receding horizon, and that my mind had a host of thoughts I never knew about, I felt a little overwhelmed with the difficulties of my enterprise. I therefore decided that it might make tha problem more manageable if I were to choose some special kind of experience and try to study that in detail. Just as in my diary I had tried to record each day's best moments, so I now set out to observe these moments more carefully, to find out what might be their cause. The first thing I noticed was that in certain moods the very simplest things, even the glint of electric light on the water in my bath, gave me the most intense delight, while in others I seemed to be blind, unresponding and shut off, so that music I had loved, a spring day or the company of my friends, gave me no contentment. I therefore decided to try to find what these moods depended upon. Could I control them myself? It did seem to me sometimes that they had been influenced by a deliberate act of mine. Particularly was I struck by the effect of writing things down. It was as if I were trying to catch something and the written word provided a net which for a moment entangled a shadowy form which was other than the meaning of the words. Sometimes it seemed that the act of writing

Source: From Joanna Field (pseudonym), A Life of One's Own. New York: Penguin Books, 1952.

The author of this article, much troubled by a constricting tendency in her personal life, courageously set herself to search for the solution. Her writings reveal a fascinating process of self-discovery, which is painful at the beginning but exhilirating at the end. [Ed.]

was fuel on glowing embers, making flames leap up and throw light on the surrounding gloom, giving me fitful gleams of what was before unguessed at.

Not only did I find that trying to describe my experience enhanced the quality of it, but also this effort to describe had made me more observant of the small movements of the mind. So now I began to discover that there were a multitude of ways of perceiving, ways that were controllable by what I can only describe as an internal gesture of the mind. It was as if one's self-awareness had a central point of intensest being, the very core of one's I-ness. And this core of being could, I now discovered, be moved about at will; but to explain just how it is done to someone who has never felt it for himself is like trying to explain how to move one's ears.

Usually this centre of awareness seemed to be somewhere in my head. But gradually I found that I could if I chose push it out into different parts of my body or even outside myself altogether. Once on a night journey in a train when I could not sleep for the crowd of day impressions which raced through my head, I happened to "feel myself" down into my heart and immediately my mind was so stilled that in a few moments I fell into peaceful sleep. But it surprised me to think that I had lived for twenty-five years without ever discovering that such an internal placing of awareness was possible.

The first hint that I really had the power to control the *way* I looked at things happened in connection with music. Always before, my listening had been too much bothered by the haunting idea that there was far more in it than I was hearing; but occasionally I would find that I had slipped through this barrier to a delight that was enough in itself, in which I forgot my own inadequacy. But this was rare, and most often I would listen intently for a while and then find I had become distracted and was absorbed in the chatter of my own thoughts, personal preoccupations. Impatiently I would shake myself, resolving to attend in earnest for the rest of the concert, only to find that I could not lose myself by mere resolution. Gradually I found, however, that though I could not listen by direct trying I could make some sort of internal gesture after which listening just happened. I described this effort to myself in various ways. Sometimes I seemed to put my awareness into the soles of my feet, sometimes to send something which was myself out into the hall, or to feel as if I were standing just beside the orchestra. I even tried to draw a little picture to remind myself of how it felt.

In my notes I find:

Last Wednesday I went to the opera at Covent Garden, *Rigoletto*. I was dead tired and could not listen at first (sitting on the miserably cramped gallery benches), but then I remembered to put myself out of myself, close to the music—and sometimes it closed over my head, and I came away rested in feeling light-limbed.

At this time also I began to surmise that there might be different ways of looking as well as of listening.

One day I was idly watching some gulls as they soared high overhead. I was not interested, for I recognized them as "just gulls," and vaguely watched first one and then another. Then all at once something seemed to have opened. My idle boredom with the familiar became a deep-breathing peace and delight, and my whole attention was gripped by the pattern and rhythm of their flight, their slow sailing which had become a quiet dance.

In trying to observe what had happened I had the idea that my awareness had somehow widened, that I was feeling what I saw as well as thinking what I saw. But I did not know how to make myself feel as well as think, and it was not till three months later that it occurred to me to apply to looking the trick I had discovered in listening. This happened when I had been thinking of how much I longed to learn the way to get outside my own skin in the daily affairs of life, and feel how other people felt; but I did not know how to begin. I then remembered my trick with music and began to try "putting myself out" into one of the chairs in the room (I was alone so thought a chair would do to begin with). At once the chair seemed to take on a new reality, I "felt" its proportions and could say at once whether I liked its shape. This then, I thought, might be the secret of looking, and could be applied to knowing what one liked. My ordinary way of looking at things seemed to be from my head, as if it were a tower in which I kept myself shut up, only looking out of the windows to watch what was going on. Now I seemed to be discovering that I could if I liked go down outside, go down and make myself part of what was happening, and only so could I experience certain things which could not be seen from the detached height of the tower. . . . One might have thought that after the discovery of such a new possibility I would have been continually coming down to look at things. Actually, however, with the press of a daily work which demanded thought, not feeling, I seem to have forgotten the fact of this new freedom, also I think I was afraid of it and loth to leave the security of my tower too often.

In these ways I began to understand that my powers of perceiving could be altered, not by directly trying to look, or trying to listen, but by this special internal gesture.

I then began to guess that not only perceiving, but doing also could be controlled in the same way. I find in my diary: "The secret of playing ping-pong is to do it with a loose arm, relaxed." A similar statement can be found, I should imagine, in almost any handbook on any athletic sport, but to admit its truth because everyone says so, and to prove it in one's own muscles are two very different matters. I could not believe when I first began to play that the placing of such an exuberant ball with a tiny bat could be accomplished without effort. For I had been brought up to believe that to try was the only way to overcome difficulty. ("Oh, Miss Smith, this sum is too difficult."—"Well, dear, just try it.") And trying meant frowning, tightening muscles, effort. So if ping-pong was difficult, one must try. The result was a stiff body, full of effort, and a jerky swipe at the ball, until someone said: "Play with a loose arm," and I tried, unbelieving. At once the ball went crisply skimming the net to the far court, not once only, but again and again, as long as I could hold myself back from meddling. What surprised me was that my arm seemed to know what to do by itself, it was able to make the right judgments of strength and direction quite without my help. Here the internal gesture required seemed to be to stand aside.

My next discovery about movement was while darning stockings. I was usually clumsy-fingered, fumbling, and impatient to be finished, but slow because I did not find the task interesting enough to keep me from day-dreaming. But one day I read somewhere that one should learn to become aware of all one's bodily movements. I did not remember what else was in the book but this struck me as intersting and I decided to try. I found I could make some internal act while darning my stocking, an act of detachment by which I stood aside from my hand, did not interfere with it, but left it to put in the needle by itself. At first I found great difficulty in restraining my head from trying to do my hand's work for it, but whenever I succeeded the results startled me; for at once there came a sense of ease and I was able to work at maximum speed without any effort. I found it was not just a momentary effect, but it returned whenever I again managed to hold my interfering brain in leash. Henceforth sewing was something to look forward to, a time to enjoy the feel of movement in my hand instead of a tiresome task to be avoided as often as possible.

Although I felt that this discovery was very important to me, I did not seem able to make use of it in the way I had hoped. Although I knew what to do I hardly ever remembered to do it, like the heroes in fairy tales who used to exasperate me by forgetting to use the charm they had been expressly given. But when I did remember to do it, I was reminded of that little one-celled animal which can spread part of its own essence to flow around and envelop within itself whatever it wants for food. This spreading of some vital essence of myself was a new gesture, more diffuse than the placing of awareness beyond myself which I had tried with music; it was more like a spreading of invisible sentient feelers, as a sea anemone spreads wide its feathery fingers. Also I saw now that my usual attitude to the world was a contracted one, like the sea anemone when disturbed by a rough touch, like an amoeba shut within protective walls of its own making. I was yet to learn that state of confidence in which my feelers would always be spread whenever I wanted to perceive.

Whether it was something in the spring weather that next reminded me of this mental gesture I cannnot tell. It was nearly a year later, an Arpil heat wave in Richmond, Virginia. One evening I saw that the half-opened leaves of trees by the dusty roadside, sycamores perhaps, made a pattern against the pale sky, like tracery of old ironwork gates or the decorations on ancient manuscripts. I had an aching desire to possess the pattern, somehow to make it mine—perhaps drawing would capture it. But I was too busy to draw and did not know how to begin even had there been time. Then I remembered to spread the arms of my awareness towards the trees, letting myself flow round them and feed on the delicacy of their patterns till their intricacies became part of my being and I had no more need to capture them on paper. The quality of the delight that followed is forgotten but I find a lame attempt to make a note of it: "Gosh, I feel there's a bird singing high in the tree-tops inside me." This was the nearest memory I could find of my delight, yet it had a too familiar ring and I was uneasy lest it was not truly my own expression, vaguely suspicious that someone else had said it before me.

After this I discovered another gesture, simply to press my awareness out against the limits of my body till there was vitality in all my limbs and I felt smooth and rounded. This time I tried a more mundane description and called it simply: "That fat feeling." Later I find a note: "That fat feeling deepens one's breathing." This interested me, particularly as it was another example of a bodily effect following what I have called a purely mental gesture. Also I was not long in finding uses for the "fat feeling," for once, when returning exhausted from a day of difficult conversations, I remembered to try the pressing out gesture and after a little time found myself completely refreshed, able to respond without flagging to the demands of the evening.

A little later I found a first clue as to what was preventing me spreading my feelers whenever I needed. It was one evening when I was trying to feel out in this way while watching the players at the Chinese Theater in New York; since there were no intelligible words to engage my attention, I was finding it difficult to keep my thoughts from wandering back to the day's preoccupations which I wished to forget. I thought how much there was of entrancing interest going on before me if I only could reach it, and how pretty and nagging were the anxieties of the day which continually distracted me. I had therefore tried deliberately to spread my feelers. No sooner had I made the gesture, however, than I became aware of a vague panic in the back of my mind prompting me to withdraw again into myself like a frightened spider who tucks in his legs, shamming dead.

All these experiences seemed to follow some special internal act, and my next discovery was that this act could be towards inactivity, a letting go. One day I was sitting in the sun alone on a ships's deck with the sea all about me and a gentle wind. I was restless and unhappy, worried because I seemed cut off from enjoying something which I had so often longed for in dark days of winter and cities. I knew that I ought to be happy now that I was having what I wanted, sun and leisure and sea. Suddenly I noticed that I was trying to think, and that I seemed to have taken it for granted that I would be happy if only I could think of something. Not that I had any special problem that needed solving at that particular moment, it was simply the feeling that one ought to have thoughts, ideas, something intersting to say about all one had seen and heard. But with the sun and the wind and the good food I was too turnip-headed to think, my body simply wanted to do nothing. Of course as soon as I became aware of this idea that one ought to have thoughts I realized how silly it was and I stopped trying to do anything, I simply "let go." At once the whiteness of sun-lit ropes against the sea leapt to my eyes and I was deeply content to sit and look.

I also found another example of the effects of passivity. I had always been vaguely interested in pictures, but worried because so often I could not say what I liked; I never seemed to know how to decide, except on a few occasions when a picture would seem to leap at me before I had begun to look at it, when I was still busy about something else. But one day I stopped in front of a Cézanne still-life—green apples, a white plate, and a cloth. Being tired, restless, and distracted by the stream of bored Sunday afternoon sight-seers drifting through the galleries, I simply sat and looked, too inert to remember whether I ought to like it or not. Slowly then I became aware that something was pulling me out of my vacant stare and the colors were coming alive, gripping my gaze till I was soaking myself in their vitality. Gradually a great delight filled me, dispelling all boredom and doubts about what I ought to like. . . . Yet it had all happened by just sitting still and waiting. If I had merely given a cursory glance, said: Isn't that a nice Cézanne?" and drifted on with the crowd, always urged to the next thing, I would have missed it all. And also if I had not been too tired to think I would have said: Here is a Cézanne, here is something one ought to like," and I would have stood there trying to like it but becoming less and less sure what I felt about it. I am reminded in writing this of another experience during fatigue, when I was too tired to think. One mid-summer morning, after dancing so late that it did not seem worth while going to bed, I had walked out alone on Hampstead Heath in the bright sunlight and lain on my back amongst the bracken watching the slow march of clouds. At once I had slipped into such a happiness as I had never known till then, for this was in the days before I had begun to watch for delights and how they came.

In the next striking experience that occurred to me I perceived a new quality. We had just returned to England after two years away, and, landing at Plymouth, were meandering across Cornwall in a Sunday train which every few miles slowed up and creaked to stillness in the quiet of a village station. At first I was deep in my own thoughts, only glancing out of the window occasionally with a sense of the utter familiarity of the country and faintly disappointed that I was feeling no great emotion of home-coming, for it all seemed a little obvious and ordinary. As so often before, my emotions were failing to live up to a romantic moment. Then something happened. Perhaps I remembered to spread myself, to feel out into the landscape. I do not remember the precise gesture. But suddenly I began to notice white cottages and lanes and tidy green fields, and something, either the colors or the shapes, or the character of the land, aroused such a deep resonance in me that I sat, as if meeting a lover, aglow with an almost unbearable delight.

At this time, remembering the vague sense of panic I had observed in the Chinese Theatre, I gradually became aware of something which seemed to be preventing me making these gestures of feeling out. Certain fears began to take form, shadowy and elusive as yet, but intense as a missed heart-beat. Chiefly there seemed to be a fear of losing myself, of being overtaken by something. One day I was lying half asleep on the sands when I saw a gull alight quite close to me, with wings stretched above its back in that fashion peculiar to great winged birds when they settle on the ground. Without thinking, I felt myself into its movement with a panic ecstasy and then turned quickly round upon my fear, for the first time framing the question: "What is this ogre which tries to prevent me from feeling the reality of things?" But I was too slow, it had vanished before I could recognize its shape.

I did not find out anything more about control of mood for another year and did not progress very far in applying what I had already learnt. Then one day, when on a holiday in the Black Forest in Germany, I discovered a more vivid power of perceiving than ever before. The weather was wet and cold, my companion was nervously ill so that we were prevented from following our plan of a walking tour, and, being unable to speak German, I had little wherewith to distract either of us from depressed brooding. I was lonely and filled with a sense of inadequacy, I longed to do something, to act, as an alternative to the ceaseless chatter of worrying thoughts, I was angry with my companion for being ill and angry with myself for being so self-centered as to grumble. I felt cramped that we must stay in a town, and my only delight was when the cold night air, blowing down empty streets, brought the smell of encircling forest. I said: "If only the sun would come out then I could rest without thinking." And one morning I woke to find that the sun was out, and I went into the forest, wandering up a path to a cottage where they served drinks on little tables under apple trees, overlooking a wide valley. I sat down and remembered how I had sometimes found changes of mood follow when I tried to describe in words what I was looking at. So I said: "I see a white house with red geraniums and I hear a child crooning." And this most simple incantation seemed to open a door between me and the world. Afterwards, I tried to write down what had happened:

. . . Those flickering leaf-shadows playing over the heap of cut grass. It is fresh scythed. The shadows are blue or green, I don't know which, but I feel them in my bones. Down into the shadows of the gully, across it through glistening space, space tha hangs suspended filling the gully, so that the little sounds wander there, lose themselves and are drowned; beyond, there's a splash of sunlight leaping out against the darkness of forest, the gold in it flows richly in my eyes, flows through my brain in still pools of light. That pine, my eye is led up and down the straightness of its trunk, my muscles feel its roots spreading wide to hold it so upright against the hill. The air is full of sounds, sighs of wind in the trees, sighs which fade back into the overhanging silence. A bee passes, a golden ripple in the quiet air. A chicken at my feet fussily crunches a blade of grass. . . .

I sat motionless, draining sensation to its depths, wave after wave of delight flowing through every cell in my body. My attention flickered from one delight to the next like a butterfly, effortless, following its pleasure; sometimes it rested on a thought, a verbal comment, but these no longer made a chattering barrier between me and what I saw, they were woven into the texture of my seeing. I no longer strove to be doing something, I was deeply content with what was. At other times my different senses had often been a conflict, so that I could either look or listen but not both at once. Now hearing and sight and sense of space were all fused into one whole.

I do not know how long I sat there in absolute stillness, watching. Eventually, I stood up, stretched and returned along the little path down the hillside, freed from my angers and discontents and overflowing with peace. But there were many questions to be answered. Which of the things I had done had been important in the awakening of my senses? Or was it nothing I had done, but some spell from the forest and the sun? Could I repeat the experience and so have a permanent retreat for the cure of my angers and self-pity? If just looking could be so satisfying, why was I always striving to have things or to get things done? Certainly I had never suspected that the key to my private reality might lie in so apparently simple a skill as the ability to let the senses roam unfettered by purposes. I began to wonder whether eyes and ears might not have a wisdom of their own.

Discovery of the "Other"

Although relaxing and watching my thought seemed to have all these advantages, I still had not learnt how to do it continually. When considering this I ran over in my mind all the occasions on which I had managed to do it, and then I realized that it had always happened when I was alone, for when with other people I seemed to tighten up and make a protective ring between myself and the world.

I remembered how, when I had first discovered that it was possible to spread wide the invisible feelers of mind, to push myself out into the landscape or the movements of a flying bird, I had felt a panic fear. Gradually, however, as I had found that nothing terrible happened, but only great delight, I had apparently lost such feelings and in the world of nature I had begun to feel safe; but apprehension still lurked in my attempts at other kinds of perception. Sometimes in listening to music I would feel myself being carried away until neither I nor anything else existed but only sound, and in spite of the delight I would clutch wildly at some wandering thought to bring me back to the familiar world of bored selfconsciousness. Once when listening to a Brahms Quartet I suddenly wanted to gasp out: "Oh, stop, stop, he shouldn't pour out his heart like that, he'll get hurt. Those are the things one hides." And then again, in looking at architecture, I discovered fear. I had never been able to find buildings as interesting as pictures, though I felt sure they must be if only I knew how to look. I used to drift round churches with other people, famous places that everyone said ought to be seen and admired, but I always found my attention wandering, always found myself wishing they would get it over quickly and come out in the sun, for my gesture of deliberate wide perceiving never seemed to work here; or perhaps it was that I could never bring myself to try it. Then, one day after I had had some practice in learning how to relax, I was taken to see some sculpture (a form of art which I had always before found rather puzzling). But this time I discovered that by keeping very still and forgetting everything I had been told, I could slip down into a world of dark tensions, stresses and strains that forged themselves into an obscure but deep satisfaction. I felt it in my bones and in my feet and in my breathing. Soon after this I happened to be in Westminster Abbey, a place I had always found vaguely tiresome, hating the litter of monuments and chairs. I was waiting for some music to begin and looked about me, trying to break through the fog of associations and to escape from my preconceived ideas of boredom in churches. Suddenly I succeeded, suddenly I managed to strip my mind clean of all its ideas and to feel through the decoration to the bare structure of the building and the growing lines of the stone. But in an instant I found a catching in my breath, for there was here an echo of terror. Here were the same stresses and strains as in the life-size sculptures but on such a superhuman scale that they seemed to threaten my very existence. It occurred to me, after this, that perhaps in order to understand architecture one needs just as good a head for masses as a mountaineer does for heights. By keeping myself immersed in the safety of personal preoccupations and ideas about, rather than feelings of, the things I was looking at, I suppose I had managed to feel secure on all my past tours round churches; and when in the streets it was easy to be so filled with purposes as to look at buildings with a blind eye. But now that I had realized this terror of trusting pillars and arches that loomed and brooded over me I found, as always before, the dread of annihilation merging into a deep delight.

After this I slowly came to understand more about the problem of relaxing when amongst other people. Just as I had once found that invisible feelers could be spread round things, so I now found that I could spread them round people as well. But here, more than ever, I needed to have some basis of security before I could do it, for so often I had a feeling that there was something to be guarded against, which time and again came between me and the people I wanted to know. It took me a long time to realize just what this fear was. Although I understood by now well enough that in the world of perception what I wanted was to lose myself in the thing perceived, yet it was too terrifying a thought to be fully admitted when it was a matter of another person. And since I could not recognize it for what it was, it remained at the level of blind thinking and kept me perpetually straining to guard against the very engulfment which I wanted.

In the end the knowledge of my deliverance came suddenly. Of course I had had many hints and part understandings of what I was trying to escape, but the full realization did not come until one day when I happened to have been looking back over all that I had discovered. I had just begun to ponder over the fact that all the things which I had found to be sources of happiness seemed to depend upon the capacity to relax all straining, to widen my attention beyond the circle of personal interest, and to look detachedly at my own experience. I had just realized that this relaxing and detachment must depend on a fundamental sense of security, and yet that I could apparently never feel safe enough to do it, because there was an urge in me which I had dimly perceived but had never yet been able to face. It was then that the idea occurred to me that until you have, once at least, faced everything you know—the whole universe—with utter giving in, and let all that is "not you" flow over and engulf you, there can be no lasting sense of security.

Only by being prepared to accept annihilation can one escape from that spiritual "abiding alone" which is in fact the truly death-like state.

I realized now that as long as you feel insecure you have no real capacity to face other men and women in that skill of communication which more than any other skill requires freedom from tension. By communication I did not of course mean only intellectual conversation but the whole aesthetic of emotional relations; and just as I had, when first beginning to examine my experience, found most of my delights in natural things, I was now finding that I chiefly reckoned each day's catch of happiness in terms of my relationships with others. Of this, wordless understanding seemed to be particularly important. Before, I had been inclined to judge the value of meeting with my friends largely by what was said. Now it was unvoiced relationship which seemed of more concern—though this was perhaps partly the result of having for eighteen months shared the life of someone who had not yet learned to talk.

Here also I began to discover a new world of direct communication, not through the symbols of words and actions and gestures, but what seemed to be an almost direct interchange of emotion which came with this spreading of invisible feelers. It was not only that my own perceptions were heightened, not only that by spreading myself out towards a person I could "feel the necessities of their being," it was that they also seemed to receive something, for in no other way could I explain the changes in their behavior. For instance, I was one day helping a very old lady from her chair to her bed. She was so old that she was past the age of reasonable understanding, and was like a child in most things, including the disinclination to go to bed. She was so heavy that I did not know how to deal with the situation at all and I felt embarrassed, tightly withdrawn, wishing it were over. Then I caught sight of her helplessly obstinate feet and something in them drew me out of myself into her problem, so that it became my problem too, and at once all her obstinacy vanished and she yielded easily to my help. Of course it was quite probable that she detected a subtle change in my clumsy efforts to help her; but there were other times when a person's mood would change when I had made no outward movement whatever, only spread internal feelers. So, when trying to persuade my baby to go to sleep I would often wait beside him, absolutely motionless, but my own heart filled with peace. Once I let impatience and annoyance dominate my mind he would become restless again. This may have been sheer accident, of course, but it happened so many times that in the end I found it very difficult to escape from the belief that my own state of mind did have some direct effect upon him.

Now also communication came to include the whole intricate texture of communal living. Just as I had once learnt to look at colors and shapes for their own sakes, I now began to see, as possible ends in themselves, actions like house-work which had before seemed to be nothing but tiresome routine because they were not "getting me anywhere." Now I was beginning to find that part of the day's happiness came while sweeping or preparing food (always before I had hated house-work because after so much time spent there was so little to show for it); I seemed to like it because it was a kind of communication, it expressed my feeling for the house I kept clean and the people who lived in it. Of course I did not always manage to achieve this disinterestedness, just as I could not always see things for their colors and shapes rather than for their use in furthering my private purposes. There were many times when I could not see my actions at all for their own sake, I must sweep from house-proudness because visitors might notice the dirt and think derogatory things, or I must cook a good dinner because that was the sort of person I liked to imagine myself. But I never found that the house-work I did for these reasons appeared in my day's list of happiness.

I now saw too how my earlier discoveries could be applied to this problem of communication. For quite early in my enterprise I had found that to want results for myself, to do things with the expectancy of happiness, was generally fatal, it made the stream of delight dry up at the source. (Of course the greater part of every day was filled with jobs which had to be done in order that something else might happen; but I am not here dealing with necessities imposed from without, only with how to manage one's actions and attitudes where there is any freedom of choice.) So now I began to find that it was no way out, as I had once hoped it would be, to want results for other people. In my exasperated self-absorption I had envied those who were always doing things for others. But as I grew more observant I began to see that this by itself was no sure way of peace, for as long as you expect results from what you do there are here even more sources of exasperation. Once you assume your right to interfere in other people's problems they become in some ways more of a worry than your own, for with your own you can at least do what you think best, but other people always show such a persistent tendency to do the wrong thing. And then it was so fatally easy to think that I knew what was good for other people; it made me feel pleasantly superior to think myself in a position to help, and also it made me feel good, feel that I was piling up some subtle advantage for myself, becoming a more admirable character. It took me a long time to learn to resist the feeling that I *ought* to interfere and try to help people for their own good. I knew others did it and so felt I ought to, although I was never too clear about what were best to be done. And then in addition to the feeling of ought, there was also the sheer pain of another person's misery, which of course grew greater, not less, as I learnt to be more perceiving. Gradually, however, I now came to understand that it was all right to do things for people as long as I did it for the sake of doing it, as a gesture of courtesy, the value being more in the act than in the result. If I sacrificed myself for others, it must be, not because I thought they really needed what I had to give (for this might be an insult, as if I were implicitly putting myself above them), but simply as a way of expressing my feelings towards them. Here the giving was enough in itself, it was not a means to an end.

So it was that I gradually came to see what great delights were to be found in those moments of detached seeing when I could recognize another mind and yet want nothing from it. Such communication did not always require contact in time and place, for sometimes from a book or a picture I caught a human meaning to add to my stock of day's delights. I came to be not at all surprised at that tiresome attitude of superiority people seem unable to avoid when they can see meaning in a difficult work of art, although I had often been irritated by it myself, and made to feel very small by people who liked music and pictures I did not understand. For now I was myself realizing a cause for this seeming arrogance, since there were times when for me too a picture or a building or a poem would suddenly come alive. These were times when I would be left so exulting in communication, exulting in the human contact with the artist, that I really did feel in that moment of shared experience a quite new and bigger person; so it was difficult not to strut just a little, for blind thinking almost had a feeling that it had done a bit in the creating of the beautiful thing itself.

17

I Resolve to Become a Jungle Doctor

ALBERT SCHWEITZER

On October 13th, 1905, a Friday, I dropped into a letter box in the Avenue de la Grande Armée in Paris, letters to my parents and to some of my most intimate acquaintances, telling them that at the beginning of the winter term I should enter myself as a medical student, in order to go later on to Equatorial Africa as a doctor. In one of them I sent in the resignation of my post as principal of the Theological College of St. Thomas', because of the claim on my time that my intended course of study would make.

The plan which I meant now to put into execution had been in my mind for a long time, having been conceived so long ago as my student days. It struck me as incomprehensible that I should be allowed to lead such a happy life, while I saw so many people around me wrestling with care and suffering. Even at school I had felt stirred whenever I got a glimpse of the miserable home surroundings of some of my school-fellows and compared them with the absolutely ideal conditions in which we children of the parsonage at Günsbach lived. While at the university and enjoying the happiness of being able to study and even to produce some results in science and art, I could not help thinking continually of others who were denied that happiness by their material circumstances or their health. Then one brilliant summer morning at Günsbach, during the Whitsuntide holidays—it was in 1896—there

Source: From Out of My Life and Thought *by Albert Schweitzer. Translated by C. T. Campion. Copyright 1933, 1939,* © *1961 by Holt, Rinehart & Winston. Reprinted by permission of Holt, Rinehart & Winston.*

Albert Schweitzer (1875–1965) gave up his successful career in Europe and went to Africa to serve as a physician. This article, an excerpt from his autobiography, is an interesting testimony for a theory of metamotivation presented in Chapter 3. [Ed.]

came to me, as I awoke, the thought that I must not accept this happiness as a matter of course, but must give something in return for it. Proceeding to think the matter out at once with calm deliberation, while the birds were singing outside, I settled with myself before I got up, that I would consider myself justified in living till I was thirty for science and art, in order to devote myself from that time forward to the direct service of humanity. Many a time already had I tried to settle what meaning lay hidden for me in the saying of Jesus! "Whosoever would save his life shall lose it, and whosoever shall lose his life for My sake and the Gospels shall save it." Now the answer was found. In addition to the outward, I now had inward happiness.

What would be the character of the activities thus planned for the future was not yet clear to me. I left it to circumstances to guide me. One thing only was certain, that it must be directly human service, however inconspicuous the sphere of it.

I naturally thought first of some activity in Europe. I formed a plan for taking charge of abandoned or neglected children and educating them, then making them pledge themselves to help later on in the same way children in similar positions. When in 1903, as warden of the theological hostel, I moved into my roomy and sunny official quarters on the second floor of the College of St. Thomas, I was in a position to begin the experiment. I offered my help now here, now there, but always unsuccessfully. The constitutions of the organizations which looked after destitute and abandoned children made no provision for the acceptance of such voluntary co-operation. For example, when the Strasbourg orphanage was burnt down, I offered to take in a few boys, for the time being, but the superintendent did not even allow me to finish what I had to say. Similar attempts which I made elsewhere were also failures.

For a time I thought I would some day devote myself to tramps and discharged prisoners. In some measure as a preparation for this I joined the Rev. Augustus Ernst at St. Thomas' in an undertaking which he had begun. He was at home from one to two P.M. and ready to speak to anyone who came to him asking for help or for a night's lodging. He did not, however, give the applicant a trifle in money, or let him wait till he could get information about his circumstances. He would offer to look him up in his lodging house that very afternoon and test the statements he had volunteered about his condition. Then, and then only, would he give him help, but as much, and for as long a time, as was necessary. What a number of bicycle rides we made with this object in the town and the suburbs, and very often with the result that the applicant was not known at the address he had given. In a great many cases, however, it provided an opportunity for giving, with knowledge of the circumstances, very seasonable help. I had some friends, too, who kindly placed a portion of their wealth at my disposal.

Already, as a student, I had been active in social service as a member of the student association known as the Diaconate of St. Thomas, which held its meetings in St. Thomas' College. Each of us had a certain number of poor families assigned to him, which he was to visit every week, taking to them the help allotted to them and making a report on their condition. The money we thus distributed we collected from members of the old Strasbourg families who supported this undertaking, begun by former generations and now carried on by us. Twice a year, if I remember right, each of us had to make his definite number of such begging appeals. To me, being shy and rather awkward in society, these visits were a torture. I believe that in these preparatory studies for the begging I have had to do in later years I sometimes showed myself extremely unskillful. However, I learned through them that begging with tact and restraint is better appreciated than any sort of stand-and-deliver approach, and also that the correct method of begging includes the good-tempered acceptance of a refusal.

In our youthful inexperience we no doubt often failed, in spite of the best intentions, to use all the money entrusted to us in the wisest way, but the intentions of the givers were nevertheless fully carried out in that it pledged young men to take an interest in the poor. For that reason I think with deep gratitude of those who met with so much understanding and liberality our efforts to be wisely helpful, and hope that many students may have the privilege of working, commissioned in this way by the charitable, as recruits in the struggle against poverty.

While I was concerned with tramps and discharged prisoners it had become clear to me that they could only be effectively helped by a number of individuals who would devote themselves to them. At the same time, however, I had realized that in many cases these could only accomplish their best work in collaboration with organizations. But what I wanted was an absolutely personal and independent activity. Although I was resolved to put my services at the disposal of some organization, if it should be really necessary, I nevertheless never gave up the hope of finding a sphere of activity to which I could devote myself as an individual and as wholly free. That this longing of mine found fulfillment I have always regarded as a signal instance of the mercy which has again and again been vouchsafed to me.

One morning in the autumn of 1904 I found on my writing table in the college one of the green-covered magazines in which the Paris Missionary Society reported every month on its activities. A certain Miss Scherdlin used to put them there knowing that I was specially interested in this society on account of the impression made on me by the letters of one of its earliest missionaries, Casalis by name, when my father read them aloud at his missionary services during my childhood. That evening, in the very act of putting it aside that I might go on with my work, I mechanically opened this magazine, which had been laid on my table during my absence. As I did so, my eye caught the title of an article: *Les besoins de la Mission du Congo* ("The needs of the Congo Mission").*

It was by Alfred Boegner, the president of the Paris Missionary Society, an Alsatian, and contained a complaint that the mission had not enough workers to carry on its work in the Gaboon, the northern province of the Congo Colony. The writer expressed his hope that his appeal would bring some of those "on whom the Master's eyes already rested" to a decision to offer themselves for this urgent work. The conclusion ran: "Men and women who can reply simply to the Master's call, 'Lord, I am coming,' those are the people whom the Church needs." Having finished the article, I quietly began my work. My search was over.

My thirtieth birthday, a few months later, I spent like the man in the parable who "desiring to build a tower, first counts the cost whether he have wherewith to complete it." The result was that I resolved to realize my plan of direct human service in Equatorial Africa.

With the exception of one trustworthy friend no one knew of my intention. When it became known through the letters I had sent from Paris, I had hard battles to fight with my relations and friends. Almost more than with my contemplated new start itself they reproached me with not having shown them so much confidence as to discuss it with them first. With this side issue they tormented me beyond measure during those difficult weeks. That theological friends should outdo the others in their protests struck me as all the more preposterous, because they had, no doubt, all preached a fine sermon—perhaps a very fine one—showing how St. Paul, as he has recorded in his letter to the Galatians, "conferred not with flesh and blood" beforehand about what he meant to do for Jesus.

My relatives and my friends all joined in expostulating with me on the folly of my enterprise. I was a man, they said, who was burying the

* *Journal des Missions Evangéliques* (June, 1904): 389–393.

talent entrusted to him and wanted to trade with false currency. Work among the savages I ought to leave to those who would not thereby be compelled to leave gifts and acquirements in science and art unused. Widor, who love me as if I were his son, scolded me as being like a general who wanted to go into the firing line—there was no talk about trenches at that time—with a rifle. A lady who was filled with the modern spirit proved to me that I could do much more by lecturing on behalf of medical help for natives than I could by the action I contemplated. That saying from Goethe's *Faust* ("In the beginning was the Deed"), was now out of date, she said. Today propaganda was the mother of happenings.

In the many verbal duels which I had to fight, as a weary opponent, with people who passed for Christians, it moved me strangely to see them so far from perceiving that the effort to serve the love preached by Jesus may sweep a man into a new course of life, although they read in the New Testament that it can do so, and found it there quite in order. I had assumed as a matter of course that familiarity with the sayings of Jesus would produce much better appreciation of what to popular logic is nonrational, than my own case allowed me to assert. Several times, indeed, it was my experience that my appeal to the act of obedience which Jesus' command of love may under special circumstances call for, brought upon me an accusation of conceit, although I had, in fact, been obliged to do violence to my feelings to employ this argument at all. In general, how much I suffered through so many people assuming a right to tear open all the doors and shutters of my inner self!

As a rule, too, it was of no use allowing them, in spite of my repugnance, to have a glimpse of the thoughts which had given birth to my resolution. They thought there must be something behind it all, and guessed at disappointment at the slow growth of my reputation. For this there was no ground at all, seeing that I had received, even as a young man, such recognition as others usually get only after a whole life of toil and struggle. Unfortunate love experiences were also alleged as the reason for my decision.

I felt as a real kindness the action of persons who made no attempt to dig their fists into my heart, but regarded me as a precocious young man, not quite right in his head, and treated me correspondingly with affectionate mockery.

I felt it to be, in itself, quite natural that relations and friends should put before me anything that told against the reasonableness of my plan. As one who demands that idealists shall be sober in their views, I was conscious that every start upon an untrodden path is a venture which only in unusual circumstances looks sensible and likely to be successful. In my own case I held the venture to be justified, because I had considered it for a long time and from every point of view, and credited myself with the posession of health, sound nerves, energy, practical common sense, toughness, prudence, very few wants, and everything else that might be found necessary by anyone wandering along the path of the idea. I believed myself, further, to wear the protective armor of a tempermament quite capable of enduring an eventual failure of my plan.

As a man of individual action, I have since that time been approached for my opinion and advice by many people who wanted to make a similar venture, but only in comparatively few cases have I taken on me the responsibility of giving them immediate encouragement. I often had to recognize that the need "to do something special" was born of a restless spirit. Such persons wanted to dedicate themselves to larger tasks because those that lay nearest did not satisfy them. Often, too, it was evident that they had been brought to their decisions by quite secondary considerations. Only a person who can find a value in every sort of activity and devote himself to each one with full consciousness of duty, has the inward right to take as his object some extraordinary activity instead of that which falls naturally to his lot. Only a person who feels his preference to be a matter of course, not something out of the ordinary, and who has no thought of heroism, but just recognizes a duty undertaken with sober enthusiasm, is capable of becoming a spiritual adventurer such as the world needs. There are no heroes of action: only heroes of renunciation and suffering. Of such there are plenty. But few of them are known, and even these not to the crowd, but to the few.

Carlyle's *Heroes and Hero Worship* is not a profound book.

Of those who feel any sort of impulse, and would prove actually fitted, to devote their lives to independent personal activity, the majority are compelled by circumstances to renounce such a course. As a rule this is because they have to provide for one or more dependents, or because they have to stick to their calling in order to earn their own living. Only one who thanks to his own ability or the devotion of friends is in worldly matters a free man, can venture nowadays to take the path of independent activity. This was not so much the case in earlier times because anyone who gave up remunerative work could still hope to get through life somehow or other, while anyone who thought of doing the same in the difficult economic conditions of today would run the risk of coming to grief not only materially but spiritually as well.

I am compelled, therefore, not only by what I have observed, but by experience also, to admit that worthy and capable persons have had to renounce a course of independent action which would have been of great value to the world, because circumstances rendered such a course impossible.

Those who are so favored as to be able to embark on a course of free personal activity must accept this good fortune in a spirit of humility. They must often think of those who, though willing and capable, were never in a position to do the same. And as a rule they must temper their own strong determination with humility. They are almost always destined to have to seek and wait till they find a road open for the activity they long for. Happy are those to whom the years of work are allotted in richer measure than those of seeking and waiting! Happy those who in the end are able to give themselves really and completely!

These favored persons must also be modest so as not to fly into a passion at the opposition they encounter; they have to meet it in the temper which says: "Ah, well, it had to be!" Anyone who proposes to do good must not expect people to roll stones out of his way, but must accept his lot calmly if they even roll a few more upon it. A strength which becomes clearer and stronger through its experience of such obstacles is the only strength that can conquer them. Resistance is only a waste of strength.

Of all the will for the ideal which exists in mankind only a small part can be manifested in action. All the rest is destined to realize itself in unseen effects, which represent, however, a value exceeding a thousandfold and more that of the activity which attracts the notice of the world. Its relation to the latter is like that of the deep sea to the waves which stir its surface. The hidden forces of goodness are embodied in those persons who carry on as a secondary pursuit the immediate personal service which they cannot make their lifework. The lot of the many is to have as a profession, for the earning of their living and the satisfaction of society's claim on them, a more or less soulless labor in which they can give out little or nothing of their human qualities, because in that labor they have to be little better than human machines. Yet no one finds himself in the position of having no possible opportunity of giving himself to others as a human being. The problem produced by the fact of labor being today so thoroughly organized, specialized, and mechanized depends only in part for its solution on society's not merely removing the conditions thus produced, but doing its very best to guard the rights of human personality. What is even more important is that sufferers shall not simply bow to their fate, but shall try with all their energy to assert their human personality amid their unfavorable conditions by spiritual activity. Anyone can rescue his human life, in spite of his professional life, who seizes every opportunity of being a man by means of personal action, however unpretending, for the good of fellow men who need the help of a fellow man. Such a man enlists in the service of the spiritual and good. No fate can prevent a man from giving to others this direct human service side by side with his lifework. If so much of such service remains unrealized, it is because the opportunities are missed.

That everyone shall exert himself in that state of life in which he is placed, to practice true humanity toward his fellow men, on that depends the future of mankind. Enormous values come to nothing every moment through the missing of opportunities, but the values which do get turned into will and deed mean wealth which must not be undervalued. Our humanity is by no means so materialistic as foolish talk is continually asserting it to be. Judging by what I have learned about men and women, I am convinced that there is far more in them of idealist will power than ever comes to the surface of the world. Just as the water of the streams we see is small in amount compared to that which flows underground, so the idealism which becomes visible is small in amount compared with what men and women bear locked in their hearts, unreleased or scarcely released. To unbind what is bound, to bring the underground waters to the surface: mankind is waiting and longing for such as can do that.

18

Productivity and Existence

MARTIN BUBER

"A remarkable and charming man, your friend," said the professor; "but what does he really *do*? I mean . . . in the intellectual sphere?"

"In the intellectual sphere . . ." I answered. "H'mm . . . in the intellectual sphere . . . he is simply there."

"How do you mean?"

"Well, his occupation is not, in fact, of a very intellectual nature, and one cannot really assert that he makes anything out of his leisure time."

"But his thoughts?"

"He contents himself for the most part with images. When they want to combine and condense into a thought, he gladly helps them and is pleased if something real comes out of them. At times, in conversation, as just now, he also shares some of these clear and fulfilled images."

"Then he does not write?"

"Oh, he once confessed to me, almost against his will, that occasionally, now and then, when his thoughts congeal, he enters a few lines in a secret book, in order, as he put it, to distinguish from then on what is actually won from what is merely *possible*."

"Then will he perhaps eventually publish something comprehensive?"

"I do not believe that he has that in mind. He has no need to enter into relation with men other than the friends life has brought him in

Source: From Pointing the Way *by Martin Buber. Translated by Maurice Friedman.* © *1957 by Martin Buber. Reprinted by permission of Harper & Row.*

contact with. He trusts life like a child. He said once that intensity is the only dimension that unceasingly rewards travelling.''

"But why do not you, his friends, persuade him to collect his thoughts and share them with the general public?'' I have heard enough of them to say with certainty that they are worth while.''

"We feel that his real unity lies in his personality and that only there can it exist. And we feel that we would injure his vitality, which means more to us than any book, if we induced him to store it between covers instead of pouring it into our souls, repaying living with living. He does not give away any part of himself; he only lends it, to receive it back transformed, so that all being then blooms in his presence as young faces, young gestures. That alone makes the blessing of his sharing; that calls up and enlivens ever new levels in him and renews him, indeed, time after time. In the sureness of our glance, in the buoyancy of our plan, in the sacrificial power of our undertaking, he reads the fiery writing of his transformed words. When one of our circle died, I marked that our friend went on reading him in an immortal sphere.''

"But the world—you forget the world! You speak as if a book were an end in itself, whereas it is only a transmitter that bears our voices to unknown ears and hearts. I write what I am inspired to; I fling it out beyond all that is personal, into the whirl of the market, and the whirl carries it into reading-rooms and lamp-lit parlours where men whom I have never seen and never will see hear my words—and perhaps really understand. Is a book not a significant mixture of the personal and the impersonal? The book works and woos out there, and yet it is also myself. Thus separated from myself, I flow into all the world—into distant houses and perhaps into distant generations also—elevating, pleasing, angering who knows, but always in some way educating the human spirit. This thousandfold journey, this victory over all limits of individual existence, this bond with the unknown—for ever misused by vanity and yet never wholly desecrated—this is the predestined way of the thinker.''

"I am familiar with this way, for at times I, too, publish a book. I know the joy of it and its terror—yes, its terror; for it is something dreadful to know that the ghost of my thought hovers in the dreams of confused and impure men, confused and impure as they. But I also know its joy—I remember how it moved me when an old bee-keeper wrote me that he had read my book every day for a week on a bench in his garden in the bright hours of the afternoon, from the coming of the apple-blossoms till their withering. And, in order to be entirely fair, I shall also recall the great and creative gifts which I myself owe to books. Now I feel wholly what they are. And yet—more powerful and more holy than all writing is the presence of a man who is simply and immediately present. He need not cry through the loud-speaker of a book to that special circle of contemporary and future readers the writer calls the world. He has spoken without a medium, from mouth to ear, silently and overpoweringly, from his countenance to an eye and to an entranced soul; he has spoken in the magic fullness of togetherness to those men he calls his friends—and who are now full of the spirit because it has laid its hands upon them. Such a man will rarely produce a book. And if he does anything of this sort, the original source of the book is the life of a man who is present only in a direct way.''

"Then all those who are not among the friends of such a man must remain excluded from his teaching?''

"Not at all, for those who are transformed through his teaching are forthwith, one and all, apostles—even though they do not repeat anything of it, nor even proclaim the name of the teacher; as transformed men, they are apostles through their existence, and whatever they do is done in apostleship, through the essence of his teaching which they express therein. In the life of his friends, in the life of all who meet him, and thus to distant generations, immediacy is transmitted.''

"You wish, then, if I understand you rightly, to regard productivity as a lower rung of existence?''

"Rather, I regard productivity, in general, as existence only when it is rooted in the immediacy of lived life. If the man whom you call productive, the one who expresses himself in a creative work, is inferior in power, in holiness, to him who only expresses himself in his life, he is still, in so far as he is grounded in immediacy, superior to him in the noble faculty of creating form. But if you consider an individual who has shrunk to mere form the streaming, living potency, there stands before us a masquerading hobgoblin who cannot form himself but can only disguise himself in forms. No, what I said of the immediate man was not said against the productive one: I was attacking the dominant delusion of our time, that creativity is the criterion of human worth. But illegitimate creativity, creation without immediacy, is no criterion, for it is no reality. It is an illusion—and I believe in the absolute eye before which it cannot stand for a moment. Only that can be a criterion from which genuine creativity arises; that is, the immediate.''

"Certainly, man can be judged only by what he is. But does not his creating, along with his acting, belong to his being?''

"Yes, when it functions as a valid organ of the living body; no, when it indicates a mere excrescence. Artifice has so much got the upper hand that the fictitious dares to usurp the place of the real. The overvaluation of productivity that is afflicting our age has so thrived and its par-technical glance has set up a senseless exclusiveness of its own that even genuinely creative men allow their organic skills to degenerate into an autonomous growth to satisfy the demand of the day. What the born deceivers never had, they give up: the ground where the roots of a genuinely lived life alone can grow. They mean, they strive for, and at last they contain nothing but creativity. Instead of bringing forth a natural creation, in a gradual selective progression from experiences to thoughts, from thoughts to words, from words to writing, and from writing to public communication, they wear themselves out turning all experience to account as public communication; they renounce true necessity and give themselves over to the arbitrary. They poison experience, for already while it is taking place they are dominated by the will to produce. Thus they prostitute their lives and are cheated of the reward for their ignominy; for how can they expect to create anything save the artificial and the transitory? They forfeit both life and art, and all that they gain is the applause of their production-mad contemporaries.''

''But it appears to me that the will to create is a legitimate part of the experience of every productive man. Thus the painter is the man who paints with all his senses. His seeing is already a painting, for what he sees is not merely what his physical sight receives: it is something, two-dimensionally intensified, that vision produces. And this producing does not come later, but is present in his seeing. Even his hearing, his smelling, are already painting, for they enrich for him the graphic character of the thing; they give him not only sensations but also stimulations. In the same way the poet creates poetry with all his senses; in each of his experiences the form in which it will be phrased is immediately announced. His perceiving is already a transformation of the thing perceived into the stuff of poetry, and in its becoming each impression presents itself to him as an expression of rhythmic validity.''

''That is indeed so. But this dynamic element that you find in the experience of the creative is no will to create but an ability to create. This potentiality of form also accompanies every experience that befalls the non-artistic man and is given an issue as often as he lifts an image out of the stream of perception and inserts it into his memory as something single, definite, and meaningful in itself. For the creative man this potentiality of form is a specific one, directed into the language of his particular art. If an intention is expressed in this direction, it is that of his genius, not that of a self-conscious resolution. The dynamic element of his experience does not affect is wholeness and purity. It is otherwise when in perceiving he already cherishes the deliberate intention of utilizing what he perceives. Then he disturbs the experience, stunts its growth, and taints the process of its becoming. Only the unarbitrary can grow properly and bear mature and healthy fruit. That man is legitimately creative who experiences so strongly and formatively that his experiences unite into an image that demands to be set forth, and who then works at his task with full consciousness of his art. But he who interferes with the spontaneity of perceiving, who does not allow the inner selection and formation to prevail, but instead inserts an aim from the beginning, has forfeited the meaning of this perception, the meaning that lies above all aims. And he who meets men with a double glance, an open one that invites his fellows to sincerity and the concealed one of the observer stemming from a conscious aim; he who is friendship and in love is cleft into two men, one who surrenders himself to his feelings and another who is already standing by to exploit them—this man cannot be delivered by any creative talent from the blight that he has brought upon himself and his work, for he has poisoned the springs of his life.''

"You wish, then, to reintroduce into aesthetics the ethical principle that we have finally succeeded in banishing from it?"

"What was banished from aesthetics was an ideology that had degenerated into rhetoric and had thereby become false. It certainly signified a conquest of sure ground when the perspective was established that evaluated a work of art—approving or rejecting it—not by its relation to the aspirations of the artist buy by its intrinsic qualities. Now for the first time we can, without promoting misunderstanding, strive towards the deeper insight: that this approval affords entrance into the outer circle only, but in the inner circle those works alone count that have given form to the meaning of being. Similarly, a gain in clarity and solidity was achieved when it was recognized that the significance of an artist does not depend upon his morals: now for the first time we can attain the deeper clarity that in inner development mastery and power accrue only to that artist who is worthy of his art."

19

The Psychology of the Scientists

ANNE ROE

Science is the creation of scientists, and every scientific advance bears somehow the mark of the man who made it. The artist exposes himself in his work; the scientist seems rather to hide in his, but he is there. Surely the historian of science must understand the man if he is fully to understand the progress of science, and he must have some comprehension of the science if he is to understand the men who make it.

The general *public* image of the scientist has not been and indeed is not now a flattering one, and at best it certainly is not an endearing one. Characterizations of scientists almost always emphasize the objectivity of their work and describe their cold, detached, impressive, unconcerned observation of phenomena which have no emotional meaning for them. This could hardly be further from the truth. The scientist as a person is a nonparticipating observer in only a very limited sense. He does not *interact* with what he is observing, but he does participate as a person. It is, perhaps, this fact—that the scientist does not expect, indeed does not want, the things that he is concerned with to be equally concerned with him—that has given others this impression of coldness, remoteness, and objectivity. (The social scientist is in a remarkably difficult position since the "objects with which he is concerned" are people, and both they and he may be more than a little ambivalent about this matter of interaction. But this is a special problem which I will by-pass here, noting only that in many ways the

Source: From "The Psychology of the Scientist," by Anne Roe, Science, *vol. 134 (18 August 1961), pp. 456–59. © 1961 by the American Association for the Advancement of Science.*

social scientist differs from the natural scientist in terms of personality and motivations.)

The truth of the matter is that the creative scientist, whatever his field, is very deeply involved emotionally and personally in his work, and that he himself is his own most essential tool. We must consider both the subjectivity of science and what kinds of people scientists are.

The Personal Factor

But first we must consider the processes of science. Suppose we take the scientist at the time when he has asked a question, or has set up a hypothesis which he wants to test. *He* must decide what observations to make. It is simply not possible to observe everything that goes on under a given set of conditions: he must choose what to observe, what measurements to make, how fine these measurements are to be, now to record them. These choices are never dictated entirely by the question or hypothesis (and anyway, that too bears his own particular stamp). One has only to consider how differently several of his colleagues would go about testing the same hypothesis to see that personal choice enters in here.

But this is just the beginning. Having decided what is to be observed, and having set up the techniques for observing, the scientist comes to the point of making the actual observations, and of recording these observations. All the complex apparatus of modern science is only a means of extending the range of man's sensory and perceptual capacities, and all the information derived through such extensions must eventually be reduced to some form in which man, with his biological limitations, can receive it. Here, too, in spite of all precautions and in spite of complete honesty, the personal factor enters in. The records of two observers will not dovetail exactly, even when they read figures from a dial. Errors may creep in, and the direction of the error is more likely than not to be associated with the observer's interest in how the findings come out. Perhaps the clearest evidence on this point comes from research on extrasensory perception. A scientist who is deeply committed to a hypothesis is well advised to have a neutral observer if the import of an observation is immediately apparent. Often, of course, such errors are minor, but they can be important, not only to the immediate problem but to society. I have wondered to what extent the disparity in figures on radioactive fallout may reflect such factors. Very few scientists, including psychologists, who have demonstrated selective perception as a laboratory excerise, take account of the phenomenon in their own work.

Once the observations are recorded, other questions are asked: When is the evidence sufficient to be conclusive, one way or the other? How important are discrepancies? What degree of generalization is permissible? Here, again, we may expect personally slanted answers. Taxonomy offers a very clear illustration of the effect of personality: One biologist may classify a given set of specimens into a few species, and another may classify them into many species. Whether the specimens are seen as representing a few or many groups depends largely on whether one looks for similarities or for differences, on whether one looks at the forest or the trees. A "lumper" may honestly find it impossible to understand how a "splitter" arrives at such an obviously incorrect solution, and vice versa. Such differences cannot be resolved by appeal to the "facts"—there are no facts which cannot be perceived in different ways. This is not to say that the facts are necessarily distorted. The problem of the criterion exists in all science, although some scientists are more aware of it than others.

The matter of personal commitment to a hypothesis is one that deserves more consideration than it usually receives. Any man who has gone through the emotional process of developing a new idea, of constructing a new hypothesis, is to some extent, and usually to a large extent, committed to that hypothesis in a very real sense. It is his baby. It is as much his creation as a painting is the personal creation of the painter. True, in the long run it stands or falls, is accepted or rejected, on its own merits, but its creator has a personal stake in it. The scientist has more at stake than the artist, for data which may support or invalidate his hypothesis are in the public domain in a sense in which art criticism never is. It may even be because of this that scientists customarily check their hypotheses as far as they can before they state them publicly. And, indeed, the experienced scientist continues to check, hoping that if errors are to be found, it will be he who finds them, so that he will have a chance to make revisions, or even to discard the hypothesis, should that prove necessary. He finds it less difficult to discard his hypothesis if, in his efforts at checking, he has been able to come up with another one.

The extent of personal commitment to a hypothesis is a prominent factor in the historical interplay between scientists. The degree of this commitment varies in an individual with different hypotheses, and varies between individuals. One very important factor here is the scientist's productivity. If he has many new ideas he will be less disturbed (and less defensive) if one fails to pan out. If he has very few ideas, an error is much harder to take, and there are many historical instances of errors which the author of the idea has never been able to see himself. I think many scientists are genuinely unaware of the extent, or even of the fact, of this personal involvement, and themselves accept the myth of impersonal objectivity. This is really very unfortunate. It is true that only a man who is passionately involved in his work is likely to make important contributions, but the committed man who knows he is committed and come to terms with this fact has a good chance of getting beyond his commitment and of learning how to disassociate himself from his idea when this is necessary. There is little in the traditional education of scientists to prepare them for this necessity, and there are many who are still unaware of it. The extent of a scientist's personal involvement in a theory can now be a matter of grave public concern. Scientists who become advisers on political or other policy have an extraordinarily heavy responsibility for achieving some detachment from their own theories. How many of them realize this?

But once one hypothesis is found acceptable, this is not the end of it. One hypothesis inevitably leads to another; answering one question makes it possible to ask other, hopefully more precise ones. And so a new hypothesis or a new theory is offered. How is this new theory arrived at? This is one expression of the creative process, and it is a completely personal process. It is personal regardless of whether one or more indivduals is involved, for in every advance made by a group, the person contributing at the moment has had to assimilate the contributions of the others and order them in his own personal way.

The Creative Process

There have been many millions of words written about the creative process, few of them very illuminating. The reason is not hard to find. The process is intimate and personal and characteristically takes place not at the level of full consciouness but at subconscious or preconscious levels. It has been inaccessible to study largely because we have not yet found any means for controlling it. Many effective scientists and artists have learned a few techniques which may reduce interference with it, but no one to my knowledge has discovered any means by which he can set it in motion at will.

It is probable that the fundamentals of the creative process are the same in all fields, but in those fields in which an advance in knowledge is sought, there is an additional requirement—or rather, one requirement receives particular emphasis. This is the need for a large store of knowledge and experience. The broader the scientist's experience and the more extensive his stock of knowledge, the greater the possibility of a real breakthrough.

The creative process involves a scanning or searching through stocks of stored memories. There seems to be a rather sharp limit to the possibility of very significant advance through voluntary, logical scanning of these stores. For one thing, they vary enormously in their accessibility to conscious recall and in the specificity of their connections, so that reliance upon conscious, orderly, logical thinking is not likely to produce many results at this stage, however essential such procedures become later in verification. This scanning is typically for patterns and complex associations rather than for isolated units. It may be, however, that a small unit acts as a sort of key to a pattern. What seems to happen, in creative efforts in science as well in every other field, is that the individual enters a state in which logical thinking is submerged and in which thought is prelogical. Such thought is described as random largely because it typically tries seemingly illogical and distantly related materials, and it often makes major advances in just this way. It is not fully random, however, because it is goal-directed and because even in this preconscious work there is appropriate selection and rejection of available connections. This stage of the creative process is accompanied by generally confused or vague states of preoccupation of varying degrees of depth; it is well described as "stewing." It is this stage which apparently cannot be hurried or controlled.

Although termination of this stage (finding a solution, or "getting insight," as it is often called) quite frequently occurs in a moment of dispersed attention, it apparently does not help to induce a state of dispersed attention in the hope of provoking a quicker end to the process. It should be added that, while insights do frequently occur "in a flash," they need not do so, and that the process is the same whether or not the insight turns out to have validity.

To acquire the necessary store of knowledge requires long and difficult application, and as science advances, the amount of information to be assimilated becomes greater and greater, despite increasing generalization in the organizing of the data. Obviously, as more experience is stored and as the interconnections become better established and more numerous, the scanning becomes more effective.

Such interconnections develop more and more readily as the process of acquiring experience takes on significance in the light of theory. This process requires not only the basic capacity to assimilate experiences but very strong motivation to persist in the effort. Strong motivation is also required if one is to continue with a search which may for a long time be unproductive. Motivation of this kind and strength derives from the needs and structure of the personality. Its sources are rarely obvious, although they can sometimes be traced. They do not necessarily derive from "neurotic problems," although they frequently do. It is no cause for dismay when they do. The ability of the human being to find in a personal problem motivation for a search for truth is one of the major accomplishments of the species.

If past experiences have brought about a compartmentalization of the storage areas, so that some portions are partially or wholly inaccessible, obviously the scientist is limited in his search. Compartmentalization of particular areas may result from personal experiences of a sort that lead to neurotic structures generally, or it may result from specific cultural restrictions, such as political or religious indoctrination. The extent to which such indoctrination will inhibit creative effort, however, depends upon how close the inaccessible areas are in content to the problems at issue. We have fairly conclusive evidence that political indoctrination need not interfere with inquiry into mathematical and physical science. Religious indoctrination can interfere strongly at any point, as history has documented very fully for us. The conclusion is no different from the basic principle of therapy: the more areas of experience there are accessible to conscious and preconscious thought, the better are the prospects for creativity.

Once an apparent answer to the scientist's question has been found, there is still a long process of pursuing and checking to be gone through. Not every man who can produce new ideas is also good at the business of checking them, and of course the reverse is also true. It is in the utilization of such personal differences as these that a "team approach" can make sense.

The Creative Scientist

This, then, is a brief review of what little we know of the process of creation. What do we know of the characteristics of scientists who can use this process effectively? Many lines of inquiry have demonstrated that the range of characteristics that are associated with creative productivity in a human being is very wide. These characteristics fall into almost all categories into which personal traits have been divided for purpose of study—abilities, interests, drives, temperament, and so on.

To limit our discussion to scientific productivity, it is clear to start with that there are great variations in the amount of curiosity possessed by different people. Curiosity appears to be a basic drive. I suspect it may vary consistently with sex, on either a biological or a cultural basis, but we have as yet no idea how to measure such drives. No one becomes a scientist without a better-than-average amount of curiosity, regardless of whether he was born with it, was brought up in a stimulating environment, or just did not have it severely inhibited.

Intelligence and creativity are not identical, but intelligence does play a role in scientific creativity—rather more than it may play in some other forms of creativity. In general, one may summarize by saying that the minimum intelligence required for creative production in science is considerably better than average, but that, given this, other variables contribute more to variance in performance. It must also be noted that special abilities (numerical, spatial, verbal, and so on) play somewhat different roles in different scientific fields, but that ability must in no case be below average. A cultural anthropologist, for example, has little need for great facility with numbers. An experimetal physicist, on the other hand, does require facility with numbers, although he need not have great facility with words.

Personality Patterns

A number of studies have contributed to the picture of the personality patterns of productive scientists, and it is rather striking that quite different kinds of investigations have produced closely similar results. These can be briefly summarized in six different groups, as follows:

1. Truly creative scientists seek experience and action and are independent and self-sufficient with regard to perception, cognition, and behavior. These findings have been expressed in various studies in such terms as the following: they are more observant than others and value this quality; they are more independent with respect to cognition and value judgments; they have high dominance; they have high autonomy; they are Bohemian or radical; they are not subject to group standards and control; they are highly egocentric.

2. They have a preference for apparent but resolvable disorder and for an aesthetic ordering of forms of experience. They have high tolerance for ambiguity, but they also like to put an end to it in their own way—and in their own time.

3. They have strong egos (whether this derives from or is responsible for their independence and their tolerance for ambiguity is a moot question). This ego strength permits them to regress to preconscious states with certainty that they will return from these states. They have less compulsive superegos than others. They are capable of disciplined management of means leading to significant experience. They have no feeling of guilt about the independence of thought and action mentioned above. They have strong control of their impulses.

4. Their interpersonal relations are generally of low intensity. They are reported to be ungregarious, not talkative (this does not apply to social scientists), and rather asocial. There is an apparent tendency to femininity in highly original men, and to masculinity in highly original women, but this may be a cultural interpretation of the generally increased sensitivity of the men and the intellectual capacity and interests of the women. They dislike interpersonal controversy in any form and are especially sensitive to interpersonal aggression.

5. They show much stronger preoccupation with things and ideas than with people. They dislike introversive and affect-associated preoccupations, except in connection with their own research.

6. They like to take the calculated risk, but it must involve nature, not people, and must not depend on simple luck.

Conclusions

How do these personality characteristics relate to the creative process in science as I have discussed it? An open attitude toward experience makes possible accumulation of experience with relatively little compartmentalization; independence of perception, cognition, and behavior permit greater than average reordering of this accumulated experience (the behavioral eccentricities so often noted are consistent with this). The strong liking for turning disorder into order carries such individuals through the searching period which their tolerance for ambiguity permits them to enter. The strong egos, as noted, permit regression to prelogical forms of thought without serious fear of failure to get back to logical ones. Preoccupation with things and ideas rather than with people is obviously characteristic of natural scientists, and even of some social scientists. This characteristic is not directly related to creativity, I think, but rather to the content of it.

I need not add that such statements as these are generalizations and that any individual case may be an exception. We may go farther, however, and generalize differences among men who follow different branches of science. That a man chooses to become a scientist and succeeds means that he has the temperament and personality as well as the ability and opportunity to do so. The branch of science he chooses, even the specific problems he chooses and the way he works on them, are intimately related to what he is and to his deepest needs. The more deeply engaged he is, the more profoundly is this true. To understand what he does, one must try to know what his work means to him. The chances are that he does not know or care to know. Indeed, he does not need to know. We do.*

REFERENCES

Kubie, L. 1956. Some unsolved problems of the scientific career. *The American Scientist,* vol. XLI, no. 4, and vol. XLII, no. 1:3–32.

Maslow, A. H. 1966. *The Psychology of Science.* New York: Harper & Row.

McClelland, D. 1964. The psychodynamics of creative physical scientists, in his *The Roots of Consciousness.* New York: Van Nostrand.

Roe, A. 1953. A psychological study of eminent psychologists and anthropologists, and a comparison with biological and physical scientists. *Psychological Monographs,* 67, no. 2.

————. 1953. *The Making of a Scientist.* New York: Dodd, Mead.

Taylor, C. and F. Barron, eds. 1963. *Scientific Creativity.* New York: Wiley and Sons.

Taylor, C., ed. 1972. *Climate for Creativity.* New York: Pergamon.

* The conclusion reached by Dr. Roe in this essay is based mainly upon her studies of physical scientists. She has reminded us here and elsewhere (Roe, 1953) that "in many ways the social scientist differs from the natural scientist in terms of personality and motivation." It has been found, for example, that social scientists are more interested in interpersonal relationships, while physical are less so.

The apparent "coldness, remoteness and objectivity" of the physical scientists, however, might be related to the commonly accepted notion of science as a purely impersonal thing. If so, it would be interesting to speculate what possible effects a "humanization of science" (Maslow, 1966) might have upon the personality dynamics of future scientists. [Ed.]

20

A Humanistic Psychologist in the Classroom*

HUNG-MIN CHIANG

In Memory of Abraham H. Maslow (1908-1970)

In the fall of 1963, I was given an unusual opportunity to assist Abraham H. Maslow with one of his educational ventures. I was asked if I would be interested in helping him with a course he was planning to offer at Brandeis University that year, Experiential Approaches to the Study of Personality. As I understood it, he was highly dissatisfied with many of the goals and methods of traditional education and was actively in search of some alternatives. I was told that the course was to be a sort of pilot study in an uncharted waterway. Maslow was eager to have its value assessed as impartially as possible.

We both felt that the best strategy for evaluating the course would be to tape record each class session so that the proceedings could be retrieved and assessed at a later date. With the consent of the other participants in the class, we recorded the weekly sessions, and the tapes were later transcribed verbatim. An early, brief report of the course has been published elsewhere (Chiang, 1968), and a comprehensive report on the subject is still in preparation. This essay is an introduction to the more extensive report yet to come and provides background information, including Maslow's basic educational philosophy.

It is widely acknowledged that Maslow, as the chief architect of Humanistic Psychology and a longtime spokesman for that approach, had a considerable impact on the theory and practice of humanistic education. But beyond generalities, what did Maslow have to say on certain key issues in education, and the teaching of psychology in particular? And how did he approach the practical problems of teaching in an actual classroom situation? In spite of his image as a banner-

*In writing this paper I am indebted to Mary Beth Horgan for many helpful suggestions.

225

bearer of a new movement in psychology and his reputation as an inspiring psychologist, surprisingly little is known about Maslow as a teacher. His voluminous writings certainly contain a wealth of stimulating ideas for any educator with a humanistic bent. But again the question is, how would Maslow himself apply those ideas in the classroom? This paper is an attempt to provide some clues to these questions.

In many ways 1963—the year the course at Brandeis was first offered—marked the start of a pivotal period for Maslow. He had just put together his notes on social psychology, which were to be published under the title of *Eupsychian Management* (1965). He was also working on the manuscript of *Religions, Values and Peak-Experiences* (1964), from which he drew a substantial amount of material for the course. The previous year had seen the publication and wide acceptance of his *Toward a Psychology of Being* (1962), which, along with his earlier work, *Motivation and Personality* (1954), was rapidly becoming a rallying ground for a growing number of humanistic psychologists. The Association of Humanistic Psychology, a brainchild of Maslow, was formed in 1963 and held its first meeting, in Philadelphia, in August of that year. The winds of change were blowing everywhere, and Maslow, the visionary, had good reason to be enthusiastic about his new educational project at that particular time.

One remarkable sign of the "humanistic revolution" that Maslow helped to spark was the mushrooming of so-called growth centers. The most famous of these was the Esalen Institute, which began operation on the rocky coast of California in 1962. The goal of the Esalen program was the integration of humanistic psychology and various forms of Eastern thought, including Zen Buddhism and yoga. At Esalen, Maslow was regarded as the father of the humanistic revolution, and many of his ideas concerning education were incorporated in the Institute's boldly experimental program. Maslow himself, considered a maverick in his home ground at Brandeis, went out of his way to praise Esalen as *potentially* the most interesting educational institution in the world.

In certain ways, the Esalen Institute came quite close to Maslow's ideal of intrinsic education. Discussing humanistic education, he wrote, "In the ideal college there would be no credits, no degrees, and no required courses. . . . The college would be ubiquitous—that is, not restricted to particular buildings at particular times, and the teachers would be any human beings who had something that they wanted to share with others." Such a college would be a kind of educational retreat where people could go to find their own identity. To Maslow, finding one's identity meant:

> . . . finding out what your real desires and characteristics are, and being able to live in a way that expresses them. You learn to be authentic, to be honest in the sense of allowing your behavior and your speech to be the true and spontaneous expression of your inner feelings.*

That degree of self-discovery is an ideal, however. The goal Maslow set for his experimental course at Brandeis in 1963 was quite modest compared to Esalen's aims. Esalen enjoyed the freedom of an independent institution, but Maslow had to contend with the structural constraints imposed by a typical university such as Brandeis. Being realistic as well as idealistic, he simply wanted to explore possible avenues for effectively teaching experiential skills in a college setting. The course description he supplied for the Brandeis calendar reads:

> A survey of efforts at self-analysis, self-therapy and self-growth. Dreams and symbol psychology; peak, mystic and psychedelic experience; archaic and prerational cognition. Recovery of the preconscious.

Officially, enrollment in the course was limited to twenty students, but it was a rule that was not strictly observed. In 1963 there were twenty-four registered for the course, and it soon became obvious that the class was too large. At one point Maslow became keenly aware of this and remarked: "It seems quite clear to me now, we're too big a group for the effort that we are making." But no real attempt was made to reduce the size of class, then or later. In 1966, for instance, there were thirty-eight participants in the class, far too many for any meaningful group interaction.

Maslow's apparent reluctance to hold the class size down reflected to a large degree his uncertainty about an optimal size for it. Nor was he quite sure of the direction or the structure of the course at that stage. It should be noted, too, that he had the course listed not as a workshop or a group therapy, but as a survey course. It was simply announced, with no promises or fanfare, as a study of methods and means of personal growth. From the very beginning, the class members were told of the nature of the course: "This is not an experimental research designed in advance on purpose. This is a sort of groping exploration into the unknown, and we don't know where we're go-

*Maslow, 1971, p. 183.

ing.'' Then he continued, ''But I would like you to think of yourselves as not so much students who are beholden to a professor, but rather as collaborators in an enterprise in which we all want to learn as much as we can so that we can pass this on to other people.''

In choosing a model for the course, Maslow had several options. He could have chosen a group model and patterned the course after the sensitivity training group (T-group), or he could have chosen a psychoanalytic model, stressing the depth dimension of personality. He weighed the pros and cons of each, and in the end he rejected both, for practical reasons.

In the summer of 1962, Maslow had visited Lake Arrowhead, California, where he observed a T-group in action for the first time. He recorded his impressions in his journal: ''My first impression in the first group that I sat in on was one of real shock and amazement. These people behaved and talked in a spontaneous and free way that I have ordinarily associated with psychoanalyzed people, that is, with people who have been under psychoanalysis for a year or two at least.''*

Maslow correctly saw the far-reaching implications of the T-group for the psychology of personal growth, and yet when he returned to Brandeis he seemed to have a number of doubts about the applicability of T-group techniques in the classroom. He felt that the long and intensive group interaction necessary for a successful T-group would hardly be feasible because of the college's regimented schedule. Also, the anonymity called for in T-groups is practically impossible to maintain in a small college community. And Maslow was concerned about the ethical question that would arise if T-groups were introduced as part of the curriculum: Should students attend such group sessions if they are less than willing? He feared that a poorly conducted group session might drive the individual against a wall, with no possibility of graceful retreat.

There were certainly many ways of overcoming some of these difficulties, and experience has shown that a nonstructured approach can be used successfully in teaching.† But there were two obstacles confronting Maslow, and one of them was the incompatibility of the roles of teacher and T-group leader. An ideal leader is accepting and nonjudgmental, whereas a teacher is necessarily evaluative and judgmental. Maslow could see no easy way to resolve the contradiction.

*Maslow, 1965, p. 157.
†See, for instance, the articles in this volume by Tenenbaum and Rogers (pp. 174–88), and by Smith (pp. 153–63).

The other stumbling block for Maslow in leading a T-group *in the classroom* was his very ability to toy with words and concepts. This ability made him a good lecturer, but in leading a T-group it was more a liability than an asset. Maslow was fully aware of this shortcoming and warned his students about it: "I'm an intellectual and you have to tone me down sometimes or the words will run away with me." However, Maslow's awareness of the problem did not always mean that he could control it. Upon the insistence of some students, a nonstructured approach was tried out in some sessions, without desired results. Everyone soon realized that Maslow simply could not remain silent in the company of students. The following exchange that occured in one of the nonstructured sessions is self-explantory. One exasperated male student told Maslow:

> *Student:* You start a question which is always directed in your own terms and . . . as far as I can tell, with no consideration of the feeling of the day, place, time, what's happening, and then when there is silence you begin talking and you keep talking.
>
> *Maslow:* Yeah, I've been told that by practically everybody.
>
> *Student:* I'm very annoyed at this, I can't stand it and I wish you wouldn't do it.
>
> *Maslow:* You speak for many.

There is no question that Maslow firmly believed in the potential benefits of the T-group. As he wrote, "the T-group is an effort to make you aware of who you really are, of how you really react to other people, by giving you a chance to be honest, to tell what is really going on inside of you instead of presenting facades or giving polite evasions."* He even made a valid comparison with psychoanalysis, saying, "there are some kinds of things that can happen in these T-groups that can *never* happen in individual psychoanalysis, no matter how long it takes. There are certain kinds of feedback we can get from other people that we simply cannot get from just one person."†

In spite of such insights, Maslow's own attitude toward the T-group can at best be described as noncommittal. He would point out the benefits of a T-group, but at the same time he would tell the students that the course was not a form of group therapy, nor was group spontaneity the goal. He would rather recommend a voluntary

*Maslow, 1971, p. 183.
†Maslow, 1965, p. 159.

T-group run by someone other than himself outside of the scheduled class hour. It is very likely that Maslow's knowledge of the T-group at that time was basically that of an observer rather than a participant since there was no indication in his writings that he was personally affected by the experience. Nor was there any hint that he appreciated the intense joy known only to the participants themselves.

Maslow's assessment of psychoanalysis, in contrast, was solidly based on his own personal experience. Earlier, he had received training as a psychoanalyst and had gone through analysis with Karen Horney. His appreciation of the experience was genuine and totally affirmative. His basic position was that psychoanalysis is the best proven tool for exploration of the self yet discovered by man. As late as 1968 he still could reflect on his personal psychoanalysis as the experience most valuable to his process of self-discovery. Said he: "Another profound learning experience that I value more highly than any particular course or any degree that I have ever had was my personal psychoanalysis: discovering my own identity, my own self."*

This is not to say that Maslow was taken up with psychoanalysis and tried it in the classroom without necessary modifications. Maslow regarded himself as an "epi-Freudian" and was fully aware of the limitations of the psychoanalytic model in education as well as in therapy. As he saw it, psychoanalysis is essentially an individual therapy and cannot be done on a large scale. Furthermore, the recovery of the id, which is perhaps justifiable in the consulting room, may not be so desirable in the classroom. Explaining that his course was not meant to be psychotherapy, Maslow cautioned the students: "What we must avoid doing in our class are the characteristics of a depth therapy. Ours is not a regression therapy, not built on transference analysis, placing no stress on dream interpretation, and there will be no speaking about our personal sex life." He was very cautious about any potential dangers and advised the participants not to push themselves to the edge of embarassment in front of the group.

What then was the goal of the course? If it was not a course in individual or group therapy, what was it? In this scheme, the main emphasis was on the recovery of experiences—in particular, the recovery of feelings, emotions, subtle impulses and inner voices. They are believed to be the essential part of human nature and yet are so easily forgotten, denied or suppressed in the course of socialization. To be experientially alive means to renew a contact with our essential nature,

*Maslow, 1971, p. 170.

and the first step in that direction is "to pay greater attention to the concrete, pre-abstract, preverbal and the unconscious." Here Maslow could have said "preconscious" instead of "unconscious," for he did distinguish between two aspects of the unconscious and the one he was primarily interested in is generally known as the preconscious.* The unconscious is said to be the seat of drives and needs—especially irrational needs—whereas the preconscious has more to do with the way of sensing (i.e., primary process cognition).

Psychoanalysis was Maslow's starting point, and though he continued using some Freudian terminology throughout that year, the main thrust of his thinking was unmistakably humanistic. He spoke of impulses, needs and sexual urges, but he postulated that the inner nature of man is neither good nor bad but is "prior to good and evil." A good psychotherapy was seen by him as an "uncovering therapy," a discovery or rediscovery of the intrinsic growth tendency in every person.

To aid the recovery of the experiences, all kinds of experiential exercises were given and the students were asked to try them out. Included in the list were exercises in sensory awareness; here-and-now, innocent perception; synesthesia; physiognomic perception; B-humor; and the unitive consciousness. Most of the exercises were either an extension or direct application of the ideas contained in his books (mentioned earlier). Maslow left a personal memo in which he listed over two dozen "experiential techniques and experiments" he used over the years. Here are a few typical ones:†

> 1. Exercises in Suchness and concrete experiencing, use the *Sense of Wonder* by Rachael Carson. A good way of recounting the ability to perceive Suchness is to do as she did, to take a little boy or a little girl to go look at the seashore or spiderwebs or surf or trees or to look through magnifying glasses at leaves or snowflakes and the like. To help the child look means to help yourself look. Also the child's reactions to what you overlook or pay no attention to may help to pull you back to seeing the world and its Suchness as a child does.
> 2. Try not to label things or ask for names on a nature walk. Just look at each bird or tree or flower or leaf in itself, per se, as if you were seeing it for the first time, or as if no other such existed in the world. Don't try to classify it or label it or name it. It makes no difference whether it's common or not; the robin or the sparrow is just as much a

*See the article by Kubie in this volume (pp. 164–73).
†The memo was dated November 16, 1967, and is reproduced here through the courtesy of Mrs. Bertha Maslow.

miracle as the cardinal or the oriole. Try the same thing with dogs. Most people don't see dogness (although children do). They think in terms of pedigrees or lines or even clip their hair in particular ways which are not doglike but are dog-owner like. They fuss about "pure lines," and then of course you can tell that such a person doesn't really like dogs, but has acquired a property. The same thing is true of flowers. Make bouquets of meadow grasses or weeds and look at them as if they were quite rare. You will see them in a different way. In such looking also be sure that you push aside all questions of usefulness or uselessness, of good or bad, danger, etc.

3. Introduce Freud's concept of free-floating attention. Pair off students in the class, one to be a talker and one to be a listener, with the listener trying to acquire the ability for evenly distributed attention, or free-floating attention, non-concentrating attention, Taoistic attention, passive receptivity, non-active listening, etc.

4. It made a very good exercise to ask the students in a group to volunteer their peak-experiences. This generally touched off other people in the group. Also it tended to be progressively more intimate, i.e., starting from rather mild and not very intimate experiences, and going on to more poignant, more emotional, more shaking experiences being reported. The same can be done for desolation experiences*. . . .

5. I tried deliberately to help the students recover the awareness of anxiety, of sadness or depression, of anger in whatever ways I could think of through the whole semester. Alan Wheelis's book, *Illusionless Man,* in this book the peak-experience quality is missing; zest, joy in life, etc. He sees everything, he is very smart, he is fully aware, but he doesn't *feel.* What would you say to him? What can one say to a person who doesn't experience emotion, or pleasure, or joy? One can talk here about the general topic of joylessness, of the non-peaker, of emotional aridity.

6. With each such class there should be a voluntary T-group, run by someone else, I believe, rather than the teacher in charge. I lectured about feedback, about here and now, about sending out signals that could be heard, of checking back your hearing of the signals with the sender to see if you received it right, the becoming aware and conscious in the T-group situation of the actual feeling of anxiety in the face of silence, for instance, etc., etc. Of course this can be expanded a very great deal.

Within the span of some twelve weeks, a wide range of topics on

---

Desolation experience is Maslow's term for a painful experience that results not in despair but rather in a heightened sense of consciousness and insight into the meaning of existence. Maslow used the term as a parallel to *peak-experience*—both lead to the knowledge of Being (see Maslow, 1964, pp. 74–81).

personal growth were introduced. Some of these topics were Zen, mysticism, general semantics, phenomenology of love, human sexuality, masculinity-femininity, authenticity, Jungian archetypes, many Freudian concepts, dreams, peak-experiences, and self-actualization. Maslow also reported his personal observations, quotations from his notes and his latest thoughts on human values, all of which he was eager to pass on. Several scores of books, dozens of articles were mentioned. Some were discussed in the class, while others were recommended for future reading. Books specifically assigned for intensive study included *Self-Analysis* by Karen Horney and *The Forgotten Language* by Erich Fromm. There were tests and interviews, and the students were also asked to keep a personal journal.

The weekly three-hour session was divided into two periods: the first two hours were a seminar, during which the course materials were presented and discussed intellectually; the remaining hour was reserved for an experiential workshop (or "Lab in Self-Knowledge," as it was called), during which the focus was on experiential reports and exercises. It must be pointed out, however, that in the 1963–64 course the distinction between the two periods was neither clear nor scrupulously observed. As a result, a substantial portion of the class hours were taken by discussions interspersed with experiential exercises.

The lectures by Maslow were often as stimulating as his writings—perhaps even more so. He spoke with the obvious pleasure and conviction of a man who had devoted his whole life to searching for truth. He loved to experiment with new ideas and learned as much from the one that didn't work as from the one that did. He even mused at his own verbosity by saying: "I'm tossing out all sorts of seeds all over the place . . . like an old-fashioned sower with wheat grains in every direction. I don't know which word comes out and the only way I can ever find out is for you to tell me." He was definitely an intellectual—a great one. But he was also quite candid with regard to his own inner world. He talked freely about his feelings, personal experiences, and, on a few occasions, offered interpretations of his own dreams.

If there is one thing that truly distinguished Maslow's course from many other similar ventures, it was its holistic orientation. The course was experientially oriented, but was unique in its two-pronged approach to personal growth. Instead of repudiating the words and concepts as the enemies of experience—as others often advised—Maslow attempted to view both experience and abstraction in a proper perspective. To be more precise, he wanted to know if the intellect could be used to facilitate or sharpen the experiential awareness. This basic position that Maslow held was far from popular among his contemporaries. Many traditionally oriented psychologists, who live in the world of numbers and constructs, would certainly frown at the experiential approach and its implications for psychology. At the other extreme, those psychologists in the vanguard of the human potential movement (such as Fritz Perls) have gone to the point of treating the intellect with suspicion and disdain.

There is an amusing story of D. T. Suzuki, a renowned Zen scholar, giving a seminar at the invitation of the Psychology Department at Brandeis when Maslow was the chairman. The story has it that no sooner had the seminar begun then a spirited discussion erupted among the participants and, amid all the intellectual excitement, the guest speaker dozed off. Suzuki was almost ninety-years of age at that time, but the incident may well be seen as his gentle, nonverbal way of making a poignant point of Zen. Not so graceful was Perls in a well-known incident at Esalen that also involved Maslow. Maslow was giving a seminar, but right in the middle of the proceedings Perls began to crawl around on his belly, totally disrupting the seminar with his "zany" acts. This might have been Perls' way of dramatizing his boredom, but he certainly failed to see the larger issue that Maslow was deeply concerned with.

The issue at stake, which has important ramifications for education at large, concerns the relationship between the two modes of knowing: experiential knowing and abstract knowing. Are the two modes mutually exclusive, or are they complementary? Can words and concepts be used in such a way as to induce or enhance our human experiential awareness? Maslow firmly believed that they could. The only question for him was, How? Maslow pointed out that human cognitive needs (which include both modes of knowing) are too important to be ignored and therefore must be fully attended to. His view, also shared by general semanticists, was that one can use language or any other form of abstraction so long as the user is fully aware of the level of abstraction he is at. Then, by freely shifting the mental gear from one mode of knowing to the other, or alternating between the experiential and the abstract as the occasion may call for, the person might make his own life much richer.

It has often been said that a map is not a territory and a label (words and concepts) must not be confused with the reality it stands for. But if we can use the map in the exploration of an external environment, why cannot we use words and concepts for the discovery of inner space? Far from shying away from words, Maslow tried to make the best of them. Maslow hoped that by exposing the students to the experiential reports of others, they might strike responsive chords within. He often read an example or two from his large collection of peak-experiences, making comments as he went along, and then encouraged personal responses from the class. As Maslow's memo indicates, he found it a very effective way to elicit a response from the audience, (see Chapter 22 in this volume for example).

A similar technique was applied to the "unitive conciousness," which was discussed at great length toward the end of the semester. *Unitive consciousness* is defined as the transcendence of basic polarities (such as "good and evil," "sacred and profane") and is said to be a distinguishing characteristic of mystics and self-actualizing people. Again, Maslow wanted to discover whether the basic skills involved in higher forms of cognition such as unitive consciousness can be taught and developed through a combination of lectures, examples and exercises.

Maslow called his approach to experiential education a *cognitive therapy* because of the emphasis he placed on cognition (in a broad sense) as a way to greater experiential awareness. It was called a "therapy" only for lack of a better term. Maslow stressed the fact that his approach was developed not for the sick but for the normal—in particular, normal college students. It is a therapy only in the sense that it is purported to bring about a change in a person's outlook on life. A natural question is, does it work? Is it a successful alternative to a traditional method (such as meditation) that requires a long and arduous effort?

In discussing the results of the course, one can think in terms of a long-term effect as well as a short-term effect. The immediate feedback from the students was quite mixed. Some students, who had anticipated a T-group situation in the course, were rather disappointed. One student wrote in his journal the following impressions when the course was half over:

> The first hour everyone had to contribute, there was a great deal of comradeship felt, frankness was displayed. It was as if we were excited travellers about to explore ourselves together. The prospect of this new exciting, perhaps terrifying business set us all aflame. Since that day, the class has been flat. The original excitement and venturousness had been lost. Now the talkers talk, the listeners listen, and the class is normal.

It nicely sums up the happenings in the couse, but only partially. It needs to be pointed out that the above entry was made at the low point in the course, and a number of meaningful things did not happen later on. There were numerous situations that involved the whole group in a meaningful way. One of them was an exercise on what Maslow has called "rhapsodic communication." A rhapsodice communication is a non-structured communication that makes use of metaphors, figures of speech, analogy, and poetic expression. In this type of communication, primary process cognition, rather than secondary process cognition, plays a leading role and the words used tend to be more connotative than denotative. Rhapsodic communication is particularly suited for the expression of feelings, and Maslow attached great importance to its cultivation.

The rhapsodic communication workshop reported on in the next chapter of this volume was undoubtedly one of the most interesting sessions of the year. There are perhaps many ways to facilitate rhapsodic communication, but in this particular instance visual materials were employed. The exercise engaged the whole class in a spirit of adventure, which is a rare achievement in a class of that size. Best of all, it offered a group approach to self-knowledge, with all the participants joining in what might be called a shared journey into the twilight zone of self. The occasion also showed Maslow in his most introspective moments, expressing his hopes and self-doubts, convictions and dilemmas. In the class, where the ultimate goal was self-knowledge, such an experience was almost an education in itself.

When the course came to an end, if only too soon, there was a general feeling among the participants that many of the materials presented could only be assimilated over a period of years, or perhaps even decades. And this was what Maslow apparently had in mind when he planned the course: education for life. There is also some evidence that the materials learned and the insights gained in such a course are not likely to dissipate easily, since participation in the course involves a change in attitudes, beliefs, values, and even a radical change in the fundamental outlook on life. To some, at least, the course became a major turning point in their lives. The following samples of feedback solicited from the participants three months after the course ended indicate the direction of that change, and these samples are by no means atypical. One student wrote of her experience:

> I enjoyed this course very much. Every class session left me with a sense of exhilaration and renewed zest for life. This course has been a major force in determining the direction I will take for a future career.

Another student also wrote of a change in personal outlook:

> It is hard to say what I learned which I value most, because so much has been assimilated in bits and pieces, all unorganized. . . . It was not any specific theory; I think I learned an *attitude,* a way of treating life. . . . My attitudes have changed much in many ways. I allow myself to be myself, and others to be themselves in many ways that I did not before.

Maslow had suggested to the students that they keep in touch with him even after graduation, and I believe many did. They were to tell Maslow how the course may have affected their lives and how they would appraise the course in retrospect. According to our original plan, this kind of participant feedback would be an important part of the follow-up study. Unfortunately, the plan was never carried out, due to the sudden death of Maslow in California in June 1970.

Although the present essay is mainly concerned with Maslow's 1963 pilot course, it may be necessary to mention one discordant note I noticed in the closing chapter of Maslow's teaching career. There are some indications that Maslow was greatly disappointed in the student reactions to some of the courses he taught in the late 1960s. In one unusually self-critical paper (Maslow, 1970), he recalled how discouraged or even angry he became during one of the courses he taught in 1968. He was exasperated because he believed he had failed to instill in the students the love of knowledge and the sense of social responsibility he himself felt so deeply. Other teachers might have shrugged their shoulders and carried on teaching, as if nothing had ever happened, but to Maslow the issue was too important to ignore. He began to question the wisdom of his remaining in the teaching profession.

In the same article mentioned above, Maslow also raised many questions he had been asking himself. While he reaffirmed his basic belief in the value of humanistic education, he wondered how it could fit in with college education. He cast a doubt on the efficiency of a nonstructured approach in dealing with content-oriented subjects, asking if these subjects might not be better taught by a traditional method. He recognized in the students a profound desire for intimacy and community feeling, and yet he asked if the college was the proper place to fulfill such basic needs as love and acceptance.

As a polemic, he even proposed to draw a distinction between what he has called "professional" education and "humanistic" education. The former is more content-oriented, factual learning, while the latter deals with the problems of personal growth, identity, and values. Professional education consists of extrinsic learning, whereas humanistic education is devoted to intrinsic learning. He further proposed that early education might be devoted to humanistic education so that college years can be spent on professional training. This suggestion of his cannot be taken as a definitive statement, however. Not only is it incongruent with the basic tenet of his theory, but also it observes the importance he assigned to experiential and motivational aspects of learning. The idea might, furthermore, accentuate the current artificial separation between the cognitive and the affective, the extrinsic and the intrinsic, which Maslow in the main wanted to eradicate.

The most definitive statement of the goals and implications Maslow attributed to humanistic education can be found in his posthumous work, *The Farther Reaches of Human Nature* (1971). In that work, Maslow envisions humanistic education as ecompassing the whole life span, a process that commences at birth and continues throughout life. Similarly, experiential learning, as an integral part of humanistic education, need not be limited to childhood only. He also suggested that education must refocus itself on the joy of personal discovery, the sense of awe and mystery in learning. The process of learning can then become as meaningful and exhilarating as those moments when we are having peak-experiences.

One of Maslow's long-cherished dreams as a psychologist had always been to immerse himself in research and writing—full-time, if possible. The wish had been latent all those years, but as he began to experience growing frustrations in teaching, his desire to follow his true inclination became irresistible. Especially after his first heart attack in 1967, he felt time was running out, and when in 1969 the Laughlin Foundation offered him a four-year grant to do exactly what he wanted to do, he promptly accepted.

By all accounts, Maslow's final year in California was one of the happiest in his entire life. Relieved now of the burdens of teaching and other academic routines, he was able to devote all his time and energy to theoretical research and writing, activities that he came to regard as his "calling." He was full of hope and zest for his work and he seemed as encouraged as ever about the future of mankind. True, he was saddened by ignorance, hostility and violence which plagued the society, but this experience only seemed to intensify his already strong determination to work out a comprehensive theory of human nature. In the spring of 1970 he wrote and urged me to join him at the Foundation, while informing me of his plans to work out a "big systematic theory of human nature and of society." It was planned as a very large expansion of the last chapter of *Toward a Psychology of Being,* titled "Some Basic Propositions of Growth and Self-actualizing Psychology."

Could a teacher like Maslow who has taught all his life give up his profession which is almost his mission? Definitely not. Even though he left his university post, Maslow's mission was still to be a teacher, and he carried on his teaching in a new form, reaching new heights. His pupils were no longer limited to those who were within the confines of the academic institution; anybody who was willing to listen and share his joy of discovery could become his pupil. He regarded his work and writings as a continuous communication and the whole world as his classroom. As he once wrote:

> Sometimes I get the feeling of my writing being a communication to my great-great grandchildren who, of course, are not yet born. It's a kind of an expression of love for them, leaving them not money but in effect affectionate notes, bits of counsel, lessons I have learned that might help them.*

REFERENCES

Chiang, H. M. 1968. An experiment in experiential approaches to personality. *Psychologia,* 11: 33–39.

Maslow, A. H. 1965. *Eupsychian Management.* Homewood, Illinois: Irwin-Dorsey.

——. 1971. *The Farther Reaches of Human Nature.* New York: Viking.

——. 1954. *Motivation and Personality.* New York: Harper Brothers.

——. 1970. Humanistic education vs. professional education: further comments. *New Directions in Teaching,* vol. 2, no. 2, Spring.

——. 1964. *Religions, Values and Peak-Experiences.* Columbus: Ohio State University Press.

——. 1962. *Toward a Psychology of Being.* New York: D. Van Nostrand.

*Editorial, *Psychology Today,* August 1970.

21

Laboratory in Self-Knowledge
A Verbatim Report of the
Workshop with Abraham H. Maslow

ABRAHAM H. MASLOW and HUNG-MIN CHIANG

Editor's Notes

The following transcript, a part of a larger, unpublished report, is a verbatim record of the Laboratory in Self-Knowledge conducted by Abraham H. Maslow. The laboratory was a part of the course, Experiential Approaches to the Study of Personality, and was recorded on tape on January 6, 1964. Participating in this particular session were some two dozen students, mostly juniors or seniors majoring in psychology. Because of a previous agreement on confidentiality, none of the participants (except Maslow) are identified in the transcript.

All the participants were seated around a large table in a dimly-lit room, ready to view the slides. The slides were made from seven "existential" cartoons by Saul Steinberg, each depicting an existential predicament of modern man. The aim of this exercise was free association rather than interpretation, and no general consensus on the meaning of the cartoons was intended. It was a workshop on rhapsodic communication, *i.e., communication in a spontaneous and metaphorical fashion.**

The workshop lasted one hour, ending 10 minutes past the normal class hour. Because of the insufficient time, a follow-up session was planned for the following week but was abandoned due to unfavorable weather. For background information, the reader is referred to the preceding chapter by Chiang.

---

*For a discussion of rhapsodic communication, see Appendix F in Maslow's *Religions, Values and Peak-Experiences* (Ohio State University Press, 1964).

240

Verbatim Transcript (January 6, 1963)

Maslow: I don't even know how to give you instructions, exactly. The vague thoughts that I've had run something like this: for one thing, I myself was very, very much impressed with Saul Steinberg's cartoons when I ran across them and I still am and I keep watching them. I think he's one of our great artists even in the classical sense. I've seen his sketches and drawings and so on. This simplicity of the line, the simplicity of the cartoons—don't take it too lightly. They condensed so very much that you couldn't put into words very easily.

I want to pass this *(Figure 1)* around; this should be interesting to you. I think I'll make a bookplate, a bookmark for myself, out of this one. I don't have a slide [so] I'll just leave it here *(on the table)* and you can look at it, because I think it expresses me very much. Somehow I identify with it.

Well, how much would I talk about it? I think if I wanted to talk about this I would have to go off on free-association really, metaphorical, figure-of-speech kind of talk; what I call in my own journal "rhapsodic" talk rather than just straight, logical, sensible talk. It seems very real and very clear, yet the explaining or describing would be quite difficult. I remember that I made these up to show one class a couple of years ago after I'd been trying to talk about existential psychology and existentialism and the existential predicament and things like that and had not succeeded very well. I didn't seem to get over somehow, and then I made these things up and said, "Well, look. That's what I'm trying to say; here it is."

Now, let's see what happens to you, if anything. Supposing I

Figure 1

asked you, "What do you think this means?" or "What is he trying to say?" Then we could talk about that. Some of you, I know, are just going to be too shy to talk about it, so then you write that for me, if you can't talk about it. But in view of the background that we've lectured on, I would like you to try to talk about it even if you look ridiculous. This is guaranteed to make you look ridiculous, to cause you to start stammering. There really aren't any good words. There's nobody who can say this well, including Steinberg. It's just ineffable, it's beyond words. Therefore, since we all start evenly, you might say we're all cripples in this respect.

I can't pass this around because it's falling apart. Supposing I put this here *(on the blackboard).* Could I ask you to take a look at this? *(Everyone goes to the front and takes a turn examining the picture, then returns).*

I choose this—it may be a little more meaningful to you, it may be a little more interesting—because this is the one that I identify with, that I want for my bookplate, that . . . It seems to be like the model of all my work. And it certainly expresses very nicely my own ambivalent feeling toward my work. I don't know if you've seen that, a certain sense of the ridiculousness of these efforts. Now the question is, What does it mean? Or, what does it say to you? Or, how do you feel about it? I've set you off, I've told you roughly how I feel about it. What does it do to you, if anything?

Student (male): I can well understand—at least I think I can— why this seems to represent you. Perhaps the best thing to do is to explain why I think it does. For one thing, there is a man charging into a whole lot of things which are pretty much unknown. You can see that there is something there, but you don't really know what you're jumping into. Yet they look interesting, they look worthy of fooling around with. On the other hand, on a symbolic level what we've been trying to do, in a sense, is to reduce all reality to very simple adjectives of sensation and so on. We've been trying to describe things in terms of, well, here it says, "Draw the smell of an onion."* And in a sense, this kind of symbolism of cubical shapes and roughness and smoothness and points and so on really is a symbolic way of experientially putting into a picture the way you might encounter any number of objects in the real world on an experiential level. This is what they might be reduced to in terms of your association and so on.

---

*"Draw the smell of an onion" is an exercise on physiognomic perception mentioned in an earlier class.

Student (female): Well, what I can see from here—I can see all the blocks and I can see the figure; that's all I saw—but when I walked up, I saw the spear for the first time and it seemed pretty funny and I kind of laughed. Good-funny—well, that's B-humor* in this sense, but because here is this man and all these things and he's charging in, armed with a spear. This is his weapon and it's powerful, yet it's absurd. You have to kind of congratulate him on his courage, even laugh at him and with him at the same time.

Maslow: That's what you get. Do you notice, in both of them, that one starts to talk about "it's this" and "it's opposite" simultaneously.

Student (female): Also, you have one man against a whole series of shapes which are basic shapes: circles, squares, triangles. He's attacking a series of basic things which are in shadows, and he's all white in outline. Also, the whole idea that he's charging on a horse, a noble steed; a noble duty, going into the unknown.

Student (male): First of all, I think of Don Quixote and the windmill, and also, I think, the very striking thing is the man on the horse is much smaller than the objects, and you know the spear is not something to defend the person. It's his means of offending, and this is what strikes up the idea of Don Quixote in mind.

Maslow: Remember, don't anybody get Freudian about this. Don't you dare!   *(Laughter)*

Student (male): I don't know about the Don Quixote thing, but I think that the B-humor and the existential thing comes out. It seems to me that those are children's blocks. They look like a set of children's blocks which are small, and the fact that the man is so much smaller. But I also think it's—the whole Don Quixote business—a rather grandiose identification of self-image, that you can tackle these great things, best things.

Maslow: You know, you keep adding things. Even my own joke about the Freudian—I never thought about Freud there at all. It suddenly dawned on me, people start talking about spears *(chuckles)*. I hadn't thought of it before, and then these things that you say, too. It might be that we could have a kind of group addition. We could function here as a group and add up to . . . Each of you have added something to what the person before did. It accumulates, put it that way. But the interesting thing about these condensations is it's very hard to contradict anything. Do you know what I mean there? That the

*A Maslowian term for an unhostile, philosophical humor that has an uplifting quality.
See Maslow, *Motivation and Personality,* 2nd Ed., p. 169.

additions—you keep on adding opposites and adding opposites, and even if they're inconsistent, it still adds on. It's hard to say no, that's not so, because practically everything is so. And I must say, already I see things in that that I didn't see, even though I've played with this a long time and hung it in my office and so on.

Student (female): I don't think that is seems like a little man penetrating into the unknown. When you think of blocks you think of something hard. It seems like a little man, a human being in a great big wide world, trying with a little, thin spear, trying to penetrate something that's impenetrable.

Student (female): I don't think the blocks are places so much as the unknown. They represent Western civilization. They're geometrical, and yet there are all sorts of theorems backing up their existence. And here you are, trying to approach things on sort of a supernatural or spiritual level.

Maslow: Did you notice the difference in style between the two? The lines are different: this is harder, sharper, stronger, firmer; the edges are definite and black. That is a little more sketchy, wavery; more poetic, perhaps.

Student (male): Like the selfishness of our society and our goals versus the doing of things in society. I think here both elements are combined. There's not just the selfishness—that the knight on the horse by himself—certainly the self-importance of the individual is there, but also the greatness of the mission is there.

Student (female): From here, it looks as if he's stopped, he can't go on. The position of the horse is as if he were almost bucking, and you have these two completely different worlds which are being forced apart and they'll never really be able to reach each other.

Maslow: That too fits with a difference in styles. If you were closer, you'd see that the lines are different, the style of the artistic line is different.

Student (male): I think at the symbolic level it would represent your desire to fight for human elements against inhuman things such as the American Psychological Association. The man on the horse is fighting something ridiculous, but from his point of view it is something worth fighting for.

Student (male): Well, I have the feeling that here are these fundamental obvious things: triangles and spheres, and here he is with a spear, and here I go. These are basic things in life that we approach. It's kind of a funny thing to go about doing, and it makes me think of a poem—I don't remember it exactly, but it's something like: The daffodils grow in the sunlight and never ask why.

Maslow: Anybody else? Take your time.

Student (female): Somebody over here set me off to thinking about what would be the next picture in free association. What would be the end of. . . .?   *(Laughter)*

Maslow: It is an interesting thought. I bet you could use this as a projective technique. If we tried to write down what is the next picture, there would be different ones.

Student (female): I can see him turn that horse and go in the opposite direction.   *(Laughter)*

Maslow: I know what my next picture would be.

Student (female): Yours would be to go ahead.

Student (female): She was right: it is bucking that way.

Maslow: That's an interesting thought. Maybe we'll try that for more slides that are coming or even for this. Let's . . . *(Then, quickly changing his mind,)* Hold it. It would spoil it, because I think if anyone spoke up then immediately that would freeze—it would suggest too much. If you have any thoughts about this next thing, could you write it for me? I'm very interested. I'm already interested to see that you've added so much to what I saw there, and I really studied this darn thing for a long time from different angles and even personally.

This could be a kind of therapeutic technique. That is, supposing you would pick out some cartoon or painting or poem or something about which you had very strong feelings, and then listen to another group of people make associations to them of the kind that you've been making. It would be almost as if they were with their objectivity . . . Greater objectivity about you than you could have about yourself might be adding to your self-knowledge. Try it, I think it would be of special personal interest to me. How different are your second pictures to the one that I clearly have in my head! It's very clear.

Student (female): Should this be a picture of what we think you would do?

Maslow: Oh, no! What you would do. This is a projective technique. I simply ask you what's coming next. Just draw the next picture.

Student (male): In action?

Maslow: Whatever it is. What's going to happen? What comes next? And then I'll leave it to you to interpret. Do you have any more thoughts for this? I'd like to try it once around for everybody before we make our second round. Does anybody, anyone of you, disagree with anything that has been said so far that seems to grate a little bit, or is not quite right, or it didn't hit the right note?

Student (female): Yeah, the Don Quixote approach, in the windmill. He was making the windmill something more than it actually was. But in this, even though the rider is romantic, there's also a realism in it because he sees just how large the task actually is. There isn't any soft illusion there.

Maslow: I think he tries. I'll tell you what it meant to me before you got started on it. Does anybody want to add anything?

Student (male): I just think it's interesting that in the picture the objects themselves are fantastic things and really have a greater aspect of reality than the horse and the rider himself.

Maslow: It's a different style and can play many different themes.

Student (male): Well, my reaction was not specific as to what those things were. They are non-specific, mysterious.

Maslow: Anything else, anybody? This is very good because there is no right and wrong. I don't have any hesitation about telling you what I saw and there's absolutely no implication of greater virtue or validity or "worthicality." It's obviously projection, and your projections are absolutely as good as anybody else's projections. So we'd be comparing in the same way as some of those exercises the creative art educators do, where there's no right and no wrong in drawing the smell of an onion. You can compare different projections of that unreal task, so to speak.

Student (male): I think a few years ago the Brandeis Handbook had a picture on the front of a little armored rider with a lance riding into the open mouth of a crane.

Maslow: That's very interesting. I don't remember it, but I must have seen it. I probably saw it.

Student (female): Even though those blocks are very definite shapes and all, I still somehow get the impression that this is somewhat a picture of something chaotic over there, anyway, even though there might be definite objects, and that this figure on the charger, this figure representing you, might want to order it up a little bit: put the circles with the circles and the triangles with the triangles and so forth. It might not so much be fighting it but straightening out the mess a little bit.

Student (male): I've just got to answer that. I think that they're not as ordered—at least from your point of view of looking at it—as cubicle, as they would be here. They're much more vague and non-specific and non-objective, more mysterious.

Student (male): I just have a suggestion for the second picture.

Maslow: No, hold this. Keep that private because that will save the personal mess of all these suggestions so they won't be contaminated by anyone else's suggestions. I can tell you what it meant to me. Now it already means more. For one thing, when I saw it first I just laughed out loud. Now you don't often do that to a picture. It just seemed so funny, so terribly funny that I laughed and laughed and then brought it to my wife and friends and so on and then hung it on the wall and thought this was the most amusing darn thing. And I think slowly identified—realized that I was sort of laughing at my own situation and reading myself into it. And it fits. For me, in the first place, the whole thing is a nonsensical situation and the whole thing is humorous, sort of funny, absurd a little bit—on both sides of it.

The way I saw it was all those geometrical things are sort of mechanistic. I think I felt much the way you said there, sort of mechanistic, cold, bloodless kind of thing, just the sort of thing that I'm fighting against in the American Psychological Association,* let's say. The quarrels that I'll have, and the debates and so on, are against the mechanistic conception of psychology. Now it's condensed there. I remember thinking, They're very strong, they're more powerful than Don Quixote and this guy here. They're sort of frail by comparison to these huge, big, blocky, solid things, which are heavier than he is and seem more solid and heavy. And yet they're also nonsensical because they're in a big clump. They're not really arranged, they're sort of tossed around, and they themselves are absurd too, or they looked absurd to me. I'm trying to remember my first look, rather than what it is now—the accretion that you've added to it.

Yet, there's something . . . Well, I can like it; that is, I could identify with this. This is clearly weaker. That is, Don Quixote, or whoever this figure with his spear is, it's all very nice. The association with me is of bravery, a kind of hopeless bravery, you might say—the ship going down with the flag flying and so on. Because this looks stronger and he can't break them—the spear isn't big enough for that—it isn't strong enough or powerful enough. So there's that kind of fundamental absurdity about the effort itself—of Don Quixote, or a Don Quixote-ish figure. I like Don Quixote, and I like that it seems like a nice thing to do. His spear will get bent, or he can't crack it or break it or anything, but the fact is that he is in a certain sense stronger, you

---

*It was somewhat ironical that he was to be elected as the President of APA only a few years later. (1967–68).

248 LABORATORY IN SELF-KNOWLEDGE

might say, because he sees how absurd all these self-important blocks are, all puffed up with pride and solidity. A kind of fake solidity because they're all in a jumble anyhow. They make no sense and he does, and even if they are stronger than he.

Now you'll be interested in the associations. Walter Weisskopf, a friend of mine, just suddenly called me up. He was in town for a meeting. I went over to talk with him and he was sort of depressed a little bit. It was the Economics Association, and in the Statler Hotel there were 4,000 economists or something and they wandered around, and he thinks of them as so blind in general. But he felt he was just one against 4,000—he felt so weak. And I kind of bucked him up a little bit and said, "The difference between the 4,000 and you is you're right"—which he is.

And then he got into a better humor and . . . I like him, I like to see him; a great mind, a wonderful mind. It's a pleasure, an aesthetic pleasure, just to watch it function. We then started playing this game about the Freudian myth you know about the horde, the *Totem and Taboo* myth.

You know that one about the sons. The primal horde consists of the dominant father, who is more powerful and strong and who has all the females for himself. So the other, younger males, lead together, and they dethroned him and kill him and, if I remember, eat him, take his courage and strength and so on. And in that way they can get a female. And this, Freud used it. The anthropologists have been kicking like mad about it but he never meant it. It's a myth. It's a kind of a way of saying something, just the way this cartoon is. He was trying to say that you have to overthrow the dominant one or else you'll never be a man, and if you're not a man you don't deserve a woman and so on. That kind of association you can make to it.

We played the game there but we turned it around. Here the horde isn't the fathers; it's the son who is weak. There is one son and 4,000 fathers around here, and this poor one son Walter Weisskopf has to fight 4,000 fathers. But in the long run he is strong because he's right.

Well, you can play that kind of game. That's the way this seemed to me. Now I would see many more things in it. And it's extremely interesting that a psychoanalyzed man, I, didn't even think of the Freudian interpretation of this. The spears and the charging on things . . . it's a very simple possibility. Your psychoanalyst would start talking about the castration fears, anxieties, and the phallic stage of fighting against the father and so on. The things you've added to it make it richer.

Well, my attitude toward my work is involved here. I don't think it shows very much in public, where I'm just sort of talking like an authority, but the scientists . . . You see, the truth is I'm also this kind of a scientist. It doesn't show to you, I don't think, much. I'm partly identified with the blocks and the squares and the calculating machines, and I love them. And I've done very careful and rigorous experiments—that's a different kind of pleasure. It is a real pleasure too, if you do something obsessional well. You might almost speak of double identification here, of the civil war within the person. This is like the dream interpretation where you should identify yourself with every part of the whole dream. Every member in the dream, every person in it, is some part of you when you've got this kind of civil war: not a civil war but the need that reflects it. It's true because I have a great disturbance over this: great guilt for not doing rigorous experiments now, which I've done all my life until recently, and feeling somehow not decent. I felt uneasy about all these big things without data, without support and all sorts of theories and hypotheses. A big, big balloon, and there's always the thought, Which needle is going to prick that balloon? That's the thing about theories on the one hand and data on the other.

So that this does reflect for me, and it made me understand in a way that perhaps you could use it for too. It made me understand a little more about my guts, about my own self, about my internal conflicts which are really not settled and never will be: it's impossible. Not till the day I die or the day you die. There's a kind of conflict in each of you: your obsessional side, your hysterical side, your impulsive side, your control side, discipline and so on; your orderliness and your anarchy and the like. They're all in you. You could play that game for yourselves. Well, that's what it means, that's what it meant to me. There were variations on this. Weren't there? A dozen at least, different from this, equally sound. We could call this a projective test, couldn't we? Where you can insert yourself, so to speak, like the ink blot.

Maslow: Well, let's try and see what we can make out of these things.* Do you want to talk about that?   *(Figure 2)*

Student (male): Can I just ask you a question? What were the letters *(in the picture)* for?

Maslow: Well, let me make it a little more clear *(Maslow adjusts the focusing).* Yes, go ahead.

*Editor's note: Figures 2-7 were all slides projected onto a screen at one end of the classroom.

Figure 2

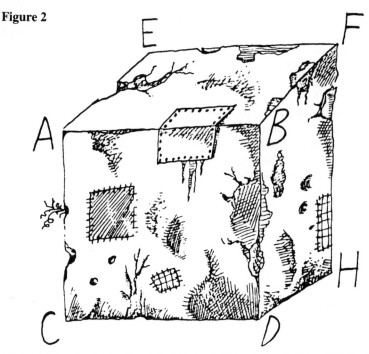

Student (female): Well, first, the letters at the angles look like geometry when you're doing geometrical shapes and you letter the angles so you can work with the figure and work along. But the shape itself is so much more interesting than the triangles. It's just filled with patches and holes and dark spots and little leaves and things coming out of it. It looks sort of like a cell, and it looks like somebody's old overalls a little bit, and all of it superimposed on a geometrical sort of framework. It looks sort of silly, absurd.

Student (female): It's the story of my life.   *(Laughter)*

Maslow: You know I just had the craziest association with that "The Czarist Russian Empire." I've just been reading about it.

Student (male): It reminds me of a Freudian defense mechanism.

Student (male): It looks to me like a sick piece of Swiss cheese.

Student (female): You might see a mouse trying to get at a piece of cheese and, you know, he has the corners labeled where you should start. And each time he goes to take a bite, something happens wrong.

Student (female): It reminds me of a map of the world where they have all of these neat longitudinal and latitudinal lines.

Maslow: So, the world.

Student (male): Well, if you think about trying to organize experience and make a code and think of what happens to a code.

Student (female): It makes me wonder whether that's really inside or the outside business or both. So what's inside?

Maslow: Okay. Let's go back to that. I think to some extent all of these overlap a little, at least to my eyes, that they have the same . . . For instance, supposing I were to ask you—you have to say it in figures of speech of course—in what respects is this similar to this thing that you just saw or, let's say, to this *(Figure 3).*   *(Pause)*

Student (female): A doctor and his patient.

Student (male): This is too Freudian.

Student (female): But just the absurdity of a man who is determined to fight or die.

Student (male): It looks to me like a man in the hands of the psychoanalyst.   *(Laughter)*

Student (female): It's someone's conscience fighting back at him.

Student (male): It looks like an atheist fighting God.

Student (female): But at least he's moving and the hand isn't.

Student (male): It controls him.

Figure 3

Student (female): Is there any significance about "Steinberg" *(signature in the picture)* being written backwards?

Maslow: No, that's my putting it wrong. *(Laughter)* That reminds me that I had hoped to invite Steinberg. I don't know where he is, but I'd certainly like to meet him. Maybe we should. How about this student government, don't they have money? We've run out of money for inviting people to our department. Why not invite Steinberg around to draw us a cartoon in public or something? Talk with us?

Student (male): Is the man's eye looking in the other direction? And afraid to fight the battle?

Student (male): It looks fierce to me.

Student (male): It's beautiful.

Student (male): It's just very wary.

Maslow: Remember you're also technicians now, so you can ask the methodological question: In what respect are you the hand and in what respect are you the person? That's the way you'd handle your own dream for instance. You're everything in this dream; this is a dream.

Maslow: Let's try this.   *(Figure 4)*

Student (male): It looks to me like a man running away from a "globbleglook." Whatever the thing on the right is, it looks like it's going to fall down. It's only balanced by the circular object on the bottom, a golf ball.

Student (male): I think the man has a problem.

Maslow: Any other thoughts?

Student (female): It kind of looks like something that has to do with the sea, at least that's the way I see it, with waves and maybe sea foliage and fishlike and, you know, a kind of sea monster. When we think of sea we think of basic origins and things. Maybe he's running away from that, maybe he sees it and he's running like all get-out.

Student (female): To me it looks like a female-type figure and he's running away from it. We did the same thing with Stride drawings years ago at Antioch in psychology class, and half the class divided as to whether a figure was male or female.

Maslow: Well, just for fun, how many of you see that figure as female and how many of you as male? Well, isn't that interesting in itself: no answer to the male.

Student (male): It isn't either one.

Maslow: How many of you see it as neither one? Supposing I forced the issue now. Make a forced choice: you must make a vote

Figure 4

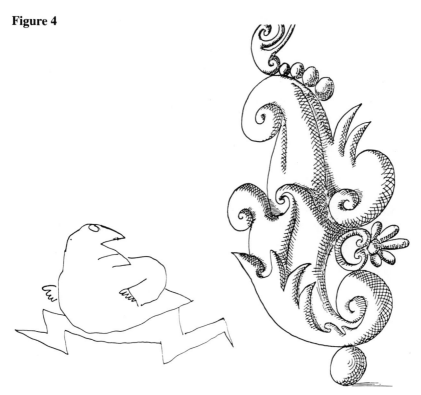

either for male or female. How many of you vote that this looks more like a female? How many of you under that forced choice will say it looks more like a male than a female?   *(Votes taken)*

That's characteristic, by the way. Remember we tried to talk about that physiognomic perception, that you'll get not a chance line-up, it's not 50/50. It's usually tipped very much one way rather than the other. Well, what's female about it?

Student (male): Fanciness and curls. A man wants a simple life. *(Laughter)*

Student (female): You may think I'm terrible . . . There's something female about it in the sense of nature, kind of. He looks like he's the type of man who thinks he has organized everything so well, and Nature just kind of gets up whenever she feels like it and becomes this fantastically complicated thing up there and he looks at it.

Student (female): Also, it looks dominating to me. It's trying to dominate him.

Maslow: That's a very common male fantasy: confronted with a primal femaleness, you know, D. H. Lawrence femaleness-type.

Student (female): He has no awareness of the little thing that she's being balanced on and I think . . . *(not clear)*   *(Laughter)*

Student (male): I think it needs something, maybe I can just point to it. I think if you put an eye—I don't know if you can do this—right there . . . I don't know how it changes [the] appearance of this whole thing.

Student (male): It makes a much more pretty girl.

Maslow: You notice again the difference in style between the two figures?

Student (female): I prefer to see [them] as neuter, though. This looks like somebody in an intense anxiety situation where they're running away from something and they don't know what. But whatever it is, it feels like it's going to fall in on them.

Maslow: Doesn't this remind you . . . Everybody here, you've had dreams like this, haven't you? Frightened at some vague, unknown?

Student (male): He looks more surprised than frightened.

Student (male): Yeah, he doesn't look like that. It would be in his mouth—more anxiety—wouldn't it? He would be more tense.

Student (female): He's not getting so well-ordered.

Student (male): It's like a modern version of a dragon, mysterious. He's sort of like a hen-pecked husband.   *(Laughter)*

Student (female): I think this is definitely Freudian.   *(Figure 5)*

Student (female): He keeps doing that to his ''no's.'' All his negative things are blocks and solid and they don't move, they have this immobility. But the ''yes'' is on wheels, and the whole thing is floating and moving and somehow much more dynamic, even if it's much more delicate and more tasteless.

Maslow: That suggestion about the Freudian thing—am I being anti-Freudian? It's obvious enough, but I hadn't seen it. Psychologists all do.   *(Maslow chuckles)*

Student (male): If you really want to be Freudian about this, if you interpret the spear coming out of the ''yes'' as a phallic symbol of some sort, it might be pointing toward the desire of sexuality with the big social ''no'' which. . . .

Student (male): Social ''no''? It's the female ''no!''

Figure 5

Copyright © 1960 by Saul Steinberg. From the book *The Labyrinth*, Harper & Row, Publishers. Originally published in *The New Yorker Magazine*.

Student (male): Well, whatever it is, I don't know. *(Laughter)*

Maslow: Well, if you could convince it, if it is. It's the female's job to say no, not the male's—in this culture anyway.

Student (male): Social "no"? It's the female "no!"

Maslow: Sure, it's a fortress. . . . *(car horn heard outside)* That's my wife. I'd better tell her.   *(He gets up and walks to the window).*

Maslow: Can you see that one now?   *(Figure 6)*

Student (male): Not too well.

Maslow: It's a pity about the light. If you look closely, you see that these are all as in A as in B. These are all paths between A and B. *(Pause)* Gee, I just hate to hurry this.*

Student (female): That looks like my husband in the upper left hand corner, and the rest looks like me.

Maslow: Do you know what I think? I think we should look at these again.

Student (male): It looks like all the complexes you go through in a relationship.

*Editor's note: Fifty minutes had elapsed since the session began. At this point, Maslow was apparently feeling the time pressure.

Student (male): Well, between A and B . . . . There's always the space between A and B. I mean, it's never one thing, it's never any one set pattern.

Maslow: Well, see what you can make out of it. I'll be back in a second.   *(Students begin talking to one another).*

Student (male): I think it's saying that there's all kinds of ways to get nowhere.   *(Maslow returns)*

Maslow: You got that alright?   *(Figure 7)*

Student (male): I think it's saying a Steinberg is out of his mind.

Maslow: I ask you how many words would it take to describe that as well?

Student (male): It's not a dialogue.

Maslow: No?

Student (male): No. Imagine what is being said.   *(Pause)*

Student (male): He's pretty busy here to save literature. *(Laughter)*

Figure 6

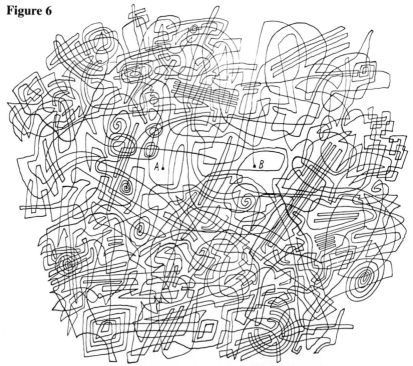

Copyright © 1960 by Saul Steinberg. From the book *The Labyrinth*, Harper & Row, Publishers.

Figure 7

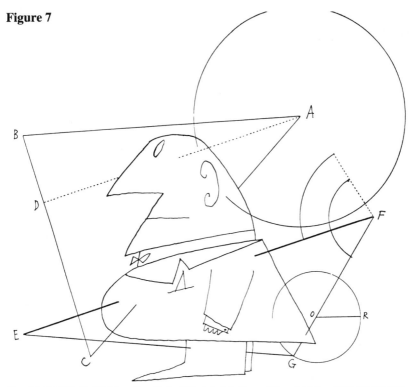

Student (male): This picture is an analysis of modern man.

Maslow: Well, again you can ask the question, How does this relate to the other? Supposing I think of this as a single series. As a matter of fact, I chose them that way. These were chosen out of perhaps several hundred. I saw . . . at least one human being saw something common in that whole series, starting with my thing that you looked at.

Student (male): What did you see in common with A and B.?

Maslow: Well, I'd rather . . . I know what I saw, how about you?

Student (female): These are like men's tools, the things he has to arm himself, you know. He takes everything. It's his knowledge. He knows about circles and triangles, his measuring devices, his compasses and things like that, what he goes to work with.

Maslow: Well, I've only got through half of them. I'd like to continue. I'd like to show you all of these things, and then also we have another kind of thing altogether that we can save for next time. I think I'll bring these slides back next time and start from the beginning. That is, I'd like to run them over again. Let's see what your unconscious can do with them in one week. Only one thing I'll say to set you going: I saw something common in all of these.

Student (female): What book are these pictures in.?

Maslow: I think these are all in his book *The Labyrinth.*

22

Peak-Experiences

Editor's Notes (H.M.Chiang)

It was Abraham H. Maslow who coined the term peak-experience to designate the happiest and most ecstatic moments in a person's life. Such an experience tends to open up and bring out the best in the person, and Maslow has appropriately called it a "transient moment of self-actualization" of the ordinary people. In collecting the reports on peak-experiences, Maslow often read the following instructions to his college subjects:

I would like you to think of the most wonderful experience or experiences of your life; happiest moments, ecstatic moments, moments of rapture, perhaps from being in love, or from listening to music or suddenly "being hit" by a book or painting, or from some great creative moment. First list these. And then try to tell me how you feel in such acute moments, how you feel differently from the way you feel at other times, how you are at the moment a different person in some ways.

—(Maslow, *Toward a Psychology of Being,* p. 71.)

The two examples of peak-experiences reproduced below were submitted to Maslow in response to such instructions. Both were written by college students and were read by Maslow in 1963 in one of his classes.

Peak-Experience 1

Two years ago, while I was attempting to do some math problems in elementary calculus that I had for homework one night, I was following the long, involved procedure for finding the derivative of functions exactly the way my teacher had told me to do. I suddenly thought I saw a quick way of finding the answer. I tried my new method, which only required inspection rather than calculation, got an answer for the next few problems, then did them again the old way. I got the same answers, showing that my perceived relationships between function and derivitive were indeed correct.

A day or so after this, going further in the math book, I saw an explanation of the way that I had discovered for myself. Finding out that mathematicians had known this method before I stumbled upon it in no way marred my pleasure. Upon finding out that my method was correct, I became very excited. I felt very proud of myself, particularly because I had been having some trouble with math during the week or so before this experience.

I ran around the house until I found my parents and showed them my findings, then I sat down by myself and looked over my work again. I suppose I could say that I felt creative. I certainly felt as if I "belonged." I now saw myself as having a right to be in the advanced math class that I was in. I did not feel guilty any longer—there were no longer any nagging fears of inadequacy.

This was not just true of my mathematical ability—no sir. I felt confident and sure of myself with respect to all of my studies. I turned to working on the homework that I had in my other subjects, and the relation from the math carried over into everything I did. It helped me with my work, but occasionally I found myself thinking about what I had done and I would grin broadly, forgetting all about the work I was then attempting to finish. I began feeling "friendly" to the study of mathematics instead of, as before, hostile to it. I also saw it as having new importance and significance. It no longer seemed to me like a boring and unnecessary discipline.

Peak-Experience 2

My peak-experience came after a night when I couldn't sleep and had been thinking. I can't remember exactly what particular situation had brought me to this point, but I felt as if I were the lowest, filthiest creature on the face of the earth. At least I was trying to convince myself that I was. The whole world was against me for no reason other than the fact that I was such a horrible person. All night long I wrestled trying to make myself believe what I knew was not true.

About 4:00 A.M. my dog came into my room and climbed into bed with me. She usually did this, but somehow this night it made me feel a sense of relief and joy that she should want to be near *me*—poor, ugly, dirty, horrible, miserable, little old me. Now I had one friend in the world, at least. On an impulse I got out of bed, dressed, and, putting her on a leash, went out of my house. I walked to a patch of woods high on the hill near our house. I sat down on the top of the hill, where the wind was blowing fiercely, and with my dog at my side I watched the sun rise. As the sky became light and there were fewer shadows, I felt a sense of wonder, puzzlement and detachment in myself. I felt small and insignificant and yet a participant in my surroundings. I suddenly saw myself and my problems in their proper perspective. My nightmare became just a part of living. I began to laugh inside and as I hugged my dog closer. I wanted to stand up and shout to the world, ''I am.''